AMBIVALENT
FRIENDS

Contributions in Afro-American and African Studies
Series Adviser: Hollis R. Lynch

AMBIVALENT FRIENDS

Afro-Americans View the Immigrant

ARNOLD SHANKMAN

CONTRIBUTIONS IN AFRO-AMERICAN AND AFRICAN STUDIES, NUMBER 67

GREENWOOD PRESS
WESTPORT, CONNECTICUT • LONDON, ENGLAND

Library of Congress Cataloging in Publication Data

Shankman, Arnold M., 1945–
    Ambivalent friends.

    (Contributions in Afro-American and African studies,
ISSN 0069-9624 ; no. 67)
        Bibliography: p.
        Includes index.
        1. Afro-Americans—Attitudes.   2. Minorities—United
States—Public opinion.   3. United States—Foreign
population—Public opinion.   4. United States—Emigra-
tion and immigration—Public opinion.   5. Public opinion
—United States.   I. Title   II. Series.
E185.615.S45   303.3'87   81-20309
ISBN 0-313-23068-4   (lib. bdg.)   AACR2

Library of Congress Catalog Card Number: 81-20309
ISBN: 0-313-23068-4
ISSN: 0069-9624

First published in 1982

Greenwood Press
A division of Congressional Information Service, Inc.
88 Post Road West
Westport, Connecticut 06881

Printed in the United States of America

10 9 8 7 6 5 4 3 2 1

CONTENTS

TABLES

ACKNOWLEDGMENTS

This book would never have been written without a National Endowment for the Humanities postdoctoral fellowship in ethnic studies at Harvard University during the 1973–74 academic year. Oscar Handlin, who supervised my work at Harvard, read early drafts of several of my essays and helped me refine my arguments and improve my style.

Many other individuals offered moral support, shared materials, and in various other ways helped me write this book. Morris Schappes, editor of *Jewish Currents*, translated material from Yiddish for me and provided constructive criticism of my work. The late Bell Wiley consistently provided encouragement for my work and shared his recollections of how Jewish merchants dealt with their black customers in Halls, Tennessee, his birthplace. David Hellwig, a scholar whose articles and dissertation have done so much to illuminate our understanding of blacks and their perceptions of immigrants, generously shared with me copies of his essays even before they were published. My conclusions sometimes differ from those of Professor Hellwig, but I have the greatest respect for the quality of his work and the depth of his research. Others who provided me with assistance include Billiana Ambrecht, Michael Chesson of the University of Massachusetts-Boston, John McCardell of Middlebury College, Mark Bauman of Atlanta Junior College, George Lamplugh of the Westminster School in Atlanta, Sue Culp Garrett, Carolyn Hoover Sung of the Library of Congress, C. Jack Tucker, Louise Pettus, Ron Chepesiuk, Adelaide Williams, Patricia Ridgeway, and Larry Mitlin, all of Winthrop College, J. Harvey Young, Harvey Klehr, and John T. Juricek of Emory University, Marcia Synnott of the University of South Carolina, Mike and Claire Gettinger,

Alicia Campi and Ruth D. Scheinberg.

I am especially grateful to Jean Morse for her expert typing of the final copy of the manuscript. Drafts of this study were typed by Judy Carter Faile, Jennie Brogan, and Vera Thomas.

Interlibrary loan and reference librarians at Harvard University, Emory University, Winthrop College, Case Western Reserve University, and the Boston Public Library were most helpful. Archivists at Harvard, Yale, the Library of Congress, the University of Michigan, Winthrop College, Emory University, the Schomburg Branch of the New York Public Library, the Western Reserve Historical Society, and Howard University greatly aided me and guided me to the materials in their collections. I am grateful to the Moorland-Spingarn Research Center at Howard University University for permission to quote from the Archibald Grimké Papers. Alan Greenberg of Winthrop College prepared the index.

Early versions of some of the material in this book have appeared in print. I am grateful for permission to use material that came from the following articles:

"Black on Yellow: Afro-Americans View Chinese Americans, 1850-1935," *Phylon* 39 (1978): 1-17. Reprinted from *PHYLON: The Atlanta University Review of Race and Culture*, 39 (First Quarter 1978): 1-17, by permission of *PHYLON*.

" 'Asiatic Ogre or Desirable Citizen'? The Image of Japanese Americans in the Afro-American Press, 1867-1933," *Pacific Historical Review* 46 (1977): 467-87.

"The Image of Mexico and the Mexican-American in the Black Press, 1890-1935," *Journal of Ethnic Studies* 3 (1975): 43-56.

"The Image of the Italian in the Afro-American Press, 1886-1936," *Italian Americana* 4 (1978): 30-49.

"This Menacing Influx: Afro-Americans on Italian Immigration to the South, 1880-1915," *Mississippi Quarterly* 31 (1977-1978): 67-88.

"Friend or Foe: Southern Blacks View the Jew, 1880-1935," in Nathan Kaganoff and Melvin Urofsky, eds., *Turn to the South: Essays on Southern Jewry* (Charlottesville, Va.: University Press of Virginia, 1979), pp. 105-23, 186-92.

Naturally, I am fully responsible for any errors of fact or interpretation that appear in this book.

INTRODUCTION

In 1972, when I first began work on a study of blacks and immigrants, I naively assumed that information on this subject would not be difficult to uncover. I did believe that what I found would relate exclusively to immigrants from Europe in the large urban centers of the Northeast, the Midwest, and possibly the West. For nearly a year, as I vainly searched through books, periodicals, and catalogs of manuscript collections at historical societies and other guides to primary sources, I began to wonder if there was any real material on this topic. Were blacks uninterested in immigrants? Was this a subject of concern to me in the 1970s but not to Negroes in the 1890s? Fortunately, I commenced reading Afro-American newspapers. Black periodicals dealt with all subjects including immigration. I discovered material not only on Jews in New York and Italians in Boston but also on Jews in Savannah and Italians in Houston. Moreover, to my great surprise, there was considerable information on Chinese, Mexican, and Japanese immigrants.

As my work progressed it became plain that I had material for a two-volume study. One would relate to blacks and their perceptions of immigrants in the North, the original project. The other would focus on how Afro-Americans viewed non-European immigrants and what they thought of Jews and Italians in the South, a region where some states had as few as 1 percent of its residents claiming birth in a foreign land. This book presents my findings on the second volume. I am still at work on my original study, which, I hope, will eventually appear as a companion to this volume.

In this book, I am concerned mainly with the years 1880–1935. Where significant primary information was uncovered for earlier years, as in the case of the Chinese, this material is included. Before 1880 there was almost no mention of Italians or Mexicans in black journals. Several factors influenced my choice of 1935 as a termination date. One was the impossibility of examining an ever-increasing number of Afro-American journals and newspapers for more than half a century. Another was that for more than a decade after 1935 comparatively few immigrants were coming to the United States from Europe or Asia. Even Mexicans were by the hundreds of thousands being shamelessly deported south of the border. Moreover, by 1935 material about such groups as Jews and Italians often concerned second or even third-generation Americans and not immigrants. A final reason was that after 1935 scholars slowly began to turn their attention to how various nationalities perceived each other. Before that date, almost no one but Emory Bogardus, Paul Taylor, and a handful of others considered such questions. It is hoped that this volume will help historians, sociologists, anthropologists, social workers, and others get a better historical idea of how minorities have perceived each other.

I have relied largely on contemporary Afro-American newspapers and journals, but I have also made use of all other pertinent sources I could locate whether book, article, dissertation, manuscript, or oral history memoir. I have been mindful—and I caution the reader to be mindful—of two things. First, the average Afro-American newspaper before 1935 was an eight- to twelve-page weekly with a rather small paid circulation. Few editors could afford the luxury of hiring reporters; many freely borrowed from other journals they received in exchange. In fact, the paste pot might well be a newspaper owner's only "reporter." In some ways, however, this has been a blessing, for I have uncovered information about immigrants from black newspapers no longer extant but quoted in a paper that has survived. On the other hand, I have sometimes come across material which editors sought to pass on as their own when there was reason to doubt this was the case. I have even come across identical "news" stories printed in the same journal in different years.

A second problem is that Afro-American newspapers were, in some ways, elitist. They catered to literate and successful blacks, and because many editors accepted subsidies from Booker T. Washington, their papers often reflected his opinions on such subjects as immigration. Nonetheless, whatever their biases and defects, the Afro-American press represents the best source of information on what Negroes were thinking and doing about critical issues during these years.

I hesitate to make many firm judgments since I am still working on a companion volume, but some conclusions are apparent. First, because Afro-Americans were insecure economically, it is only logical that they worried about immigrants competing for their jobs or serving as strike-breakers. Where there was such competition tensions plainly were manifest. Chinese laundrymen, Japanese railroad car porters, Mexican field hands, and Italian barbers represented very real menaces. This caused some black editors to project images of Chinese as idolatrous opium smokers, Japanese as disloyal, Mexicans as lazy, and Italians as bomb-throwing anarchists. If these negative stereotypes corresponded to what many Americans were saying about the immigrants, so much the better.

There was a special bitterness to black comments, however. For if there was a consensus that newcomers were less than completely desirable, immigrants with adequate funds usually could attend first-rate colleges, stay in quality hotels, attend the theater and not be consigned to the balcony, and purchase first-class railroad tickets. These were rights often denied blacks.

Blacks were, for the most part, evangelical Protestants. They looked with disfavor on the unfamiliar religious customs of the Chinese and Japanese. They also considered some of the religious practices of Roman Catholics from Mexico and Italy as superstition. Even Southern Jews, the people of the Bible for whom blacks had a special affinity, were occasionally accused of killing Jesus Christ.

Since in recent years the complex question of black anti-Semitism has been the subject of thousands of pages, much of it polemical, it is important to give this matter an historical examination. Of all the groups I consider in this book, blacks held Southern Jews in the highest regard. Unlike the Italians or Chinese, Jews seldom competed with Afro-Americans for jobs.

Southern Jews, in fact, sometimes hired Negroes, and they treated Afro-Americans better than most whites in Dixie. I know of no Japanese or Mexican philanthropist who helped Negroes, but in many rural Southern communities the name of Julius Rosenwald was revered. Thus, although blacks found some qualities worthy of emulation in every immigrant group, they tended to find more admirable traits in Jews than in Italians, Chinese, Japanese, or Mexicans.

All but the last chapter in this volume have appeared in print over the past seven years. In every case, each essay was completely revised for publication in this book. Earlier judgments were modified if I uncovered information warranting such changes. New material was incorporated to take advantage of sources previously overlooked and of the most recent scholarship. My work has given me a great appreciation of the Afro-American experience in the United States and has caused me to wonder why scholars have not made greater use of black newspapers and periodicals.

Arnold Shankman

AMBIVALENT
FRIENDS

1 THE CHINESE

In 1865, a Boston magazine aimed at the freedmen of the South featured an article on the Chinese. Conceding that Orientals were accomplished artisans and inventors, the writer of the story nonetheless observed that they were superstitious people with primitive religious beliefs. "We must not laugh at them," he cautioned, "but pity and pray for them and save some of our money to send teachers who shall tell them of a better way." The feature concluded by praising a Negro lad, who instead of spending his meager allowance on oranges, contributed to a Chinese mission box. When questioned about this, the boy supposedly responded, "Why, mother, if [the three cents] . . . only buys one leaf of a Bible to tell some poor heathen about Christ and save his soul . . . the good lasts forever."[1]

Over the next seventy years, hundreds—if not thousands—of black boys and girls contributed their pennies to China mission boxes to save the "heathens." But this was not the only contact American Negroes had with the Chinese. Tens of thousands of Chinese, seeking to make their fortunes in the United States, journeyed across the Pacific and settled in the West, New York, Illinois, Massachusetts, and even some parts of the South. On occasion, blacks and Chinese came into direct contact with each other. Despite a common heritage of persecution, contemporary evidence suggests that, on the whole, blacks consistently displayed noticeable antipathy towards Orientals.

Doubtless the first blacks to encounter Orientals were those few thousand who lived in California and other Western states in the 1850s, 1860s, and 1870s.[2] Relations between the two groups were mixed. In the 1850s, some blacks hired Chinese as domestics, and in Sacramento a black hotel keeper employed three Chinese. Rudolph Lapp, the historian of Afro-American life in nineteenth-century California, has found evidence that in Sacramento the Chinese permitted blacks to worship in their chapel while the Negroes were organizing their own church.[3] Lapp also notes some signs of cordiality between Chinese and blacks in the mining areas of California but admits there was also friction. Proof of friction came in 1853 near Sonora, where ten blacks and 100 Chinese engaged in fighting, and in Auburn, where a black man killed a Chinese man.[4]

Unlike whites, blacks rarely mistreated Chinese in California, but on the whole, they were generally unimpressed with Orientals. Some Negroes found the Chinese to be a peculiar and super-stitious people who were "filthy, immoral and licentious—according to our notions of such things." For example, a New Orleans black newspaper alleged that Chinese religious services consisted mainly of having priests shout, yell, and groan to the sound of gongs and drums. Equally repulsive to California blacks was the "grotesque appearance" of the Chinese. The "wretched looking" Orientals shaved their heads with "the exception of the top [of] the hair from which is formed . . . a plaited tail, resembling 'pig tail tobacco'." Furthermore, a San Francisco Negro complained, a Chinese man's "vacant Know Nothing face is expressive of nothing but stupidity."[5]

When we consider these negative views, it is not surprising that blacks expressed shock when California and Nevada pro-hibited Oriental, Negro, and Indian children from attending the same schools as Caucasians. In many communities, all non-white pupils were placed together in segregated schools.[6] Dr. W.H.C. Stephenson, a black living in Virginia City, Nevada, objected to having his children go to the same schools as the "idolatrous heathens." He was not motivated solely by prejudice, he insisted, for he would also oppose having his sons or daughters attend classes with "the scum of the community, let them be white, black, yellow or red." Moreover, he delcared, he would willingly allow his children to associate with Chinese pupils living with "good, honest, respectable white families."

Similar sentiments were expressed in 1873 by an unidentified San Francisco man who called for an intensive program to Americanize the children of Chinese immigrants. Once the children learned English, they would readily cast aside paganism and "their forefathers' customs and opinions." Within a short time, he thought, they would become "true Californians and dress in the American fashion."[7]

Others also objected to Chinese religious beliefs, but not all agreed that the Chinese immigrants or their progeny could ever rid themselves of heathen superstition. To W. H. Hall, who encountered the Chinese in Nevada and California, they were a degraded people "without any regard for the sanctity of the Christian oath," who "for three thousand years have maintained a wall of superstition and error against our revealed religion." Because of their pagan ideas, a San Franciscan added, there was no hope that the Orientals could ever become respectable citizens. On the contrary, they would continue to be "inhuman in their traits . . . scurrilous [in] . . . their feeling . . . [and] illiterate in intellectual education and of the doctrine of morality." Even Philip Bell, editor of the *San Francisco Elevator*, who tried to see positive elements resulting from the Chinese influx, reluctantly concluded that the Asians were people whose "habits, customs, modes of living, manner of worship (faith or religion it cannot be called) are all at variance with our ideas."[8]

Everywhere blacks looked in San Francisco they saw evidence of the evils of tolerating Chinese immigrants in their midst. On the streets of the Chinese section of town, blacks complained, one could "find filth actually personified and the stench which arises and penetrates the olfactory nerves is something perfectly horrible." This was proof that Orientals were "particularly adapted to sordid, insolubrious [sic] localities and places of abode." Gambling, prostitution, and theft—these were what the Chinese had brought with them to America. Was it any wonder that foreigners visiting the United States returned to their homes and told their friends that the Chinese quarter of San Francisco was "the most filthy and disgraceful place they had ever seen?"[9]

It was generally believed that the Chinese were unacquainted with American customs, and, considering themselves sojourners in the United States, they had no real desire to become naturalized. They intended, most people thought, to make their fortunes in America and then, "return home to venerate heathen worship." Both blacks and whites in California were suspicious of a transient people who were unwilling to Americanize themselves. How perverse the Chinese were to be so devoted to the "flowery kingdom" that they refused to consider America their home! Whenever a Chinese immigrant died, his relatives made elaborate plans to ship his bones back to China. This so repulsed one black that he called upon the California legislature to prohibit "the exportation of the Chinese dead." This, he thought, would discourage temporary immigrants. Orientals would be "less odious and onerous" if they came "with the intention of remaining."[10]

Most of the blacks in California, like most of the Chinese, were laborers, and often the two groups competed for the same jobs. At first, Philip Bell believed there was enough work for all, but as time passed he became displeased with the Chinese. The "hordes" of Orientals were willing to work for subsistence wages, forcing the whites and blacks to toil for "starvation prices of the beggars in London and the serf[s] of Moscow." Bell recommended that his readers withdraw their patronage from all who hired the Chinese. "Let our citizens," he urged, "agree not to employ the Chinese nor purchase goods from them." He further suggested that blacks help elect political officials willing to deal with this "thorn in the flesh . . . which must sooner or later there fester." As for the Chinese, Bell concluded, they would have to "paddle their own canoe."[11]

Despite such feelings, most blacks believed that no matter how bad the habits of the Chinese were, "these vices do not justify the whites in oppressing them." When a riot erupted on the streets of San Francisco and a Chinese was murdered, Bell cautioned his readers to avoid participating in such acts of violence. To do so would eventually work to the disadvantage of the Negroes. Similarly, mindful that many Negro women were earning their living by taking in washing, he strongly opposed heavy licensing taxes on laundries. Instead, he proposed that a *"burdensome* tax" be levied on all foreigners and that we "then instruct our tax collectors to discriminate and collect only from the offensive [Oriental] element." He further suggested that a fee be extracted from "all persons who *employ* Chinese or buy fish from them or have their clothes washed by them." If such legislation were enacted, blacks need have no reason to fear Asians.[12]

W. H. Hall also worried about the menace of Chinese labor. In 1869, he began a letter-writing campaign to alert blacks to the evils of Chinese immigration. He was elected to represent California and other Western states at the National Labor Convention of Colored Men held in December of that year at Washington, D.C., but did not attend the meeting. Nonetheless, he made his views known in a written communication in which he strongly denounced the Chinese as "fit subjects for that class who persistently adhere to the doctrine of inferiority of races." There was no doubt in his mind that unless immediate action were taken, the number of Oriental immigrants would increase geometrically. China, he declared, was "so over-crowded and dense" that there was "no limit" to the number of coolies she could send over. The other delegates at the convention attentively listened to his philippics and obediently endorsed his resolution calling for an end to "imported contract coolie labor and appeal [ing] to Congress to enforce the Act of 1862, prohibiting coolie importation." Hall was confident that he had properly represented the sentiment of Western blacks.[13]

Other Negro delegates at the convention and others who met in 1869 were more favorably disposed towards the Chinese and invited "John Chinaman" to join black labor organizations. To some Afro-Americans it was important to cultivate the friendship of the Chinese.[14]

The *Christian Recorder,* on July 24, 1869, warned California blacks to "Keep their garments clean" and avoid oppressing the Chinese. The editor recognized that those who would persecute individuals with yellow skins would just as easily cheat and discriminate against persons with black skins.[15] These words of caution had little impact on California's black population. One reason why California Negroes remained hostile to the Chinese was that, like whites, they were unfamiliar with Chinese history and customs. Stuart Creighton Miller well summarizes the case in the observation that Californians and most other Americans (including blacks) saw the "Chinese as uniquely enslaved to an idolatrous ancient tradition, politically servile, morally depraved, and loathsomely diseased. China was viewed as singularly impervious to nineteenth century ideals of progress, liberty, and civilization to which an emergent America was fervently committed."[16]

Moreover, blacks and Chinese were serious job competitors.[17] In 1876, about 8,000 California Chinese worked as domestics or launderers, jobs blacks had once considered to be their monopolies. Philip Bell regularly urged Afro-Americans to come to California and displace the Chinese servants and laundrymen. As late as 1902, one Washington, D.C. paper sadly noted: "San Francisco had the smallest Negro population of any large city in the country because of cheap labor performed by the Chinese."[18]

But there were more subtle reasons why blacks disliked the Chinese and sought to disassociate themselves from them. California Negroes were insecure, unsure about their proper place in society. Before the Civil War California blacks, like Negroes in most other states, had been unable to testify in civil and criminal cases, and in 1858 a bill prohibiting the immigration of Negroes to the state was nearly enacted into law. Many of those who opposed the Chinese had no love of blacks. A resident of Sonoma, for example, claimed that "one white man is worth two Chinamen; that one Chinaman is worth two negroes, and that one negro is worth two tramps." Another Californian insisted that the Chinese were biologically and culturally superior to blacks, and Professor Luther Spoehr has concluded that California whites in the 1870s had more positive stereotypes of the Chinese than of blacks.[19]

In 1867, Governor Henry Haight opposed granting suffrage to blacks on the grounds that this action would eventually lead to the enfranchisement of Chinese. Never would Californians consent to allow either group to "vote or hold office," he declared in his inaugural address, for both were "inferior races."

Realizing that sentiment against Chinese voting was widespread, blacks sought to show that they were different from the Asians. Unlike the yellow men, they were Christians well acquainted with American habits and customs. Furthermore, they had fought for their freedom and for the preservation of the Union; the United States was the land of their birth and the only home they had ever known or wanted to know. The Chinese, on the other hand, were sojourners of dubious morality who did not need or particularly want the vote; foreign treaties could adequately protect their civil rights.[20] Constitutional amendments extended the vote to blacks, but as anti-Oriental agitation became more intense, Negroes continued to find it prudent to avoid expressing sympathy for the Chinese.

Apparently, some residents of Nevada shared Haight's prejudice. Less than three months after the California governor denounced proposals to enfranchise blacks, a group of whites met in Pine Grove, Nevada, to form the National Democratic Club. Membership in this group was limited to those "opposed to Negro and Chinese social equality in the United States."[21]

Anti-Chinese sentiment in the 1860s and 1870s was not limited to the West; it also existed in the South. In Dixie, however, this antipathy was based almost entirely on economic grounds. Some white settlers in California who had been born in the South wrote their relatives and friends about the desirable qualities of Chinese servants and laborers. A Louisiana native in San Francisco assured the readers of the *New Orleans Daily Picayune* that he could state "from experience" the Chinese "work well and faithfully and I would prefer them every time to black labor, and I think they will be a success on the Southern plantation."[22] Another white, John Thrasher, published a letter in which he, too, contrasted the supposedly idle Negroes with the industrious Chinese he had observed in Cuba. His letter was widely read.[23]

To whites, who professed to be dissatisfied with allegedly inefficient and unreliable Afro-American laborers, importing diligent workers with no interest in social equality or political rights sounded quite attractive. Both R. Izard Middleton, a South Carolina planter, and William Lawton, chairman of a committee investigating the value of Chinese immigrants, felt that plantations—rice plantations especially—would be better served by Chinese laborers than by blacks. Godfrey Barnsley, a New Orleans factor, predicted in 1869 that Chinese workers would soon replace black field hands, and even William Tappan Thompson, a Savannah journalist, concluded that the Chinese were first-class laborers.[24]

In 1867, some Louisianians, who had resided in Cuba, imported a few Chinese to determine whether they would make good field hands. Two years later, Arkansas planters organized the Arkansas River Valley Immigration Company, and soon they hired Captain George Gift to serve as a labor agent to obtain laborers from China or California. In a parallel move that same year, the Vicksburg (Mississippi) Chamber of Commerce sent General W. R. Miles to San Francisco to investigate the desirability of importing Chinese labor. The *New Orleans Daily Picayune* and the *Vicksburg Times* showed great interest in these schemes, and between 1866 and 1870 perhaps 500 to 1,000 Chinese aliens moved to Louisiana, Texas, Mississippi, and Arkansas.[25]

At first, blacks professed to be unconcerned. Some insisted that the Southern whites were bluffing, trying to scare their employees and to keep wages down. Others, repulsed by the Chinese, thought that Oriental labor in the South would teach Dixie to appreciate its Negro help. A few believed that the South was underpopulated and did in fact need more agricultural workers. Either Chinese or Europeans would be imported, the *San Francisco Elevator* predicted, and "we would sooner see the freedmen contending against the Mongolian than the Celt." Editor Philip Bell insisted that no more than 50,000 Chinese would ever immigrate to the South in any one year, and he maintained that Dixie "could easily give remunerative employment to a million more" than she had in her fields. In similar vein, Frederick Douglass doubted that the South really wanted to encourage the settlement of large numbers of coolies. Even the *Charleston* (South Carolina) *Missionary Record* announced that it was not alarmed over the anticipated Oriental influx, for it argued that it would cost more to import and keep Chinese laborers than black workers. Moreover, if the importation of Asians forced blacks to purchase and farm their own land, the influx might even be beneficial to Negroes.[26]

As the first boatloads of Chinese arrived in the late 1860s, Afro-Americans quickly changed their minds. Negro papers in Louisiana and Arkansas denounced the whites who sought to supplant them and demanded that the "coolies" be sent back to China. The presence of Chinamen would lead to lower wages and promote widespread unemployment. W. H. Hall, who had no use for Orientals in the West or South, solemnly warned that unless speedy action were taken, hordes of Chinese would over-run the South. He further predicted that Orientals would cor-rupt the Southern Afro-Americans; their "accumulated vices and pagan practices would creep into the habits of our illiterate race, checking their present advancement and hastening . . . a war of races."[27]

Such fears proved groundless. Because of the illegality of con-tract labor and high cost of transportation and other related ex-penses, Chinese labor was more expensive than anticipated.[28] As Nell Painter has pointed out, the Chinese Six Companies in San Francisco let it be known that they would not send Chinese workers to the South for the low wages paid blacks.[29]

Initially, the Chinese newcomers were slower workers than the blacks. Mississippi planters discovered, to their dismay, that Orientals had no familiarity with handling mules, working with plows, or using cotton gins. Futhermore, the Chinese had no intention of remaining sharecroppers or field hands once they be-came aware that they would not be treated fairly. On one plantation a white employer shot several of his "unruly" Oriental workers, and on another Chinese laborers tried unsuccessfully to lynch the man responsible for their coming to Louisiana. William Tappan Thompson revised his opinion of the Chinese "pagans" downward and decided that the best agricultural workers for the South were European immigrants. More blunt was the *Dallas* (Texas) *Herald*, a white newspaper. "We want neither niggers or Mongolians—we want white men." Others, however, decided that docile blacks were, after all, the best field hands.[30] In the words of Governor J. W. Throckmorton of Texas, "The nigger is good enough for us and . . . will make a better laborer than China or any other place can send."[31]

Chinese sent to Meridian, Mississippi, in 1871 to work on the Alabama and Chattanooga Railroad proved to be so costly and troublesome that company officials sent them to the Chattanooga end of the line. Chinese laborers on the Houston and Texas Central Railroad were considered more satisfactory, but after a few months they were let go because Irish immigrants refused to work with them. Oriental sharecroppers, some coming from China and others from Cuba, soon abandoned cottonfields near Calvert, Texas, for the herbal shops and laundries of Galveston and El Paso. Although Floridians sometimes spoke about the need for Chinese laborers to supplant blacks, there was no great influx of Asians in that state. As early 1869, the Tennessee legislature considered a law prohibiting the importation of Chinese. Eleven years later, Louisiana lawmakers over-whelmingly endorsed a resolution declaring that the needs of the state did not require the importation of Chinese immigrants. Some Chinese did remain in the Mississippi Delta counties, but most of these quickly abandoned farming to become house servants or self-employed grocers or dry goods merchants. In addition, nearly 200 Chinese came to Augusta, Georgia, before 1900 to work on a canal expansion project. Those remaining in the city once the work was completed, like their compatriots in Mississippi, opened up small stores and laundries.[32] Few, if any, of them ever engaged in agricultural labor in Georgia.[33] Before long, it was apparent that the Chinese were not a direct threat to black agricultural labor in the South.

But if the Chinese gradually gained tolerance from blacks in Dixie, their compatriots in the West were not so lucky. Many Westerners actively sought to repeal the Burlingame Treaty of 1868 which had granted the United States and China "the mutual advantage of free migration of their citizens and subjects respectively from the one country to the other for the purpose of curiosity or trade as permanent residents."[34] In 1880, a new treaty abrogated the 1868 agreement, and within two years Congress passed the first Chinese exclusion act.[35] Only a few black newspapers were willing to support the various exclusion acts. The *San Francisco Vindicator*, hoping to promote "a great field for colored labor," insisted that the Chinese had to go. "They are polluting the air and everything else. In fact, to come into contact with them at all is to be polluted." Similar sentiments were expressed by the *Washington Colored American*, which proclaimed: "There is no room in this land for the disease-breeding, miserly, clannish and heathen Chinese."[36]

When we consider the hostility blacks manifested towards the Chinese during the 1860s and 1870s, the views expressed by these two journals do not seem shocking. When compared with the anti-Chinese editorials of Irish-American newspapers, they seem rather tame. What is surprising is that most black newspapers opposed restrictions on Chinese immigration.[37]

Typical of the views of the Negro press was that of the *Washington New Era*. According to its editors, Americans had no more right to close their doors to the Chinese than to the Irish and Germans. "As between the peaceably disposed, industrious and frugal Chinaman and the lazy, drunken and revolutionary anarchist," asked the *New York Freeman*, "which is the more desirable class of immigrants?" Not only was such legislation "directly at variance with our free institutions," added the *Trenton Sentinel*, but it was also a "disgrace to free America and a sop thrown to the barbarous, unchristian prejudice of hoodlums." Even the *New Orleans Louisianian*, published in a state where several hundred Chinese had settled, insisted that, although the Chinese had their faults, "this land is the common heritage of all races."[38] Not only editors but also prominent black leaders condemned legislation to exclude Chinese immigrants. Senator Blanche K. Bruce of Mississippi, representing a state where blacks and Chinese had briefly been agricultural competitors, felt obliged to condemn proposed Chinese exclusion acts as unnecessary, and, on at least one occasion, he voted against their adoption. Frederick Douglass and D. Augustus Straker, who taught at Howard University, refused to give their assent to legislation discriminating against any race. Even Booker T. Washington, whose opinion of the Chinese was somewhat unfavorable, publicly condemned Chinese exclusion acts as contrary to American ideals. Equally outspoken was the Reverend George Woodbey, a socialist, who refused to believe that keeping any immigrant group out of the United States, whether the group was Oriental or European, was good for America.[39]

Why had blacks expressed opposition to the various exclusion laws? Certainly it was not because of any great respect for the Chinese, for Orientals continued to be represented unfavorably in the Negro press. One answer is that some black journalists felt obliged to attack any legislation that was "barbarous in spirit and brutal in execution." Even if the Chinese were of dubious value as settlers, it was unjust and un-American to treat them as subhumans. John E. Bruce, writing under the pen-name of Bruce Grit, castigated those statutes "born of a spirit of narrowness and caste prejudice." In his opinion, racial prejudice on the part of whites explained why the Chinese had been singled out for exclusion, and it would be best for Negroes to disassociate themselves from discriminatory legislation. Perhaps most important to blacks was the belief that officially sanctioned mistreatment of Orientals was but a prelude of what was in store for Negroes. "The party that endorses the unjust laws against the Chinese," warned the *New York Weekly Witness*, "will not be just to the colored man or anyone else, except when it is convenient." As David Hellwig has noted, laws excluding nonwhite immigrants reinforced the idea that all non-Europeans should be subjugated, and this profoundly worried blacks.[40]

Negro sentiment on Chinese exclusion was atypical. In general, blacks of the late nineteenth and early twentieth centuries found the "moon-eyed Celestials" to be "absurd, unwholesome, and unacceptable [for] . . . Americanization." Less than six years after the enactment of the 1882 Chinese Exclusion Law, one Minnesota journal denounced both the "interdicted Celestials" and unscrupulous San Francisco customs inspectors for working in partnership to evade the law. According to this paper, numbers of Chinese regularly secured certificates enabling them to return to China. These documents supposedly were never used for the purposes intended; instead, they were illegally sold "to parties shipping fresh loads" of Chinese to the United States.[41] Given these sentiments, it was not surprising that the *Appeal* rejected the pleas of Chinese for the same sort of protection Americans were given in China. Ignoring massacres of Orientals in Wyoming, Oregon, and California, the April 2, 1893, issue of the *Appeal* acidly commented, "We cannot hire a bodyguard to protect every Chinaman."

The more Negroes came into contact with the "inscrutable" and "crafty" Chinese, the more they became persuaded that Orientals were not like other immigrants and were therefore of dubious value as Americans. Hard as he might try to understand the Chinese and as vigorous as he might be in opposing legislation excluding them from entry into the United States, Timothy Thomas Fortune, editor of the influential *New York Age*, admitted he could not rid himself of the belief that "there is something uncanny and frightening about Chinamen." Another black reiterated these views, announcing that the residents of San Francisco's Chinatown were "blocking up" the city's "sewers so as to manipulate the sewerage for manuring purposes."[42]

After the San Francisco earthquake of April 18, 1906, one black magazine reported that workers clearing the rubble in the Chinese quarter came upon scores of hidden opium dens and houses of prostitution. That some of these infamous places had been located in caves and tunnels hidden below the streets made the Chinese appear especially sinister, mysterious, and alien. In fact, from 1880 to 1935 almost every time the Chinese were mentioned in the black press, it was in connection with intrigue, prostitution, murder, the sale of opium or children for money, fan tan games, lotteries, smuggling, superstitious practices, shootings, or tong wars.[43] Therefore, it was only natural that one Los Angeles newspaper warned gullible Afro-Americans to avoid the omnipresent Chinese lottery proprietors who were "waxing fat off Sambo."[44]

Few blacks expressed disapproval of discriminatory naturalization laws that made it impossible for alien Chinese to become citizens. After all, many thought, these "moon-eyed strangers" were so very different from all others living in America. Had not one Chinese in Kansas seriously suggested that the barbarous custom of binding the feet of women "would be a good one to inaugurate in America?" And had it not been reported that Ah Fong, a Chinese millionaire, attempted to foment revolution in Hawaii in the 1880s, "his alleged purpose being to appropriate anything he c[ould] get his hands on during the excitement?" How could one grant citizenship to people upon whom Christianity has [not] made the least percepti[ble] impression," asked

Samuel S. Scottron, a black writer and inventor. After his return from a visit to the Chinese community of Phoenix, Arizona, in 1911, Booker T. Washington wrote, "the thing that most impres[sed] me . . . in regard to the Chinaman was the extent to which he is an alien in this country. I doubt whether any other portion of the population remains so thoroly [sic] foreign as is true of the Chinaman." Washington's observations were remarkably similar to those of Levi Coffin, a black bishop, who toured San Francisco in the 1890s and who concluded that the opium-smoking Chinese were not likely ever to adjust to the American way of life. As late as 1922, the *Chicago Whip*, which quite possibly was then the most militant black newspaper in the country, found itself unable to believe that the "backward" Chinese could ever absorb American civilization. Chinese people, it said, "come into this country and retain eating sticks, sandals, and queues for many years and they always think as Chinese."[45]

Even when the Chinese outwardly appeared to have been assimilated, insisted Mason Roberson, a newspaper writer, they still secretly retained their peculiar customs and strange beliefs. In 1932, after passing through San Francisco's Chinatown, Roberson reported his impression of the "dark, sinister, silent" section of town. At first glance, he admitted, Chinatown did not appear to be any great menace to the city. Tourists passing down Grant Avenue saw only speciality shops, restaurants, and exotic buildings. "China's immense filth and its overpowering symphony of odors have been diluted by a metriculous [sic] Board of Health," and so the typical visitor might well return to his home without any awareness of what was really going on in Chinatown. If however, the tourist examined the alleys hidden between the restaurants and ventured into houses and stores where the "windows are blinded with carefully drawn shades," as Roberson had done, he would "find vice in all its brutish pathos." Here one could see "old men sit[ting] in tiny sidewalk stores and blank inscrutable eyes behind jars of shark fins, snakes, and candied rice." Even worse, he might see the sleeping rooms of the Chinese, which Roberson luridly described as follows:

The air is a fog of cheap tobacco and opium. The smell of bodies long unwashed mingles with the odors of stale sweat and whiskey. Dirty ragged figures crouch around a fan-tan table under a single sickly electric light.

Along the shadowy wall, filthy mattresses without bedclothes hold emaciated figures, bony caricatures of men and women lost in poppy dreams.

A man slides in from the night, shivering horribly from nerves that burn for dope. His shaking fingers exchange silver for a package of "snow" and he disappears into the obscurity of a shadowfilled corner and watching over it all a fat proprietor glides silently about, seeing all, expressing nothing in the oily mask that is his face.

Little wonder that Roberson concluded that Chinatown was "not a pleasant place."[46]

Why did such unfavorable stereotypes persist for so long in the black press? No single factor can fully account for this hostility, but in part the answer lies in the way blacks viewed China. Periodically, articles appeared in Negro publications praising the Chinese for their inventiveness, their artistic contributions, their willingness to rent rooms to blacks, and their knowledge of medicine and drugs,[47] but more common were stories about overpopulation, brutality, famine, and poverty. According to the *Philadelphia Tribune*, food in China was so scarce in 1919 that some parents had been forced to sell their infants for sums as small as 60 cents. Writing in the *Norfolk Journal and Guide*, Timothy Thomas Fortune, who had visited the Far East, commented that "wages are so low in China that there are things to eat and the like which are purchased for the fraction of a penny." As late as 1934, S. A. Haynes, an Afro-American newspaper columnist, confidently asserted that "in China blood baths are as common as floods. War lords, bandit chieftains, and ambitious generals are tricked into pacts by so-called friendly rivals and assassinated without much ceremony."[48]

Two things about China especially bothered blacks. One was that the country was the object of so much wasted missionary activity. Untold sums of money were being sent to save the Chinese, who had no real desire to become Christians. Blacks felt that this money might better be spent on educating Negro Americans. Second, and more importantly, blacks resented the obsequiousness of the people living in China. In their own homeland, it was reported, the Chinese had fewer rights than the Europeans who exploited them. Foreigners paid no taxes, respected no Chinese laws, and tolerated no Oriental customers in their restaurants. Any Chinese could even be booted off a train if a barely literate alien desired his seat. And to curry favor with these unworthy foreigners, some Chinese agreed to bar Afro-Americans from their restaurants and hotels, even though this decision would arouse the "enmity of blacks and affect the whites not at all." According to Afro-Americans, the only time the Chinese had ever voiced strong objections to outside intruders was during the Boxer Rebellion. This puzzled and disgusted blacks, who subconsciously might have been simultaneously chastising themselves for having to put up with similar indignities in the United States.[49]

Perhaps because black adults had such a low opinion of the Chinese, they did not seem to object when their children openly taunted Orientals. Mary Church Terrell, the distinguished black civil rights activist, remembered seeing Negro youth join their white peers in singing crude doggerel about the alleged Chinese penchant for eating rats. Walter Stevens, a black who worked for the government, confessed that when growing up in Boston in the early 1900s, he would sometimes surprise a Chinese man and grab and tug at his pig tail.[50]

Yet another reason for hostility to the Chinese was that in some parts of America they continued to be economic competitors. In many towns in the United States, there was a Chinese laundry, and this took away business from Negro washerwomen. This was no trivial problem, for in some communities as many as a third of the adult black female workers were listed as washerwomen. In addition, it became increasingly fashionable for whites to replace their black maids, cooks, and butlers with Chinese domestics.[51] In Colorado, during the 1880s, several Denver restaurants fired their black waiters, janitors, and dishwashers and hired "John Chinaman" to take their places. Even in some barbershops, Afro-Americans were losing out to the Chinese.[52]

White employers alleged that the Chinese were cleaner, politer, more industrious, and more reliable than Negroes. Blacks retorted that these claims were false and that the "non-consuming Chinese" had been hired solely because they would work for "five cents a day," which was "less than human beings [*sic*] can do." No one who wanted an attractive "home and who insist[ed] upon ample food for his family," complained the *Washington Colored American*, was able to toil for the starvation wages of the Chinese. So, as had been true three decades before, blacks denounced the "Celestials" for representing a menace to American labor.[53]

On at least four occasions, Chinese were employed as Pullman club car porters to prevent blacks from unionizing. Because of these activities, Robert Abbott, editor of the influential *Chicago Defender*, sharply castigated Pullman Company officials. Asa Philip Randolph, the organizer of the sleeping car porters, expressed alarm that "the introduction of . . . [nonunionized] Oriental laborers [represented] . . . a threat to American standards of health and decency." Pressure from Afro-Americans, Sinophobes, and Northern politicians courting Negro votes forced the Pullman Company to back down. But until the 1930s Negro porters were frequently warned not to join any union lest they lose their jobs to Orientals.[54]

Yet another reason blacks disliked the Chinese was that they believed the Orientals were prejudiced against Afro-Americans. Apparently, there was some basis for this commonly held belief. Negro newspapers frequently reported that Chinese restaurant owners refused to serve black customers. Even in the 1950s, blacks told Harold Isaacs that they considered the Chinese to be "international Uncle Toms, bootlickers of the white men," because they aped the Jim Crow practices of whites. Negroes told Chinese sociologist Rose Hum Lee that the Chinese were as prejudiced as whites. Professor Lee's research substantiated their claim. She found that Chinese were reluctant to hire blacks, to have Negro neighbors, or to develop friendships with Afro-Americans. Other scholars have also found evidence that the Chinese were quick to absorb American prejudices.[55]

Afro-Americans did not need sociologists to tell them that the Chinese did not like them, for they clearly sensed this antipathy.

"It is quite remarkable," acidly commented the *New York Age* of January 26, 1905, "how easily Chinamen and other foreigners catch on to the notion that it is money in their pockets to treat Afro-Americans [with] . . . disdain." "The Chinese," added the March 27, 1909, issue of the *Indianapolis Freeman*, "seem to polarize about the white race" and to hinder "the Negro's progress."

In Washington, D.C., in the spring of 1906, a black was nearly lynched after a Chinese accused him of stealing. Several years later, in Cleveland a Negro was shot to death when a Chinese restaurant owner mistakenly thought he was pilfering food. The *Chicago Defender* was indignant to learn in 1921 that a Chinese prisoner refused to share his jail cell with a black. The *Defender* concluded that the Chinese learned he would lose status by not scorning blacks. Additional unpleasant incidents were occasionally mentioned in the black press.[56] It was probably fortunate that blacks did not know that since there is no Chinese word for Negro or African, they were frequently called *hok guey* or "black devils."[57]

It would be unfair to conclude that the Chinese were never given any favorable coverage in the black press. To be sure, unfavorable items did predominate, but Negroes did find some Chinese qualities to be admirable and worthy of emulation. Perhaps most impressive to blacks was the willingness of the Chinese to cooperate with each other and to work together for their common good. Negro periodicals frequently warned their readers that constant bickering among black leaders was retarding the progress of the race. Thus, it was only natural that the "supreme willingness [of the Chinese] to help one another" would appeal to Afro-Americans. Admittedly, the status of Orientals in America was low, Negroes conceded, but because the Asians stuck "close together in all their social and business relations," they were making significant economic gains.[58] "We ought to learn something from the Chinese," commented the *Pittsburgh Courier* of April 7, 1928. "Although a small group in this country, they control more restaurant business catering to the general public in any large city than the Negroes have in the entire country."

What accounted for this remarkable success of Chinese restaurants and laundries? First and foremost, it was noted in the black press that the Chinese were polite and industrious. Attentive to every need of their customers, they gave good service and were able to win repeat business. Moreover, unlike many Negro merchants, they actively sought white customers, for they realized that their prosperity depended upon making money from the "dominant" element of society. Equally important was that because the Chinese were thrifty, they were able to reduce their prices—and overhead—to such a level that they could undersell their competitors and therefore attract business from bargain hunters. It would, therefore, be wise for the enterprising black businessman to study their methods and borrow those of their techniques suitable for his store.[59]

Stories about Orientals traditionally represented them as being parsimonious—even stingy—but there were a few exceptions to this unflattering view. After the 1906 San Francisco earthquake, the *New York Age* reported that Chinese-Americans contributed $2,700 for the mayor's relief funds. This, the *Age* observed, contrasted greatly with "the brutal treatment" they experienced on the Pacific Coast.[60]

An even more celebrated example of Chinese generosity concerned one Lemon Lee Sing, an elderly Chinese laundryman in New York. Sing won the attention of the black press when it became known that he had applied for permission to adopt Firman Smith, a black boy he had found sleeping in a hallway. The child apparently had been abandoned by his parents and had no place to go, and Sing had taken him into his home, fed him, clothed him and enrolled him in the local public school. Although the judge assigned to the case originally was reluctant to give custody of the boy to a sixty-eight-year-old man, he was so moved by the testimony he heard that he agreed it would be best to allow Sing to adopt the boy.[61] Circulation of this story improved the image of the Chinese in Afro-American journals, but its effect was only temporary.[62]

Equally temporary was Afro-American interest in the problem of the Mississippi Chinese. Some descendants of the Chinese who migrated to Mississippi after the Civil War, and their

relatives later brought to the state, continued to live in Mississippi
Delta counties in the twentieth century, A few of the Chinese
merchants had families and sought to educate their children in
white schools. In 1920, the attorney general of Mississippi
ruled that Chinese were "colored" and had to attend the same
schools as blacks. Four years later Gong Lum, a wealthy and
respected businessman in Rosedale, sued the Coahoma County
School Board in an effort to have his progeny enrolled in the
local white schools. The Mississippi district court ruled in favor
of Gong Lum, but this verdict was overturned by the state
supreme court. The U.S. Supreme Court also ruled against
Gong Lum. To prevent Orientals from losing face by having to
attend black schools, Rosedale and several other communities
eventually established separate schools for the Chinese.[63] When
compared with the interest blacks manifested in the Japanese
school problems in California discussed in the next chapter, it is
noteworthy that few Afro-American newspapers commented
extensively on the problems of the Mississippi Chinese. As
might be expected, since the Chinese objected to the stigma of
attending schools with blacks, there was little reason to be
sympathetic with their grievance.[64]

What then was the general image of the Chinese in the black
press from 1850 to 1935? Despite periodic praise as expressed in
the Lemon Lee Sing case, the image of the Chinese during these
eighty-five years was a negative one. As suggested above, there
were several reasons for the emergence of this unfavorable stereotype. First and foremost, blacks feared Chinese economic competition, believing that the Asians "degrade labor because their
wants are so few that they can afford to work for a third of what
is necessary to support an American."[65] This fear was not an idle
one, for Chinese domestics,[66] laundrymen, and even Pullman
porters sometimes competed with Afro-Americans and occasionally, the availability of Orientals as laborers—and strike-
breakers was used as an excuse to pay Negroes lower wages.

Even in areas like Phoenix, Arizona, where Negroes and
Chinese were not engaged in economic competiton, the two
races eyed each other suspiciously. Although Booker T. Washington admired the industriousness of Chinese merchants, he

was perplexed by the customs of the Arizona Chinese. The more he observed the Chinese, the more he concluded that blacks and Chinese were different. Unlike the "sojourners" from China, the Afro-Americans had "the same moral and political standards as the white man." Washington's view was repeatedly expressed by Negro journalists who maintained that the Chinese "cannot or will not become a part of occidental civilization." Blacks saw themselves as more "American than the orientals."[67]

Furthermore, many blacks were devout Protestants affiliated with fundamentalist sects, and they were unable to rid themselves of the image of the Chinese as heathens who smoked opium, conducted gambling lotteries, desecrated the Sabbath, engaged in the white slave trade, and participated in tong wars. Not content to confine their vices to Chinatown, one Afro-American San Francisco newspaper complained, Chinese lottery proprietors, eager "to pile up huge bank accounts," sought to corrupt gullible Negro dishwashers and bootblacks by teaching them to waste their hard-earned "nickels and dimes."[68]

Finally, the blacks disliked the Chinese because they believed that the Chinese were prejudiced against Negroes. As far as is known, there are no data on Chinese views of Afro-Americans during the eighty-five years studied. Evidently, sociologists never considered this question until after World War II. However, every study located for the years after World War II indicates that social mixing between the two was infrequent. These works also indicate that there was notable anti-Negro bias in the Chinese community. There is no reason to believe that this prejudice suddenly developed after 1945. Thus, Afro-Americans before World War II were probably correct in sensing that the Chinese had accepted the whites' prejudices against them.[69]

Altogether, therefore, it is not surprising that in 1928, when sociologists first began to ask blacks to rank various ethnic groups,[70] the Chinese were not considered desirable either as marriage partners or as friends. Over the next thirty years, blacks consistently ranked the Chinese among the most undesirable of all the ethnic groups surveyed. When the historical origins are considered, the results of these surveys should come as no surprise. The historical background, however, has generally been neglected in studies of social interactions between Chinese and blacks.[71] The next chapters of this study examine black perceptions of the Japanese and Mexicans, and of Italians and Jews in the South.

NOTES

1. *The Freedman* (Boston) 2 (June 1865): 1.

2. In 1860, there were 4,086 Negroes in California, about 1,000 of whom lived in San Francisco. The black population of California grew at a slow rate until the twentieth century. On the other hand, the Chinese population of California grew rapidly in the 1860s, and by 1870 there were nearly 60,000 Chinese in the state. Eugene Berwanger, *The Frontier Against Slavery* (Urbana, Ill., 1967), p. 74; Betty L. Sung, *Mountain of Gold: The Chinese in America* (New York, 1967), p. 42.

3. Rudolph Lapp, *Blacks in Gold Rush California* (New Haven, Conn., 1977), pp. 104–5, 109–10. See also the positive comments on the Chinese in James Williams, *Life and Adventures of James Williams, a Fugitive Slave* (Philadelphia, 1893), p. 109.

4. The black murderer was not prosecuted because there were no white witnesses to the crime. At that time only testimony from whites was acceptable in court. Lapp, *Blacks*, p. 88.

5. Letters from "Nubia" of San Francisco, August 10, 1854, and February 28, 1855, quoted in *Frederick Douglass' Paper*, September 23, 1854, and April 6, 1855; Leon Litwack, *North of Slavery* (Chicago, 1961), pp. 167–68; *New Orleans Tribune*, November 12, 1864, cited in David Hellwig, "Black Reactions to Chinese Immigration and the Anti-Chinese Movement: 1850–1910," *Amerasia* 6 (1979): 34, hereafter cited as "Chinese."

6. In the mid-1860s, the California legislature enacted a law requiring school districts to establish a separate school for Negroes, Mongolians, and Indians if there were ten or more of these children in a school district. In 1870, school boards were no longer required to educate Chinese children. Two years later, white schools had to admit black and Indian children if there were no separate schools for these youngsters in a district. Segregated schools lasted in San Francisco until 1875. Fifteen years later, in 1890, in the case of *Wysinger* v. *Crookshank* all segregated schools in California were outlawed. See, for example, Robert Heizer and Alan Almquist, *The Other Californians* (Berkeley,

Calif., 1971), pp. 62-63, 133-34, 175-76; Charles Wollenberg, *All Deliberate Speed: Segregation and Exclusion in California Schools, 1855-1975* (Berkeley, Calif., 1976), pp. 14, 33; Elmer Rusco, *Good Time Coming* (Westport, Conn., 1975), pp. 82-85; W. Sherman Savage, *Blacks in the West* (Westport, Conn., 1976), Chapter 8.

7. W.H.C. Stephenson to editor, June 5, 1867, *San Francisco Elevator*, June 21, 1867; E. T. to editor, May 23, 1873, ibid., May 31, 1873; Gary BeDunnah, *A History of the Chinese in Nevada 1855-1904* (San Francisco, 1973), p. 83; Kenneth Goode, *California's Black Pioneers* (Santa Barbara, Calif., 1974), pp. 82-84; Rusco, *Good Time*, p. 84.

8. Hall to editor, *San Francisco Elevator*, November 19, December 17, 1869; C. P. of San Francisco to editor, ibid., March 29, 1873; ibid., May 24, 1873. See also *San Francisco Pacific Appeal*, May 17, 1862, February 10, 1872.

9. *San Francisco Elevator*, November 19, 1869, March 29, 1873. See also Douglas Daniels, *Pioneer Urbanites: A Social and Cultural History of Black San Francisco* (Philadelphia, 1980), pp. 32, 34.

10. *San Francisco Elevator*, August 30, 1867, August 27, November 19, 1869, July 9, 1870, May 24, 1873. See also *Washington Bee*, March 14, 1885: *Nicodemus* (Kansas) *Western Cyclone*, April 14, 1887.

11. *San Francisco Elevator*, December 17, 1869, July 9, 1870, March 29, April 26, May 3, 17, June 14, 1873. See also letter from T. D. of Idaho City, Idaho, August 6, 1867, quoted in *San Francisco Pacific Appeal*, August 17, 1867; Harris Newmark, *Sixty Years in Southern California*, ed. by Maurice and Marco Newmark, 3d. ed. (Boston, 1930), p. 123; Leigh Johnsen, "Equal Rights and the Heathen 'Chinee': Black Activism in San Francisco, 1865-1875," *Western Historical Quarterly*, 11 (1980): 61, 68.

12. Letter from "Nubia" of San Francisco, February 28, 1855, quoted in *Frederick Douglass' Paper*, April 6, 1855; *San Francisco Elevator*, May 3, June 14, 1873; *San Francisco Pacific Appeal*, May 31, 1873; Francis Lortie, *San Francisco's Black Community, 1870-1890* (San Francisco, 1973), pp. 5, 11-12, 37-38, 40, hereafter cited as Lortie, *San Francisco*.

13. *San Francisco Elevator*, October 15, 24, 1869; letter from Hall to President and Members of the National Labor Convention of Colored Men of the United States, ibid., November 19, 1869; letter of Hall to editor, ibid., December 17, 1869; *New York National Anti-Slavery Standard*, December 18, 1869; Rusco, *Good Time*, p. 110.

14. Philip Foner and Ronald Lewis, eds., *The Black Worker*, 5 vols. (Philadelphia, 1978), 2: 12-13, 54.

15. *Christian Recorder*, quoted in ibid., 1: 389. Frederick Douglass

expressed similar sentiments in 1881, when he noted that those who hated the Chinese were the same people who also disliked blacks. Philip Foner, ed., *The Life and Writings of Frederick Douglass* 5 vols. (New York, 1954), 4: 350; Hellwig, "Chinese," p. 31.

16. *The Unwelcome Immigrant: The American Image of the Chinese, 1785-1882* (Berkeley, Calif., 1969), p. vii. See also *Sacramento Record-Union* (n.d.), quoted in *Topeka Kansas State Ledger*, February 2, 1894; Gunter Barth, *Bitter Strength, a History of the Chinese in the United States, 1850-1870* (Cambridge, Mass., 1964); Sung, *Mountain of Gold*, pp. 22-42; Johnsen, "Equal Rights," pp. 67-68.

17. According to the 1920 census, as late as that year blacks and Orientals continued to compete for jobs as porters, servants, waiters, laundresses and laundry operators, janitors, and garden laborers. The 1920 figures combine totals for Japanese and Chinese, but it is reasonable to assume that the Chinese represented serious job competitors in at least half of these occupations. J. McFarline Erwin, *The Participation of the Negro in the Community Life of Los Angeles* (San Francisco, 1973), pp. 25-26. See also Daniels, *Pioneer Urbanites*, pp. 34, 67; Paul Ong, "An Ethnic Trade: The Chinese Laundries in Early California," *Journal of Ethnic Studies* 8 (1981): 95, 99-108.

18. Alexander Saxton, *The Indispensable Enemy: Labor and the Anti-Chinese Movement in California* (Berkeley, Calif., 1971), pp. 4-5; *San Francisco Elevator*, October 24, 1874; *New Orleans Weekly Louisianian*, June 26, 1875; *San Francisco Pacific Appeal*, May 31, 1873; *Washington Colored American*, March 8, 1902; Lortie, *San Francisco*, pp. 11-12, 49. See also "Kelly Miller Says," *Philadelphia Tribune*, July 28, 1927; Lucy Salmon, *Domestic Service* (New York, 1897), p. 176 n. 1.

19. Rudolph Lapp, "Negro Rights Activities in Gold Rush California," *California Historical Society Quarterly* 45 (1966): 5-13; Miller, *Unwelcome Immigrant*, p. 199; Luther Spoehr, "Sambo and the Heathen Chinese: Californians' Racial Stereotypes of the Late 1870s," *Pacific Historical Review* 43 (1973): 196 n. 32; Cheng-tsu Wu, ed., *"Chink!"* (New York, 1972), pp. 12-13, 114-15, 124-27; Rusco, *Good Time*, p. 106. For an interesting discussion on the image of the Chinese, see Ronald Takaki, *Iron Cages* (New York, 1979), Chapter 10, especially pages 216-17.

20. Haight eventually changed his mind about black suffrage, but he continued to oppose giving the vote to the Chinese, Spoehr. "Sambo," p. 197; Cheng-tsu Wu, ed., *"Chink!,"* pp. 109-13; Barth, *Bitter Strength*, p. 42; *San Francisco Elevator*, August 30, December 20, 1867, March 29, 1873.

21. BeDunnah, *Chinese in Nevada*, p. 6.

22. "Willie Wild to editor," June 20, 1869, quoted in *New Orleans Daily Picayune*, July 11, 1869. See also Wild's letters of January 19 and April 28, 1869, in ibid., February 7, May 18, 1869; Lawrence D. Rice, *The Negro in Texas, 1874-1900* (Baton Rouge, La., 1971), p. 161; Robert Athearn, *In Search of Canaan: Black Migration to Kansas, 1879-1880* (Lawrence, Kans., 1978), p. 105; Jean Scarpaci, "The Italian Immigrant: An Answer to Louisiana's Post War Plantation Labor Problem" (unpublished paper presented at the Citadel Conference on the New South, 1978), p. 4.

23. Lucy Cohen, "Entry of Chinese to the Lower South from 1865 to 1870," *Southern Studies* 17 (1978): 11.

24. In 1869, there was a conference in Memphis that considered the question of Chinese immigration. James Roark, *Masters Without Slaves* (New York, 1977), p. 166; Carl Osthaus, "From the Old South to the New South: The Editorial Career of William Tappan Thompson," *Southern Quarterly* 14 (1976): 258, Takaki, *Iron Cages*, p. 219.

25. Despite the claim that the Chinese were infidel, the first Chinese brought to Louisiana in 1865 were from the Philippine Islands and were likely Christians. Cohen, "Entry of the Chinese," p. 13-18, 22; Scarpaci, "Italian Immigrant," p. 6; *New Orleans Daily Picayune*, June 5, July 7, 13 1869; Vernon Lane Wharton, *The Negro in Mississippi* (New York, 1965), pp. 97-99; George F. Seward, *Chinese Immigration in Its Social and Economic Aspects* (New York, 1881), p. 421; James W. Loewen, *The Mississippi Chinese: Between Black and White* (Cambridge, Mass., 1971), p. 22; Joe Gray Taylor, *Louisiana Reconstructed* (Baton Rouge, La., 1975), p. 391.

26. Frederick Douglass never seriously worried—not even in the 1880s—that the Chinese would drive the Negro from the sugar and cottonfields of Louisiana and Mississippi. Foner, *Douglass*, 4: 325; *San Francisco Elevator*, December 3, 1869; *Charleston* (S.C.) *Missionary Record* (n.d.), quoted in ibid., November 26, 1869; Barth, *Bitter Strength*, pp. 189-90; Hellwig, "Chinese," pp. 26-27.

27. *Little Rock Arkansas Freeman*, October 5, 1869; *New Orleans Daily Picayune*, June 5, July 7, 1869; letters from Hall, August 17, October 22, 1869, to editor, *San Francisco Elevator*, August 27, October 29, 1869; Hall to President and Members of the National Convention of Colored Men of the United States, ibid., November 19, 1869; Miller, *Unwelcome Immigrant*, p. 152. See also *Nicodemus* (Kans.) *Western Cyclone*, May 12, 1887.

28. Lucy Cohen estimates that in 1867 it cost $50 to $60 to bring a Chinese laborer to Louisiana, Cohen. "Entry of Chinese," pp. 18, 31.

29. Nell Painter, *Exodusters* (New York, 1977), p. 237.
30. Osthaus, "Old South to the New South," p. 258; *Herald*, quoted in Winston Kinsey, "Immigrants in Texas Agriculture During Reconstruction," *Agricultural History* 53 (1979): 137-38; Claude Nolen, *The Negro's Image in the South: The Anatomy of White Supremacy* (Lexington, Ky., 1967), p. 174; Taylor, *Louisiana Reconstructed*, p. 391; Loewen, *Mississippi Chinese*, pp. 1-2, 25-26; Scarpaci, "Italian Immigrant," p. 5; Wharton, *Negro in Mississippi*, pp. 97-99, 125; *New Orleans Weekly Louisianian*, November 2, 1871; William Ivy Hair, *Bourbonism and Agrarian Protest: Louisiana Politics, 1877-1900* (Baton Rouge, La., 1969), p. 95; Edward Rhoads, "The Chinese in Texas," *Southwestern Historical Quarterly* 81 (1977): 1-6.
31. Throckmorton quoted in Kinsey, "Immigrants in Texas," p. 137.
32. Wharton, *Negro in Mississippi*, pp. 97-99; Hair, *Bourbonism*, p. 95; Salley Ken, "The Chinese Community of Augusta, Georgia from 1873 to 1971," *Richmond County History* 4 (1972): 51-60; E. Merton Coulter, *The South During Reconstruction* (Baton Rouge, La., 1947), p. 105-6; Rhoads "Chinese," pp. 6-7; George Pozzetta, "Foreigners in Florida: A Study of Immigration Promotion, 1865-1910," *Florida Historical Quarterly* 53 (1974): 171.
33. As late as 1904, Georgia editors and planters were warning about the perils of importing Chinese laborers to the state to replace blacks. Edward Gaston, "A History of the Negro Wage Earner in Georgia, 1880-1940" (Ph.D. dissertation, Emory University, 1957), p. 158. See also Willard Gatewood, "Strangers and the Southern Eden," in *Ethnic Minorities in Gulf Coast Society*, Jerrell Shofner and Linda Ellsworth, eds., (Pensacola, Fla., 1979), p. 3.
34. Quoted in R. D. McKenzie, *Oriental Exclusion* (Chicago 1928), p. 27.
35. The Chinese Exclusion Act of 1882, which barred nearly all immigrants from China for a period of ten years, was renewed in 1892. Ten years later, in 1902, the provisions of the act were extended indefinitely, and, in 1924, Congress passed an even more rigorous exclusion act.
36. *San Francisco Vindicator*, June 25, November 17, 1887; *Washington Colored American*, December 28, 1901; *Nicodemus Western Cyclone*, May 12, 1887, Lortie, *San Francisco*, p. 37, 39, 43.
37. Even the *Pacific Appeal* had reservations about the justice of excluding all Chinese from the United States. The paper seemed to fear that once the Chinese had departed, white laborers would insist "that the 'Negro must go also.' " *San Francisco Pacific Appeal*, May 31, 1873; March 1, 15, 1879; February 28, 1880. For the anti-Chinese position of the Irish press, see *Boston Pilot*, June 24, 1876.

38. *Washington New Era,* July 14, 1870; *New Orleans Weekly Louisianian,* March 8, 15, 1879, April 8, 15, May 20, 1882; *Huntsville* (Ala.) *Gazette,* April 8, 1882; *Trenton* (N.J.) *Sentinel,* April 15, 22, May 18, 1882; *New York Freeman,* May 15, 1886 *New York Age,* August 3, 1905; *Atlanta Independent,* October 19, 1907.

39. *Congressional Record,* 45th Congress, 3d Session (February 14, 1879), pp. 1314, 1400; David Hellwig, "Building a Black Nation: The Role of Immigrants in the Thought and Rhetoric of Booker T. Washington," *Mississippi Quarterly* 31 (1978): 543, 545; Philip Foner, *American Socialism and Black Americans* (Westport, Conn., 1977), pp. 165–66 and Foner, *Douglass,* 4: 117; Hellwig, "Chinese," pp. 28–31, 36.

40. *New York Age,* August 3, 1905; "Bruce Grit's Column," *Washington Colored American,* July 14, 1900; *New York Weekly Witness* (n.d.), quoted in *New York Globe,* July 12, 1884; *Leavenworth Advocate,* August 3, 1889; *Washington Bee,* September 30, 1905.

41. *St. Paul* (Minn.) *Western Appeal,* April 14, 1888; *Topeka Kansas State Ledger,* September 21, 1901; *Washington Colored American,* December 28, 1901. In the 1890s, the *Western Appeal* shortened its title and became the *St. Paul Appeal.*

42. *New York Age,* August 10, 1905; *San Francisco Vindicator,* June 25, 1887; Hellwig, "Chinese," p. 42.

43. *San Francisco Vindicator,* June 11, 1887; *San Francisco Pacific Appeal,* October 25, 1879; *Chicago Times* (n.d.), quoted in *Topeka Tribune,* October 22, 1880; *Indianapolis Freeman,* April 2, 1892; November 13, 1907; *New York Age,* November 1, 1890, May 2, 1912; *New York Commercial Advertiser* (n.d.), quoted in *Washington Bee,* November 22, 1884; *Washington Bee,* March 14, 1885; *Baxter Springs* (Kans.) *Southern Argus,* July 23, 1891; *Des Moines Iowa Bystander,* July 27, 1900; *Topeka Kansas State Ledger,* September 21, 1901; *Alexander's Magazine* (Boston) 2 (May 1906): 21; *Philadelphia Tribune,* June 29, 1912, May 3, 1919; *Baltimore Afro-American,* December 24, 1920; *Chicago Whip,* August 12, 1922; *Los Angeles California Eagle,* October 14, 1916, October 12, December 28, 1918, December 17, 1921, June 13, 1924, May 22, 1925, June 24, July 1, December 9, 1927, July 19, 1929; *Chicago Defender,* August 1, 1925, April 20, 1927, December 29, 1934; *Kansas City* (Kans.) *Call,* May 23, 1930; *Houston Informer,* March 22, October 4, 1930.

44. *Los Angeles California Eagle,* April 27, 1918.

45. *Wichita National Reflector,* November 6, 1897; *St. Paul Western Appeal,* July 16, 1887; *Washington Bee,* November 22, 1884; *Washington Colored American,* July 28, 1900; S[amuel] Scottron, *Chinese vs. Negroes as American Citizens* (New York?, 1899?), pamphlet found in Widener Library, Harvard University; Booker T. Washington, "The Race Prob-

lem," in *The Independent* 71 (October 26, 1911): 911; *Indianapolis Freeman*, June 20, 1914; *Chicago Whip*, August 26, 1922; Hellwig, "Chinese," p. 34.

46. Mason Roberson, "Seeing San Francisco: Chinatown," *San Francisco Spokesman*, November 10, 1932.

47. *Medical and Surgical Reporter* (n.d.), quoted in *San Francisco Vindicator*, May 2, 1887; *Baltimore Afro-American*, September 16, 1905, January 14, 1933. Chinese-American doctors and druggists regularly advertised in some black journals. See, for example issues of the *San Francisco Pacific Appeal* for summer 1878, the *Topeka Times-Observer* for summer 1892, the *Topeka Kansas State Ledger* for spring 1899, the *Oakland Sunshine* for 1915, and the *Atlanta Independent* for 1928–1931. In San Francisco, black musicians sometimes took rooms in Chinese-owned lodging houses. Daniels, *Pioneer Urbanites*, p. 97.

48. *San Francisco Pacific Appeal*, January 16, 1875; *Indianapolis Freeman*, December 21, 1907; *Philadelphia Tribune*, May 3, 1919; *Omaha Progress*, June 21, 1890; *Fortune*, "The Way of the World," *Norfolk Journal and Guide*, March 5, 1927; *Cleveland Gazette*, February 13, 1932; S. A. Haynes, "World Horizon," *Philadelphia Tribune*, August 2, 1934.

49. *New York Age*, December 26, 1891; *Baltimore Afro-American*, July 4, 1925; *Chicago Defender*, January 28, 1928, March 11, 1933.

50. Hellwig, "Chinese," p. 35.

51. Newmark, *Sixty Years*, p. 123; *Washington Bee*, November 29, 1884; *Savannah Tribune*, January 9, 1892; *Baltimore Afro-American*, September 14, 1895, June 12, 1925; *Indianapolis World*, May 1, 1897; *Washington Colored American*, December 28, 1901; Lorenzo Greene and Carter G. Woodson, *The Negro Wage Earner* (New York, 1969), pp. 96–97.

52. *Washington Bee*, July 25, 1855; *Denver Argus* (n.d.), quoted in ibid., July 9, 1887, *Pittsburgh Courier*, April 7, 1928. Until the 1900s, whites regularly patronized black barbers.

53. *Washington Colored American*, December 28, 1901; *Voice of the Negro* (Atlanta), 3 (1906): 621; *Richmond Planet*, February 19, 1909); Greene and Woodson, *Negro*, pp. 96–97.

54. *New York Age*, January 14, 1928; *Kansas City Call*, May 31, 1929; *Los Angeles California Eagle*, April 11, 1930; *Philadelphia Tribune*, May 1, 1930, June 3, 1933; Roi Ottley, *The Lonely Warrior: The Life and Times of Robert S. Abbott* (Chicago, 1955), p. 137. For the view that the menace of Chinese porters was overemphasized, see Loren Miller, "On Second Thought," *Los Angeles California Eagle*, March 3, 1933.

55. See, for example, Harold Isaacs, *Scratches on Our Minds* (New

York, 1958), pp. 83, 87, 394; Melford Weiss, *Valley City, a Chinese Community in America* (Cambridge, Mass., 1974), pp. 126-27, 240; Rose Hum Lee, *The Chinese in the United States* (Hong Kong, 1960), pp. 111-12, 371-72; D. U. Yuan, "Voluntary Segregation: A Study of New York Chinatown," in Milton Barron, ed., *Minorities in a Changing World* (New York, 1967), pp. 263-76; Louis Wirth, "The Problem of Minority Groups," in Robert K. Yin, ed., *Race, Creed, Color or National Origin* (Itasca, Ill., 1973), pp. 49-54. See also Hellwig, "Chinese," pp. 37, 43.

56. *New York Age*, April 12, 1906; *Philadelphia Tribune*, September 13, 1913; *Cleveland Gazette*, February 16, 1924; *Chicago Defender* article cited in David Hellwig, "Afro-American Reactions to the Japanese and Anti-Japanese Movement, 1906-1924," *Phylon* 38 (1977): 103. For cases of blacks murdering Chinese, see *Philadelphia Tribune*, October 2, 1930, and BeDunnah, *Chinese in Nevada*, p. 76.

57. The Chinese also had an unflattering name for whites. Ben Fong Torres, "Introduction," to Cheng-tsu Wu, ed., *"Chink!,"* pp. ix-x. See also *Topeka Kansas State Ledger*, July 15, 1899.

58. *Los Angeles California Eagle*, February 28, 1914; *New York Age*, April 2, 1914. See also Roy Wilkins, "Talking It Over," *Kansas City Call*, September 16, 1932.

59. *Baltimore Afro-American*, September 23, 1911; William Jones, "Day by Day," ibid., April 24, 1925; Ralph Matthews, "Baltimore Has a Chinatown Too," ibid.., June 26, 1926; Washington, "Race Problem," p. 910; *New York Age*, May 23, 1907; April 2, 1914; *Atlanta Independent*, February, 7, 1914, March 27, 1915; *Kansas City Call*, September 20, 1919; *Negro World* (New York), June 24, 1922; "Kelly Miller Says," *Philadelphia Tribune*, July 28, 1927; George Schuyler, "Views and Reviews," *Pittsburgh Courier*, September 3, 1928.

60. *New York Age*, April 26, 1906.

61. *Chicago Defender*, October 22, 1927; *Pittsburgh Courier*, October 22, 1927. There was also praise for Der Jong, "a trusting old Celestial" who always gave free food to those "down on their luck," and for Sam Lee, a Chinese restaurant owner in Washington, D.C. Despite threats on his life, Lee refused to fire one of his black employees. These threats were not always idle ones, for after one Chicago Chinese restaurant served Afro-Americans it was dynamited. See *Baltimore Afro-American*, August 4, 1928; *Chicago Defender*, October 26, 1929; *Philadelphia Tribune*, April 7, 1932.

62. Black newspapers made no mention of the trials and tribulations of Charley Sing, a Chinese laundryman, in getting permission to marry Lillie Lambert, a black woman, in Mobile, Alabama. See *Mobile Register*

(white newspaper), October 15, 1913. In San Francisco, Jean Ng, a black woman who had married a Chinese man, was buried in a Chinese cemetery. Daniels, *Pioneer Urbanites*, p. 97.

63. The U.S. Supreme Court decision so offended the Lum Family that they moved to Elaine, Arkansas. Separate schools for Chinese existed in Mississippi for more than two decades. Loewen, *Mississippi Chinese*, pp. 66–67; *Tulsa Star*, February 28, 1920.

64. *Chicago Defender*, October 22, 1927; *Pittsburgh Courier*, October 22, 1927.

65. Letter from "Nubia" of San Francisco (n.d.), quoted in *Frederick Douglass' Paper*, April 13, 1855.

66. Salmon, *Domestic Service*, p. 176.

67. Washington, "Race Problem," p. 911; *Washington Colored American*, December 28, 1901; *Chicago Whip*, August 26, 1922. See also Roger Daniels and Harry Kitano, *American Racism* (Englewood Cliffs, N.J., 1970), p. 71.

68. *San Francisco Spokesman*, October 19, 1933.

69. See notes 55 and 57 above.

70. Typically, students are asked anonymously to list traits they ascribe to various ethnic groups. Responses are tabulated and each group is ranked; the more positive the stereotype, the higher the rank.

71. For examples of these surveys, see Emory Bogardus, *Immigration and Race Attitudes* (Boston, 1928), quoted in Eugene and Ruth Hartley, *Fundamentals of Social Psychology* (New York, 1959), p. 434; Max Meenes, "A Comparison of Racial Stereotypes of 1935 and 1942," *Journal of Social Psychology* 17 (1943): 327–36; J. Stanley Gray and Anthony H. Thompson, "The Ethnic Prejudices of White and Negro College Students," *Journal of Abnormal and Social Psychology* 48 (1953): 311–13; Alvin Goins and Max Meenes, "Ethnic and Class Preferences Among College Negroes," *Journal of Negro Education* 29 (1960): 128–33.

2 THE JAPANESE

As was the case with the Chinese, most blacks had little direct contact with the Japanese. Less than 1 percent of Afro-Americans lived in California, the home of nearly all Japanese in the United States.[1] (See Table 1.) Nonetheless, from time to time the Negro press did consider the Japanese question as it did all issues of national importance. As the *Indianapolis Freeman* observed about one of the incidents promoting discord between Issei and American, "The Japs seem to be furnishing the United States [with a] second race question."[2]

Apparently, the first black newspaper to concern itself with the Japanese was the *San Francisco Elevator*. Extant issues of the journal, which was edited by Philip Bell, do not mention Japanese immigrants to California, but in 1867 the paper printed letters from Peter K. Cole, an American in Yokohama, who provided the *Elevator*'s subscribers with their first look at the way people lived in the "Mikado's kingdom." On the whole, Cole's portrait was unflattering. He conceded that the Japanese were a pleasant people, eager to learn about science, economics, and foreign "virtues," and even about the Gospel, but he was obsessed with what he considered their unscrupulous business habits. Yokohama merchants and importers, he alleged, were condescending and dishonest. Possessing an "oily tongue," they delighted in "outrogu[ing]" the foreigner. Not infrequently, he declared, they would "evade receipt" of American goods they had ordered and forfeit the security deposits they had paid. They resorted to this practice if they could later purchase a consignment of the same goods at an auction for a lower price. So frequent was this obnoxious practice that Cole felt obliged to issue a warning:

Table 1   Selected Minority Population of Los Angeles, Oakland, and
San Francisco, 1900–1940

	1900	1910	1920	1930	1940
LOS ANGELES					
Black	2,131	7,599	15,579	38,894	63,774
Chinese	1,885	1,954	2,062	3,009	4,736
Japanese	152[a]	4,238	11,618	21,081	23,321
Mexican[b]	817	5,611	21,598	97,116	c
		(5,632)	(29,757)		
OAKLAND					
Black	1,026	3,055	5,489	7,503	8,462
Chinese	805	2,522	3,821	3,048	3,201
Japanese	200	1,336	2,709	2,137	1,790
Mexican[b]	95	249	1,026	3,200	c
		(252)	(1,278)		
SAN FRANCISCO					
Black	1,654	1,642	2,414	3,803	4,846
Chinese	10,762	6,914	7,744	16,303	17,782
Japanese	1,852	4,191	5,358	6,250	5,280
Mexican[b]	1.459	1,763	3,793	7,922	c
		(1,792)	(3,908)		

a. The figure given obviously is so low as to be meaningless. The number
should be around 1,200.
b. Various census reports are inconsistent in listing Mexican population.
Alternative population listed in parenthesis.
c. In the 1940 census, Mexican are listed as whites.

SOURCE: Census Reports.

[American] merchants should be very careful how they send over grain, sugar, and rice at this time because the Japanese are beginning to be far-seeing sharp traders—so sharp in their dealing with the foreigners as to know when they best can slide from under an agreement which does not suit their preconceived arrangements.[3]

Japanese business practices were not the only Japanese topics found in the Negro press of the late nineteenth and early twentieth centuries. On occasion there appeared reports on the exotic customs of the "Nipponese," and these stories, like Cole's letters, freely mixed fact and fiction and frequently presented Asians in an unfavorable light. According to these articles, the Japanese were a polite, patient, careless, superstitious, and occasionally cruel people. Readers were told that the "Nipponese" were courteous to guests, but they were "not a demonstrative people, and kissing is unknown among them." Brave and loyal to their family and friends, they would undergo almost any test to prove their fidelity to their loved ones. Sometimes this devotion took extreme forms. In feudal Japan, one story alleged, whenever a prominent man died, his immediate relatives allowed themselves to be buried alive so that they might continue to be of assistance to him in the next world. Even though such customs had long been abandoned, the Japanese remained a superstitious people, who burned lights in dark rooms to ward off ghosts and who feared the howling of a dog, thinking that such sounds portended death. But what most impressed travelers was the patience of the Japanese. They never seemed to lose their tempers, and they could concentrate on almost any subject for hour after hour. At Japanese theatrical productions, which frequently lasted six to eight hours, no one seemed bored, and rather than miss any of the performance, patrons would bring their lunches with them.[4] Absolutely no effort was made to check the veracity of these accounts of the "heathen" Japanese, and, as noted in the introduction to this volume, nearly all such stories were lifted from other papers.

The black press's negative image of Japan and its people changed abruptly in 1905, when Russia lost the Russo-Japanese War. No longer were the Japanese described as improvident, ignorant, careless, or superstitious. Instead, they were seen as a courageous people, who did "not fear death in any form."[5] As early as 1898, one paper had predicted that "Japan is moving into the front rank among the nations"; others remained less certain until tiny Japan humbled mighty Russia. Blacks, who had often heard about the alleged inferiority of the darker races, exulted in the Japanese victory: "white is not always the conqueror when pitted against other races."[6]

This sentiment greatly impressed John T. Campbell, a black living in Lafayette, Indiana. Campbell had been outraged in November 1906, when Theodore Roosevelt discharged the Brownsville soldiers.[7] Campbell predicted that the Japanese, who had humbled Russia, might now seek to humble America for mistreating her nationals in the United States. One way for them to seek revenge, he warned, would be for the Japanese secretly to employ "the discharged and disgraced soldiers of the Twenty-Fifth Infantry." These men might be sent to the South to recruit alienated Negroes who would be asked "to quietly meet" at some place on our Pacific coast to join a Japanese Army." Campbell readily acknowledged that such an army would be defeated, "but it would be a troublesome problem." He warned that unless Negroes were given "cause to be patriotic rather than alien," it might not take long before Japanese and blacks began to fraternize.[8]

There is little evidence of the variety of fraternization that Campbell predicted. Yet, a new image of Japanese appeared in Negro journals. From the end of the Russo-Japanese War to the attack on Pearl Harbor, stories about Japan in the black press deemphasized the supposedly backward characteristics of its people. No longer was it considered a primitive nation, and Afro-Americans marveled that it was able to achieve in sixty years what other countries had taken thousands of years to do. If the Japanese had rejected the advances of Christian missionaries, they did so not because they were ignorant pagans, but rather because they "avoided" all the "ludicrous follies of the white man." Negroes observed the *Washington Bee*, would do well to imitate the Japanese and adopt "the good of white American civilization, improve on the indifferent, and reject the bad."

Booker T. Washington also thought that blacks could learn much from Orientals. "The Japanese race," he observed in 1906, "is a convincing example of the respect which the world gives to a race that can put brains and commercial activity into the development of the resources of a country."⁹

Even Kelly Miller, a professor at Howard University, who did not believe that the Japanese had contributed to the glory of America and who refused to link the well-being of blacks and Japanese, was impressed with the progress of Japan. He marveled at the way her people "wove the woof of alien attainment upon the warp of native culture." Japan, he declared, "has opened the eyes of the world and has convinced the weaker races that culture is not an attribute of color and that the white race cannot claim a monopoly of those facilities of mind and soul which make for advancement and civilization." The Howard University professor concluded that Japanese progress had been self-imposed; had Europe colonized Japan "as a means of developing the natives, like progress would have been delayed by many centuries, if not made entirely impossible."¹⁰

Several black editors agreed with Washington and Miller. Looking at the activities of Japanese businessmen in the United States, they found much to emulate. According to one story, Japanese merchants in the 1880s were among the most successful in New York City. Courteous, cultured, and contented, the 200 Japanese of Gotham attended performances of the most popular plays, visited the fanciest resorts, worshipped at fashionable Christian churches, and even intermarried with respectable white women. "All the Japanese thirst for knowledge and culture," commented the *Boston Colored Citizen*. So well assimilated were these newcomers that it was hard for some to believe that "they had [not] been with us from the first instead of only since the [Civil W]ar."¹¹

Even in those parts of the country where they were not assimilated, the Japanese proved to be successful entrepreneurs. In Los Angeles, where blacks outnumbered Japanese after 1910, the Japanese operated nine times as many businesses as blacks. The reason for this, the *Los Angeles California Eagle* speculated, was that "the Japanese have learned not only to organize 'man' but have been taught the lesson of organizing 'money.' "¹²

Considerably less impressed with Japanese merchants was the *San Francisco Spokesman*.[13] It complained that the city's Negroes were purchasing too many of their goods in "little Tokyo" from people "who spoke a language only God and themselves understood and . . . have faces about as expressive as a plate of soup [even] . . . when you try to insult them." Like many whites in the San Francisco area, the editor of the *Spokesman* was quick to note the shortcomings of the Japanese. Perhaps he thought that by so doing he would win favor for blacks living in California. At any rate, he printed a letter from a reader who castigated the Negro patrons of Japanese restaurants. According to R. F. Pope, Japanese restaurants served inferior food and refused to employ black help. Therefore, in his opinion, Afro-Americans would do well to eat elsewhere.[14]

Several years before Pope voiced his complaint, another writer in a California black newspaper reported why he disliked the Japanese:

We have no sympathy for the Japs because as soon as they open a place of business anywhere along the coast of the inland states they draw their color line as tightly as a Georgia cracker, unless it be a house of gaming or some dirty dive of a place.[15]

If blacks had ambivalent feelings about Japanese businessmen, they had little but scorn for Japanese laborers and domestics, who, the *St. Paul Appeal* incorrectly insisted, were flocking into the country at the alarming rate of 100,000 per year. Periodically, rumors would circulate that boatloads of Japanese maids and butlers were being imported into the United States and that these foreigners would displace Negro domestics. "About all the American Negro knows about the Japanese," a feature writer complained in 1933, "is that they are rather silent and ofttimes take jobs from them as butlers and chauffeurs, especially in the west coast."[16]

That Negroes would fear competition from Japanese domestics was only natural. After all, in several Northern and Southern cities, over two-fifths of the adult black population earned its livelihood by working as maids, butlers, coachmen, restaurant and hotel employees, or washerwomen.[17] Stories that Orientals were monopolizing hotel work in California or yardboy and coachmen's jobs in Texas provided ominous reading for black bellboys and chauffeurs in the East. Even more frightening were accounts, like the story in the *St. Paul Appeal*, that "our strenuous brown brother . . . bids fair to excel the Afro-American" or the report in the *Cleveland Gazette* that "Japanese servants are more and more in demand every year in New York. They are looked upon as more capable than any other kind of domestic help." Such stories prompted black newspapermen to warn white employers of the alleged dangers of relying exclusively on Japanese servants and workers. Orientals, several newspaper editorials announced, were "ambitious and discontented with servitude" and would not be able to do a proper job. Moreover, they could "not be induced to treat . . . women with respect." Unlike the Chinese, Japanese servants, one editor insisted, did not hesitate to steal from their employers, and the "Japanese criminal will as quickly . . . assault or murder an American as one of his own nationality."[18] But with the passage of time, this type of editorial disappeared, probably because few black domestics and butlers lived in areas that had enough Japanese to displace them.[19]

Yet another group that feared Japanese competition was the black agricultural worker of the South. Millions living in Dixie earned their livelihoods by laboring for white planters or by renting or sharecropping land from them. White landowners frequently complained that their Afro-American help was inefficient, improvident, and unreliable. During the first quarter of the twentieth century, there was talk of importing Japanese laborers to work the cotton and rice fields and the fruit orchards. The *Southern Cultivator*, a white agricultural magazine, reported in 1903 that it knew of a planter who hoped to replace Negro workers with Japanese. In 1904, some Japanese were given jobs in the pine forests of Mississippi. Less than a decade later the *New Orleans Picayune*, an influential white daily, said that Southerners should consider whether eventually 10 million or more Chinese and Japanese would be needed to replace the whites and blacks who were leaving Dixie's farms.[20]

Around 1904 about fifty Japanese families established a 67,000-acre colony called Yamato[21] in Dade County, Florida, and experimented in the growing of rice, silk, tobacco, and pineapples. A decade later, another colony was established at Middleburg in Florida's Clay County. Around the same time, other groups of Japanese began to purchase tracts of land in Texas, especially near Houston, Galveston, and Brownsville. Some of the more prosperous of these farmers hired Afro-Americans and Mexicans to help them harvest their crops. Reports in 1924 that rice and vegetables could profitably be grown in Dixie caused a Japanese diplomat to accompany W. R. Tucker, a farm extension agent of a railroad company, on a trip through south Georgia and Florida. The purpose of the journey was to find suitable lands for Japanese farmers wishing to leave California. The railroad hoped that Tucker could convince the Japanese to buy abandoned rice plantations it owned near Darien, Georgia. This land supposedly was well suited for truck farming.[22]

Just one year later, stories circulated that 50,000 Japanese, dissatisfied with conditions in California, planned to move to Crittenden and Mississippi counties in Arkansas.[23] Blacks represented a majority of the farm workers in these two counties, and some of them feared that "the thrifty Japanese [would] absorb some of the Brother's American birthright." Admittedly, these rumors proved to be erroneous, but the Afro-American press gave careful consideration to the "menace" of Japanese competition in Dixie.[24]

A few black newspapers professed to be happy about Japanese migration to the South, for they expected the "Asiatic ogre[s]" to teach Dixie a much needed lesson. The Japanese worker might appear to be contented and industrious, they warned, but actually "he'll work hard in those peach orchards [only because] . . . he'll count on getting hold of them sooner or later." Roscoe Conkling Simmons, a columnist for the *Chicago Defender*, predicted that southern country store merchants who expected to get rich from extending credit to the newcomers would probably be disappointed. "Japanese," he noted, "work and save, attend to their business, [but they will] run no accounts." Others insisted that the Japanese, being proud and sensitive, would not tolerate the insults that blacks were regularly forced to put up with. If necessary, the Japanese would organize strikes, fight back against those who cheated them, and protest to the Japanese government any time they felt mistreated.[25]

Even though most of the Japanese who moved to the South to work Dixie's agricultural fields soon abandoned these tracts because of poor soil and scanty harvests, many Afro-Americans continued to worry about being displaced by Orientals. An effort was made to persuade whites that importing Japanese, who could subsist on "fifty percent of the requirements of white Americans," was not worth the monetary savings. Blacks hoped to do this by projecting an image of the Issei and Nisei as strike-breakers, heathens, and vindictive men, who, if cheated, would readily complain to the Japanese government and call international attention to conditions in the South. If Southern whites accepted these arguments, the newspaper writers concluded, they would be less likely to speak out about the alleged inefficiency of their Negro fieldhands.[26]

Black periodicals viewed the Japanese as more than economic competitors; they also saw them as fellow sufferers in a society that offered first-class citizenship only to those whose skins were white. Proof that people of Asian origin were considered different came on October 11, 1906, when the San Francisco School Board passed a resolution requiring the ninety-five Japanese pupils enrolled in the city's schools to attend classes with the Chinese in a segregated Oriental school. Initially, the blacks denounced the resolution as a flagrant violation of the Constitution and the Gresham-Kurino Treaty of 1899, but they expected that the Japanese would eventually be forced to submit to Jim Crow education. Protests continued, however, and warnings of a Japanese boycott of American goods seemed so ominous to exporters that President Theodore Roosevelt, in the words of the *Chicago Journal*, "threaten[ed] California with federal action and the big stick unless the yellow children of aliens [we]re placed on equal footing with the grandsons of forty-niners."[27]

When the president forced the San Francisco School Board to reverse its segregation policy, sympathy for the Japanese in some black papers turned into hostility. To be sure, this was not true of all journals, for the *New York Age, The Voice* (Chicago), *Horizon*, and the *Colored American Magazine* expressed satisfaction that, for the first time, the United States had found a "colored" race that merited respect. These journals saw a definite connection between anti-Japanese sentiment and Jim Crow legislation. Other periodicals, however, saw no such connection. They were less pleased about the turnabout and criticized Roosevelt. The *Indianapolis Freeman*, for example, had no desire to see Japanese turned away from white schools whether in California or in Dixie, but the paper refused to concede that Asians merited consideration denied blacks. The *Freeman* dismissed talk that Roosevelt acted out of a desire to avoid war with Japan. "The Japs are brave fellows," it conceded on June 15, 1907, "but really they can't mean to tackle Uncle Sam." Others were displeased with Roosevelt, and they, too, saw no likelihood of impending conflict. What bothered them was that the president championed the cause of the Japanese and then remained silent when the U.S. Supreme Court ruled that Berea College in Kentucky could prevent Negro applicants from matriculating. Furthermore, they noted, Roosevelt had never voiced any objections to school segregation in the South. Why should alien Japanese attend integrated schools in California when Dixie blacks had to go to segregated schools. The reason, another paper commented, was that unlike the Japanese, the blacks had no powerful foreign government prepared to champion their cause and, if necessary, to teach "a lesson to . . . their Anglo-Saxon neighbors."[28]

While they were willing to commiserate with a fellow sufferer forced to attend a separate school, blacks were angry that "the wishes of yellow aliens from . . . Japan [are] of more consequence to this nation than [those of] its loyal Negro citizens."[29] Cabinet members had spoken out in favor of integration in San Francisco, but they were silent about segregation in Dixie. Resentful of this double standard, blacks took out their frustrations in criticisms of the Japanese.

For the next few years, Afro-Americans displayed noticeable antipathy towards the Japanese. Their newspapers featured stories about illegal Japanese aliens entering the United States from Mexico and Canada, about regiments of Japanese soldiers, disguised as laborers in Hawaii, and about armed Japanese residents of the Pacific Coast states. Most ominous was a lurid story printed in a Minnesota black newspaper about the arrest of a Japanese band in Seattle. According to the *St. Paul Appeal*, when police searched the residences of the prisoners they uncovered large quantities of explosives. Authorities also supposedly discovered one regulation army rifle and one Japanese army uniform in each of the approximately two dozen houses they searched.[30]

On the other hand, considerable sympathy for the Japanese was expressed in 1913, when Californians enacted a law preventing Japanese—or, as they were called, aliens ineligible for citizenship—from acquiring more land in the state. This legislation disturbed blacks, for it punished the Japanese for being "a bit smarter that the average Yankee" and for being able to take "so-called unproductive California land[s] and Ma[k]e them yield bumper crops." Because the native white American horticulturists were unable to "compete with a race which works from sunrise to sunset [and one] in which every member of the family contributes his share to the toil," they were foolishly trying to restrict the productivity of the industrious Japanese. How ridiculous this was, for by reclaiming swamp lands and by "mak[ing] two blades of grass grow where one was accustomed to grow before," the Japanese were enriching the state and proving that "when it comes to brain power they take a back seat [t]o no group."[31]

With obvious delight, blacks noted that hypocritical whites were punishing the Japanese for not being Bolshevik assassins or Mafia criminals, like the "trash that comes from European soil," or being white slavers or improvident paupers. No, these were not the offenses of the Japanese. Their "crime" was that they were skilled farmers "only asking to be left alone to extract the best living they can out of the soil by their own labor." What terrified the envious Californians was that the incredible success of the Japanese truck farmers had proved that white superiority was a myth. "The Japanese succeeds," observed Robert Bagnall, an official of the National Association for the Advancement of Colored People, "where the whites fail. He is

their superior . . . and so they would debar him from competition." If allowed equal rights, added Floyd Calvin, a syndicated
Negro columnist, the industrious Japanese would outshine their
rivals and "might in time own" most of the land in California.[32]

The "shrewd and efficient" Japanese were able partially
to circumvent the discriminatory land laws. Purchasing farm
acreage in the names of their native-born children, the Nisei,
who were American citizens, they nearly tripled their landholdings in California between 1913 and 1920.[33] From 1909 to
1919, the value of the agricultural products that the Japanese
raised in California jumped from $6 to $57 million; the $57
million figure represented fully one-tenth of the total value of
the state's fruit and vegetable produce for that year.[34] Even more
remarkable, 70 percent of the land the Japanese cultivated in
1921 had previously been considered useless. James Weldon
Johnson, the black poet and writer, marveled that in California

one can ride for miles and miles and see nothing but Japanese
at work on the land. One can arrive at a station and see car after
car being loaded with berries; and all of the loading, all of the
shipping, and all of the clerking, all of the handling both of the
berries and the money being done by the Japanese.[35]

To many blacks the success story of the Japanese, who suffered
from race prejudice and from restrictive legislation, was remarkable. Some thought that the wise Negro would do well to
emulate the perserverance, temperance, and efficiency of the
Issei and Nisei. In fact, declared the *Chicago Defender*, unless
restrained by further legislation, they "will soon own all of the
best lands in California! At whose door does the fault lie? Why
[do we] not gobble up the best ourselves and not go to sleep on
the job as we apparently are doing?"[36]

Not a few journals believed that the most important lesson
to be learned from the Japanese was their practice of protesting
loudly whenever mistreated, thereby calling attention to their
plight. Moreover, unlike Negroes, the Japanese openly manifested racial pride and, thus, "successfully challenged white
supremacy." For example, noted the *Los Angeles California*

Eagle, the Japanese vigorously protested when local theaters showed a movie, *The Cheat,* which portrayed Orientals as sly and sinister. Negroes, on the other hand, seldom condemned movies degrading blacks. Worse, yet, declared Frank Crosswaith in the *Savannah Tribune,* the Afro-American press featured advertisements for such products as "Get White Overnight Grease," and, in Crosswaith's opinion, these ads were offensive. No Japanese paper, he insisted, would dare insult its readers' "racial pride" by running such advertisements.[37]

Others praised the Japanese for their unity, contrasting this closeness with the constant bickering of Afro-Americans. According to one report, when a Japanese speaker at a black college was asked how his people viewed the Negro, he allegedly responded, "[they have] no money, no organization, hence [they are of] no consequence." The Japanese, however, did have organization and stuck together, helping one another in time of crisis, patronizing merchants sympathetic to their cause, and boycotting their enemies' businesses. The Japanese had made themselves a "necessary" people without whom the nation would be in trouble. By withholding their "labor at the critical stages of the fruit crop," they could ruin American agriculture. So terrified were some Western farmers "that the weaker ones among the native population have been told neither to sell nor lease to the Japanese." In contrast, blacks were not indispensable to the country; they were "not [yet] a necessary people."[38]

Not all whites agreed that the Japanese were "a necessary people." Senator Hiram Johnson of California, for example, was a vociferous critic of Japanese rights. His position disturbed *The Half-Century Magazine,* which warned that in time a man prejudiced against one dark race would likely display similar prejudices against other nonwhites.[39] In similar vein, Senator James D. Phelan of California never missed an opportunity to attack what he termed America's "yellow peril." Not only did he oppose the naturalization of Japanese immigrants, but he also urged that the native-born Nisei be denied citizenship. Several black journalists denounced Phelan and demanded proof that the Japanese represented "a troublesome or a disturbing element in any community." They argued that such evidence did not exist, for the Japanese, whether of native or of foreign birth, were not "bolshevi[k]s, dynamiters or followers of the red flag."[40] Neither could it be proven, declared the *Baltimore Afro-American* on October 1, 1920, "that the Japanese are any more undesirable than the Jews or the Croats and Slavs of Southern Europe, who are slow to adopt the English language [and who] maintain a lower standard of living . . . than [American] working men."

Equally vigorous denunciations of American racism appeared in the black press when the U.S. Supreme Court upheld a law preventing Japanese immigrants from taking out naturalization papers. Senator Phelan's rantings were dangerous, but they were not as damaging as the verdict of the highest tribunal in the land. The *Baltimore Afro-American* observed that the decision would bar from citizenship a man who had served in the U.S. Coast Guard for ten years. Although men like Hidemitsu Toyota of Massachusetts were good enough to fight for the United States and to "sacrifice [their] . . . li[ves] for America," they were unworthy of being accorded the rights given to American draft dodgers. William Pickens, a National Association for the Advancement of Colored People (NAACP) official, was also outraged at the verdict. "Because the seed which produced him was planted in Nippon and not in fly-infested streets of Naples," Pickens sneered, "this man is accounted lower than the human beings of nearly all the rest of earth." Such court rulings heaped insult on top of injury and caused misunderstandings abroad. The *Chicago Defender* grimly predicted that "the little yellow fellows will not swallow this bitter pill with a smile and if the smile should come, back of it will be a determination to even up scores at some future date."[41]

Denial of citizenship was a blow to the immigrants from Japan. Even more shattering was the determination of many, if not most, Americans to exclude Japanese immigration entirely. By 1920, Congress prepared to restrict European immigration, and many Californians hoped that the lawmakers would also bar Orientals from coming to the United States. Blacks favored immigration restriction, for they were persuaded that the steady influx of foreigners was an obstacle to their own economic advancement. Nonetheless, they almost universally condemned any immigration laws that would prevent the black and yellow people from Asia and Africa from entering the country solely because their skins were not white. "To exclude a people from anything on account of race, color, creed, or nationality," the *Messenger* insisted, "is a slap in the face which no [p]eople who are fit to live will accept or tolerate." Similar sentiments came from the leaders of a conference of African Methodist Episcopal bishops which met in 1924. According to the bishops, Japanese exclusion was contrary to the principles of the American government.[42]

Some black newspapermen denounced the advocates of racist immigration laws as arrogant fools. Their thinking, mused the *Kansas City Call*, "savors of the spirit that made kings feel they were divine and lords treat their subjects as so much cattle." White supremacists seemed eager to make racial clashes "inevitable." According to the quota system proposed by the immigration law, Japanese aliens admitted to the United States would number less than 500 per year. Thus, discriminatory legislation, Afro-Americans noted, had been unnecessary.[43]

A number of black journalists predicted that racist immigration legislation would lead to war between Japan and the United States.[44] Even if such a conflict did not immediately erupt, it would eventually come, for as the June 7, 1924, issue of *Negro World* noted, "the Japanese have long memories and nurse a wrong until they are ready to avenge it, and they smile and look pleasant while doing so." Some years before, on February 27, 1908, the *Galveston New Idea* had made a similar comment when anti-Japanese legislation was being proposed. It noted that "the pages of history are written with the testimony of governments that lost their strength for war by mistreating those who live within their control."

A few Negro newspapers, like the *Chicago Defender*, openly favored the exclusion of the Japanese, provided this was not done exclusively for racial reasons.[45] The *Defender* objected to the Japanese because they were "less assimilable than any other nationality" in the country. Their customs, manners, and traditions were different, and they were so fiercely nationalistic that "once a Japanese always a Japanese." Evidence that they were not like others could be seen in the Japanese districts of California, where Buddhist temples dotted the countryside. "Their religion is not our religion," observed the *Defender*. "Our civilization and culture is [sic] not theirs."[46]

The *Defender* doubted that the Japanese could ever be assimilated. When the Hawaii legislature passed a bill requiring Japanese children to attend public schools, *Defender* columnist Roscoe Conkling Simmons predicted that the law would be ineffective in Americanizing the youngsters. For a few hours a day, he conceded, the children would be told how great America was. The rest of the time, however, they would "unlearn it all." Japanese teachers, parents, and friends would tell them not to believe half of what they heard. "Blood is thicker than water," Simmons concluded, "and Japanese children will remember the words of their own flesh and make faces at the red, white, and blue."[47]

Before long, Congress made up its mind to bar Asian immigrants completely. On May 26, 1924, a somewhat reluctant Calvin Coolidge, aware of the international implications of what he was doing, signed the Japanese Exclusion Bill into law. Negro newspapers suggested that overpopulated Japan send its surplus laborers to Mexico and Brazil, where they were likely to prosper. Several journals urged blacks to investigate working conditions in California and see whether they might be able to fill the vacuum they expected to be created by the suspension of Japanese immigration. Negroes were told that they would enjoy living on the Pacific Coast, where the weather was mild, much like that of the South. Blacks would also discover that they could find work in California. The *Los Angeles California Eagle* spread the word that jobs as farm laborers were easy to find. It predicted that some Negroes would even be able to establish businesses of their own. Nothing more could be done to help the Japanese, and Afro-Americans might just as well be the beneficiaries of changed conditions.[48]

As the *California Eagle* had predicted, following the enactment of the new immigration law, job opportunities for most California blacks improved, and thousands of Afro-Americans left the

South to move to San Francisco, Oakland, and Los Angeles. One group, however, the California railroad workers, continued to fear loss of their jobs to the Japanese. During the 1920s and 1930s, Asa Philip Randolph began to unionize black porters, and worried Pullman Company officials decided that strong action would have to be taken to stop his activities. Some officials remembered that in 1916 the company had avoided a strike by Afro-Americans for higher wages by hiring a few Japanese porters and threatening to fire all blacks who walked off their jobs. Pullman spokesmen reminded Randolph of this incident and warned that they were ready once again to employ Japanese.[49]

Randolph ignored their threats and continued to enroll members in the Brotherhood of Sleeping Car Porters. In 1933, the Pullman Company hired scores of Japanese porters, but Randolph refused to back down. Afro-American newspapers supported him and launched an "Employ Americans First" campaign. According to the *Pittsburgh Courier* of February 18, 1933, "American industries owe it to the American man to hire him first, last and always." Besides, it added, the Japanese were "physically disqualified" to serve as porters because they were "too short to make down the upper berth without a ladder."[50] Whether or not they were convinced by these arguments—or, as was more likely the case, by the threat of a U.S. senator to propose legislation prohibiting foreigners from working on the railroads—officials backed down, and eventually the Negroes regained their jobs.[51] After 1933, there was no major attempt to replace Afro-American porters with Japanese.

As economic competition lessened, mention of the Issei and Nisei virtually disappeared from Afro-American newspapers. Black domestics, porters, and farm workers no longer viewed the Japanese as ready to steal their jobs and deprive them and their children of food. Newspaper coverage once given to the Japanese was now devoted to the New Deal programs of Franklin Roosevelt, the efforts of the interracial Southern Tenant Farmers' Union to organize sharecroppers in Arkansas, and the "Don't Buy Where You Can't Work" campaigns being conducted in urban ghettos.[52] Not until the late 1930s did stories about the Japanese reappear in the black press. Tensions were mounting in Southeast Asia, and many thought that conflict between the United States and Japan was inevitable. War, of course, did come, and the image of the Japanese in Afro-American periodicals after 1941 was that of a sinister enemy. Things had gone full circle, for some of the stories about the Japanese that had appeared in Negro newspapers in the late nineteenth century would not have been out of place in black periodicals of the early 1940s.[53]

How does one account for the mixed image of the Japanese in the black press from 1867 to the 1930s? It is not difficult to explain the essentially negative portrayal of the Japanese prior to 1905. Japan was a distant, exotic country, and Afro-Americans unquestionably believed stories that its people were super-stitious heathens, scheming businessmen, and cruel warriors. That this image would improve when a "colored" power humbled mighty Russia was predictable.

It is more difficult, however, to explain the mixed image of the Japanese that consistently appeared in Afro-American news-papers during the twenty-eight years following the conclusion of the Russo-Japanese War. That there should have been some sympathy for the Japanese was only natural. American society plainly was racist, and many agreed with the *Portland* (Oregon) *Times* of January 11, 1919, that "the Japanese question is a curse in the West like the Negro question is in the South." The Japanese, like Afro-Americans, were subjected to indignities that would never be inflicted upon whites. Japanese farmers were punished not for their improvidence or criminality, but rather for their productivity and perserverance. Some blacks feared that anti-Japanese legislation might serve as a precedent for the enact-ment of anti-Negro laws. If the Japanese could be prevented from purchasing or leasing land, what would stop a racist legislature from barring Negroes from buying land?[54]

As already noted, blacks, unsure about their status in American society, were worried about economic competition from Japanese domestics, field hands, and porters. In retrospect, this may have been misplaced anxiety, but blacks were not willing to take any chances. White employers, eager to trim their labor costs, occasionally threatened to import Orientals if their Negro workers would not agree to paycuts. Possessing few marketable skills,

Afro-Americans saw the Japanese as a real threat. They believed that it was in their best interest to project an image of the Japanese as heathens, labor agitators, and radicals. If these negative stereotypes corresponded to what many Americans were saying about the Asians, so much the better. Southerners were prone to ethnocentrism, and perhaps they could easily be persuaded that the Japanese were in fact undesirable.[55]

· Not to be overlooked in explaining black antipathy towards the Japanese is the element of jealousy. On more than one occasion, there seemed to be justification for believing that Nisei "received more consideration and respect from the Government of the United States and its people than d[id] the 10,000,000 Negro citizens." Japanese traveling in the South, noted syndicated columnist George Schuyler, could ride in a Pullman car, eat in a quality restaurant, and get reservations for a first-class hotel, "while the Christian Negro is huddled in a crowded jim crow half-coach and dare not ask for accommodations due a citizen and which he is willing and able to pay for."[56] Mary Church Terrell, the distinguished black clubwoman and wife of a judge, was even more indignant than Schuyler. In the nation's capital, where she lived, she complained, "Japanese and representatives of any other dark race can find hotel accommodations if they can pay for them." The black man or woman, on the other hand, was "thrust out of the hotels . . . like a leper."[57] Laura Bartlett, who wrote a letter to the editor of the *Baltimore Afro-American*, was upset that even houses of worship differentiated between the races. "Our leading white churches," she observed, "gladly welcome Chinese and Japanese . . . but if a respectable colored person should dare to enter the so-called House of God, he would not be allowed inside."[58]

A perusal of scores of black newspapers yields yet another reason for black hostility towards Japanese: Afro-Americans believed that Issei and Nisei were quick to show contempt for Negroes. According to Phil Brown, a writer for the *Chicago Defender*, "the Japanese have no more interest in the Americans of our race than has the passing grandee of the Mississippi plantation. When they squeal for racial equality they do not mean us; they mean equality for themselves." "No people other than the American whites," insisted the *Cleveland Gazette*, "are more prejudiced against the Negro than . . . [the] Japs, who have shown it thousands of times in this country if not elsewhere." Mary Church Terrell met a Japanese delegate at the Washington Disarmament Conference of 1920–1921. She noted that he and his compatriots avoided blacks whenever possible and were quite unfriendly when they did have any contact. Perhaps the position of blacks was best stated by the *St. Paul Appeal*. "We would sympathize more with the Japs," it admitted, "were it not for the fact that they manifest the same prejudice against the Afro-American [as the whites]."[59]

These allegations were not completely without foundation. Black journals occasionally reported that Japanese restaurant owners refused to serve black patrons "on account of [thei]r race" and that Los Angeles Japanese merchants insulted "colored women who would perchance go to some of their places of business to make purchases." A Japanese American writing a letter to the *New York Sun* protested that he was denied citizenship, which was freely given to the European "foreigners who swarm to these shores and *to the Negro of acknowledged inferiority*." His letter was noted by blacks, and it was reprinted in at least one Negro newspaper.[60]

Blacks were not quick to forget these insults, and a few, like celebrated Negro physician Charles Purvis, frankly confessed that they had no fondness for the Japanese. In 1924, a letter to the editor of the *Baltimore Afro-American* expressed pleasure that Orientals were to be excluded from America, and the writer asked, "Can you show me . . . anything that the Jap or any other nation has done for the Negro but turn up their nose[s] at them?"[61]

The image of the Japanese in the black press was clearly an ambivalent one. To some, like W.E.B. Du Bois, who spoke for himself and the NAACP, the "fight of the Japanese for equal rights is similar to the fight the Negroes are making for their rights." Others insisted that "Japan is by no means a champion of the darker race. Only the putrid mind of a sick Negro bourgeois[i]e," acidly commented the *Cleveland Gazette*, "could imagine Japan in the role of champion of the oppressed colonial masses when Japan is herself openly pursuing a policy of robbery and oppression of the Korean"[62] Yet a third group accepted the validity of white stereotypes of the Japanese. So assimilated had these Afro-Americans become that they shared the dominant white view of the Japanese.

NOTES

1. John Modell has discovered that in Los Angeles Negroes and Japanese lived in the same neighborhoods. Modell concludes that, on the whole, blacks lived in "superior" housing. Modell, *The Economics and Politics of Racial Accommodation: The Japanese of Los Angeles, 1900–1942* (Urbana, Ill.; 1977), p. 59 n. 85.

2. *Indianapolis Freeman*, March 9, 1907.

3. Cole to the editor, August 23, 1867, in *San Francisco Elevator*, September 27, 1867. See also Cole to the editor, April 10, 1870, in ibid., May 27, 1870.

4. *New Orleans Weekly Pelican*, July 20, 1889; *The Earth*, n.d., quoted in *Lawrence* (Kans.) *Historic Times*, October 17, 1891; *Baltimore Afro-American*, August 3, 1894; *Westminster Gazette*, n.d., quoted in *Baltimore Ledger*, September 3, 1898; *Indianapolis World*, April 15, 1899, March 19, 1904.

5. *Baltimore Afro-American*, March 4, 1905; *Washington Bee*, July 4, 1914; "William Pickens Says," *Houston Informer*, February 20, 1932.

6. *Wichita Tribune*, September 24, 1898; *Indianapolis Freeman*, June 3, 1905.

7. The Brownsville Affair took place on August 13–14, 1906, when residents of that Texas city alleged that Negro soldiers from the first batallion of the 25th Infantry Regiment, Companies B, C, and D shot up their town. One man was killed in the affray, and another was wounded. Although a local grand jury was unable to come up with evidence warranting an indictment, President Theodore Roosevelt sent a commission to investigate the charges. The commission concluded that blacks were guilty of murdering and wounding the citizens of Brownsville. In November, the president summarily dismissed without honor the entire three companies. This decision caused an uproar in the black community, and some whites also denounced Roosevelt for his arbitrary action. See Thomas Dyer, *Theodore Roosevelt and the Idea of Race* (Baton Rouge, La., 1980), pp. 114–16; Marvin Fletcher, *The Black Soldier and Officer in the United States Army, 1891–1917*

(Columbia, Mo., 1974), Chapters 7-8; Jack Foner, *Blacks and the Military in American History* (New York, 1974), pp. 95-103; Ann J. Lane, *The Brownsville Affair* (Port Washington, N.Y., 1971); John Hope Franklin, *From Slavery to Freedom*, 5th ed. (New York, 1980), pp. 315-16.

8. Campbell, "Justice to the Negro," *Indianapolis Freeman*, July 13, 1907.

9. *Atlanta Independent*, April 6, 1918; *Washington Bee*, November 3, 1917; Booker T. Washington, *Putting the Most into Life* (New York, 1906), p. 33.

10. Kelly Miller, *The Everlasting Stain* (New York, reprint ed., 1968), pp. 96-97, 100-101, 163; David J. Hellwig, "Afro-American Reactions to the Japanese and Anti-Japanese Movement, 1906-1924," *Phylon* 38 (1977): 96-97, hereafter cited as "Japanese."

11. *Washington Bee*, May 26, 1893; *Indianapolis World*, August 1, 1903; *Boston Colored Citizen*, February 4, 1905.

12. *Los Angeles California Eagle*, January 6, 1917, July 4, 1924, and February 26, 1926.

13. The *Spokesman's* position on the Japanese was very much like that of the typical white American. For the attitudes of whites toward their Asian neighbors, see Yamato Ichihashi, *Japanese Immigration: Its Status in California* (San Francisco, 1915); Bill Hosokawa, *Nisei: The Quiet Americans* (New York, 1969); Roger Daniels, *The Politics of Prejudice* (Berkeley and Los Angeles, 1961); Herbert Johnson, *Discrimination Against the Japanese in California* (Berkeley, Calif., 1907); Dennis Ogawa, *From Japs to Japanese* (Berkeley, Calif., 1971); Harry H.L. Kitano, *Japanese Americans* (Englewood Cliffs, N.J., 1969); H. A. Millis, *The Japanese Problem in the United States* (New York, 1915); Eldon Penrose, *California Nativism: Organized Opposition to the Japanese, 1890-1913* (San Francisco, 1973); T. Iyenaga and Kenoske Sato, *Japan and the California Problem* (New York, 1921); Bradford Smith, *Americans from Japan* (Philadelphia, 1948); Hilary Conroy and T. Scott Miyakawa, eds., *East Across the Pacific* (Santa Barbara, Calif., 1972).

14. Pope to editor, in *San Francisco Spokesman*, May 24, 1925. See also ibid., July 6, 1933; and R. P. Edward's editorial on the Japanese in the *Los Angeles California Eagle*, June 21, 1924.

15. Unidentified black California newspaper quoted in *Indianapolis Freeman*, April 8, 1911.

16. *Indianapolis World*, May 19 and June 23, 1900; *Chicago Broad Ax*, June 16, 1900; *St. Paul Appeal*, June 15, 1907; Ras Hammurabi, "What Will Negro[es] Do if Japanese Attack America?" *Philadelphia Tribune*, June 15, 1933; Modell, *Economics and Politics of Racial Accommodation*, p. 35.

17. Charles E. Hall, *Negroes in the United States 1920-32* (Washington, D.C., 1935), pp. 289-92; Chicago Commission on Race Relations, *The Negro in Chicago* (Chicago, 1922), pp. 358-359; David Katzman, *Seven Days a Week* (New York, 1978), pp. 245-46.

18. *Washington Bee*, February 29, 1908; *St. Paul Appeal*, June 15, 1907; *Cleveland Gazette*, March 3, 1900; *Philadelphia Tribune*, May 31, 1912; *Indianapolis Freeman*, March 9, 1907.

19. However, whenever there was talk of Japanese displacing blacks, some Negroes became worried. "As a competitor in the labor markets of America," admitted the *Chicago Defender* on January 15, 1921, "we find it extremely difficult to hold our own with them [the Japanese]. The white man does not want him for economic reasons, neither do we."

20. *Southern Cultivator*, 61 (August 15, 1903): 301; *Boston Transcript*, November 1, 1904; *New Orleans Picayune*, March 6, 1912. Southerners hoped that Japanese agricultural workers would introduce vegetable growing in areas formerly devoted to the cultivation of cotton. Kelly Miller thought that the Japanese were ideally suited to truck gardening since, because of their small stature, they could easily work on their knees. Miller, *Everlasting Stain*, p. 161.

21. Yamato is the ancient name of Japan.

22. Robert Wilson and Bill Hosokawa, *East to America: A History of the Japanese in the United States* (New York, 1980), pp. 96-99; George Pozzetta, "Foreigners in Florida: A Study of Immigration Promotion, 1865-1910," *Florida Historical Quarterly* 53 (1974): 171-72; *Atlanta Constitution*, July 18, 1924; Robert Ward Immigration Clippings, Harvard University.

23. *Richmond Planet*, January 24 and March 14, 1925.

24. *Indianapolis World*, August 1, 1903; *Baltimore Afro-American*, March 23, 1907; *Nashville Globe*, September 20, 1907; *Washington Bee*, February 29, 1908; *New York Amsterdam News*, March 18 and May 20, 1905.

25. *Nashville Globe*, September 20, 1907; Simmons, "The Week," *Chicago Defender*, April 11, 1925; *Norfolk Journal and Guide*, May 2, 1925.

26. See sources listed in note 25 and Wilson and Hosokawa, *East to America*, pp. 96-99. See also Elijah Hodges to the editor, in *Philadelphia Tribune*, May 31, 1912; *Chicago Whip*, May 6, 1922.

27. The Gresham-Kurino Treaty of 1899 guaranteed Japanese aliens in the United States the same treatment as immigrants from the "most favored" nations of Europe. *St. Louis Palladium*, October 27, 1906; *Portland* (Ore.) *New Age*, January 5, 1907; *New York Age*, February 7, 1907; *The Voice* (Chicago), 4 (1907): 93; *Colored American Magazine* 11

(1906): 285; *Chicago Journal*, February 10, 1909, quoted in *Chicago Broad Ax*, February 13, 1909; *Hosokawa*, Nisei, pp. 85-86.

28. *Chicago Chronicle*, n.d., quoted in *St. Paul Appeal*, January 5, 1907; *Horizon* (Washington, D.C.) 1 (1907): 14-16; *Southern Workman*, 36 (1907): 69; *The Voice* 4 (1907): 287; *Chicago Broad Ax*, February 13, 1909; *New York Age*, February 18, 1909; *Indianapolis Freeman*, November 10, 1906, June 15, October 5, November 9, 1907; Hellwig, "Japanese," p. 94. Robert Heizer and Alan Almquist, *The Other Californians: Prejudice and Discrimination Under Spain, Mexico and the United States to 1920* (Berkeley, Calif., 1971), pp. 181-82.

29. *Indianapolis Freeman*, November 10, 1906.

30. *St. Louis Palladium*, December 15, 1906, and May 4, 1907; *St. Paul Appeal*, April 4 and 11, 1908. The *Palladium* subsequently admitted that some of its stories were based on erroneous information.

31. *Washington Bee*, July 4, 1914; *Indianapolis Freeman*, June 7, 1913; Hellwig, "Japanese," p. 95; *Philadelphia Tribune*, July 18, 1914; James Weldon Johnson, "Views and Reviews," *New York Age*, July 12, 1919, September 22, 1923, April 19 and May 3, 1924; *Baltimore Afro-American*, January 18, 1924; *Norfolk Journal and Guide*, June 2, 1924; *Negro World* (New York) January 3, 1925; J. Max Bond, "The Japanese in California," *The Crisis* 40 (1933): 133-34; Hosokawa, *Nisei*, pp. 101-102; Penrose, *California Nativism*, pp. 98-103.

32. *St. Paul Appeal*, January 12, 1907, April 19, 1913; *The Crisis* 1 (1913): 74; James Weldon Johnson, "Views and Reviews," *New York Age*, July 12, 1919; *St. Louis Argus*, June 25, 1920; *Chicago Defender*, January 15, 1921, September 15, 1923; *Pittsburgh Courier*, April 26, 1924, Robert Bagnall, "The Spirit of the Ku Klux Klan," *Opportunity* 1 (1923): 267; *Philadelphia Tribune*, April 26, 1924; Kelly Miller, *Everlasting Stain*, p. 161.

33. *Savannah Tribune*, February 10, 1917; *Cleveland Advocate*, October 9, 1920; *Tulsa Star*, November 20, 1920; *The Competitor* (Pittsburgh) 2 (1920): 175-76.

34. Hosokawa, *Nisei*, p. 106; Millis, *Japanese*, pp. 104-108; Iyenaga and Sato, *Japan and the California Problem*, pp. 122-23, 132; *Los Angeles California Eagle*, May 2, 1924.

35. Johnson, "Views and Reviews," *New York Age*, July 12, 1919; *Chicago Defender*, September 17, 1921; Hosokawa Nisei, pp. 61-62, 105.

36. *Chicago Defender*, September 18, 1920; *Norfolk Journal and Guide*, June 21, 1924; *Richmond Planet*, January 24, 1925; *Pittsburgh Courier*, September 2, 1933; Bond, "Japanese," pp. 133-34; Hellwig, "Japanese," p. 98.

37. *Los Angeles California Eagle,* January 29, 1916; Frank Crosswaith, "Race Pride vs. Profit," *Savannah Tribune,* April 25, 1929; Hellwig, "Japanese," pp. 97–100.

38. *Baltimore Afro-American,* May 24, 1913, February 28, 1919, November 30, 1923, January 1, 1927; *Portland* (Ore.) *Times,* January 11, 1919; *Chicago Broad Ax,* November 28, 1914; *Chicago Defender,* September 17, 1921, and July 20, 1933.

39. See the discussion of Johnson and the *Half-Century Magazine* in Hellwig, "Japanese," p. 96.

40. *Chicago Whip,* July 9, 1919, December 10, 1921, November 18, 1922; *Chicago Defender,* September 18, 1920; Hellwig, "Japanese," p. 96.

41. *Chicago Whip,* November 18, 1922; *Chicago Defender,* November 25, 1922; *Baltimore Afro-American,* September 18, 1920. Pickens quoted in Hellwig, "Japanese," p. 95.

42. *Philadelphia Tribune,* April 26, 1924; *Baltimore Afro-American,* April 18 and December 27, 1924; *Chicago Defender,* October 23, 1920, November 25, 1922, April 19, May 10, June 28, 1924; *Negro World,* April 26 and June 21, 1924; *The Messenger* (New York) 6 (1924): 178–79, 247; Hellwig, "Japanese," p. 94.

43. *Kansas City* (Kans.) *Call,* June 6, 1924; *Chicago Defender,* April 19 and May 3, 1924.

44. See, for example, *Chicago Whip,* November 18, 1922; *Chicago Defender,* September 22, 1923; *Pittsburgh Courier,* April 26 and June 14, 1924; *Baltimore Afro-American,* January 31, 1925; John Bruce, "Present Tendencies" (1919?), John Bruce Papers, Schomburg Branch of the New York City Public Library; *Galveston New Idea,* February 27, 1908; Miller, *Everlasting Stain,* p. 67; Hellwig, "Japanese," pp. 97,. 99.

45. William Britton, a columnist for the *Norfolk Journal and Guide,* expressed a similar view. He hoped that President Calvin Coolidge could find a way to sign restrictive immigration legislation that would not offend the Japanese. "We entertain no ill-will toward the Japanese nor any other race of people," he wrote, "but restricted immigration is imperative, without the Japanese exclusion provision if possible, but with it if that be the only way." Britton, "Review and Comment," *Norfolk Journal and Guide,* May 24, 1924. On March 6, 1909, the *Indianapolis Freeman* stated that a large influx of Asian immigrants would be bad for the country.

46. *Chicago Defender,* October 23, 1920, January 15 and September 17, 1921, April 19, 1924. See also *St. Paul Appeal,* October 12, 1907.

47. Simmons, "The Week," *Chicago Defender,* December 29, 1923.

48. *Los Angeles California Eagle,* May 2 and 30, December 26, 1924;

Kansas City Call, May 31, 1924; *Negro World*, June 21, 1924; *Norfolk Journal and Guide*, June 21, 1924. See also Noah Thompson, "These 'Colored' United States: California," *The Messenger* 6 (1924): 215, 220-21; *Richmond Planet*, January 12, 1924; Hellwig, "Japanese," p. 99.

49. *Chicago Defender*, September 16, 1916; *Los Angeles California Eagle*, April 29, 1916; Braisford Brazeal, *The Brotherhood of Sleeping Car Porters* (New York, 1946), pp. 114-16. In 1912 and 1913, the several railroads briefly replaced Negro waiters and cooks with Japanese but soon hired the blacks back. *Indianapolis Freeman*, March 9, 1912; *Savannah Tribune*, August 9, 1913.

50. *Pittsburgh Courier*, February 18, 1933. David Hellwig notes that after 1924 black journalists saw no value in equating the plight of blacks and Japanese. Hellwig, "Japanese," p. 97.

51. *Philadelphia Tribune*, June 3, 1933; Brazeal, *Brotherhood*, pp. 114-16.

52. For the issues worrying blacks in the 1930s, see August Meier and Elliott Rudwick, *From Plantation to Ghetto* (rev. ed., New York, 1970), pp. 239-44.

53. Roger Daniels and Harry Kitano assert that because of Japanese reluctance to mix with blacks there was some satisfaction among West Coast Negroes when the Japanese were interned. Several blacks were able to secure work at jobs vacated by Japanese. On the other hand, a study conducted in 1942 showed that 18 percent of blacks polled believed they would be treated better under Japanese rule than under American rule. About 31 percent said treatment would be the same, and 23 percent expressed no opinion. A mere 28 percent declared that treatment would be worse if the Japanese ran America. Daniels and Kitano, *American Racism* (Englewood Cliffs, N.J., 1970), p. 72; Charles Marden, *Minorities in American Society* (New York, 1952), p., 308. Dominic Capeci, "The Harlem Riot of 1943" (Ph.D. dissertation, University of California at Riverside, 1970), p. 69.

54. See R. P. Edwards's editorial in the *Los Angeles California Eagle*, June 21, 1924.

55. See notes 18 and 25.

56. *New York Age*, May 22, 1913, February 5, 1921; Schuyler, "Views and Reviews," *Pittsburgh Courier*, January 16, 1926.

57. Terrell, "What it Means to Be Colored in the Capital of the United States," *The Independent* 62 (January 24, 1907): 181-86; Gerda Lerner, ed., *Black Women in White America* (New York, 1972), p. 379.

58. Laura Bartlett to the editor, *Baltimore Afro-American*, December 2, 1933.

59. *Colored American Magazine* 11 (1906): 285; Brown, "Japan for the Japanese," *Chicago Defender*, January 15, 1921; *Cleveland Gazette*, March 22, 1919; *St. Paul Appeal*, January 5, 1907; *Baltimore Afro-American*, October 1, 1920; Terrell quoted in Hellwig, "Japanese," p. 103.

60. *Philadelphia Tribune*, June 27, 1910; *Los Angeles California Eagle*, September 23, 1922; *New York Sun*, n.d., quoted in *New York Age*, July 31, 1913 (emphasis added).

61. Purvis to Francis Grimké, January 14, November 6, 1921, in Carter G. Woodson, ed., *The Works of Francis J. Grimké* 4 vols. (Washington, D.C., 1942), 4: 296–97, 339; Isaiah Dorsey to the editor, *Baltimore Afro-American*, April 25, 1924.

62. *Cleveland Gazette*, February 6, 1932; *Chicago Defender*, May 24, 1913. Du Bois conceded that "Negroes of the Pacific Coast who are in competition with the Japanese laborers are decidedly against the yellow men," but he hastily added that this was not true of "the more cultured people of California."

3 THE MEXICANS

A few Southerners in the 1870s saw Mexicans as potential replacements for Negro field hands, but there is no evidence that there was then any influx of Mexicans to pick cotton or plant corn.[1] Therefore, before 1900 few black agricultural laborers seriously worried about being supplanted by Mexicans.

One major difference in the way blacks viewed Mexico from the way they viewed China or Japan is that, whereas few Afro-Americans visited Asia, several thousand Negroes traveled to Mexico. During the antebellum years, an undetermined number of slaves ran away to Mexico, where slavery was outlawed. A handful of free blacks, including William Leidesdorff, a business-man, settled in San Francisco in the early 1840s and took out Mexican citizenship. After the Mexican War, blacks and Mexicans in California occasionally worked together in the mines, socialized with each other, and sometimes even intermarried.[2]

Negroes never contemplated moving to Asia, but some did consider relocating south of the Rio Grande. The first known effort to promote black colonization in Mexico, however, was not the idea of Afro-Americans. In 1861 and again in 1862, Robert W. Schufeldt, the American consul stationed at Havana, Cuba, suggested that a colony of blacks be established on the Tehuantepec Isthmus in Mexico. This was not proposed for humanitarian reasons but rather to block any potential move-ment of France into Guatemala. Schufeldt thought that if American blacks lived in Tehuantepec, which was near Guatemala, the French, who were preparing to send troops to Mexico, would moderate their colonial ambitions. In 1861, when Montgomery Blair, Lincoln's postmaster general, discussed the subject with

Matias Romero, the Mexican chargé d'affaires in Washington. he was told that Mexico was interested in plans to colonize Negroes in Yucatan and Tehuantepec. Romero noted that there would not be much race prejudice against blacks in his country. By the fall of 1862, the Mexican government had reconsidered the matter and blocked efforts on the part of the United States to purchase Cozumel Island off the eastern coast of Yucatan as a potential colony for Negroes. Apparently, the Mexicans concluded that the existence of an Afro-American colony in Mexico would provide the United States with an excuse to intervene in their internal affairs. Moreover, the proposed colonists would not be as desirable as Romero originally thought for they would be unable to speak Spanish, would likely be Protestant in religion, and would be unfamiliar with Mexican customs.[3]

Insofar as can be determined, the blacks' first effort to resettle in Mexico came in 1888, more than twenty years after the end of the Civil War. In 1888, the Mexican Land and Development Company, which claimed to own seven million acres of land in the Mexican state of Tamaulipas, near Brownsville, Texas, offered to sell shares of its stock to interested blacks for $5 per share. Prospective investors and potential settlers were assured that Mexico was "richly endowed by nature in the resources of the soil, the forest, field and mine and [was] blessed with all of the advantages of a salubrious climate and geographical location." Unfortunately, it is not known whether the Mexican Land and Development Company was a financial success, for it was not mentioned in the black press after September 8, 1888.[4]

Whatever its fate, it was but one sign of Afro-American interest in the United States's neighbor to the south. Another was the establishment in 1893 of the Colored Colonization Company of San Diego, California. This second firm was formed by James Fowler, a black who proposed to sell shares of his company for a dollar apiece. According to Fowler, he had arranged to purchase land in Mexico between the Colorado River and the Gulf of Mexico. This territory, he said, was ideal for farming, fishing, and mining and would quickly be "gobbled up" by the intelligent Negro seeking to "worship God under . . . [his] own vine and fig tree with none to make [him] afraid." For over a year, Fowler regularly advertised the sale of his stock in the *Indianapolis Freeman*, actively soliciting funds from investors and would-be colonists.[5]

This colonization scheme intrigued the Afro-American population of San Diego, and one California writer happily noted, "The Mexican Emigration fever is rife here." A. L. Allen, another black resident of San Diego, was ecstatic about the virtues of living in Mexico. In his opinion, the soil south of the Rio Grande was unusually fertile, the mines were full of valuable minerals, and the sun was always shining. Since the Mexican government was eager to develop its resources, Allen asserted, it "would hail our coming with delight" and might even supply farmers with free land. In Mexico, the Negro would not have to fear discrimination, for there "you are a man among men, where your color is not known, where any position to which you aspire is open to you. All depends upon your merits, not your skin."[6]

Less than a month after Allen wrote his ode on Mexico, Fowler announced that he would lead a band of colonists south of the Rio Grande before the end of May 1895. Unable to believe that his colony could fail, he anticipated staging a gala celebration in Mexico on June 19, 1895, to commemorate the success of the venture. Unhappily for the historian, Fowler's note of January 9, 1895, was his last letter to the *Indianapolis Freeman*. Nothing more is known about the fate of his colonization scheme.[7]

In February of that year, approximately 800 blacks from Georgia and Alabama, fed up "with the indignities of discrimination," settled in Tlahualilo, 30 miles east of Mapimi, in Durango, Mexico. Responsible for the settlement of the colony was W. H. Ellis, an enterprising Afro-American businessman. On December 11, 1894, Ellis had entered into an elaborate contract with the Agricultural, Industrial, and Colonization Company of Tlahualilo, better known as the Mexican Land Corporation. The corporation, headed by Juan Llamedo, a wealthy Mexican businessman, had been founded earlier that year. The company owned 2.5 million acres of land in the Mexican state of Durango. Most of this land was used for ranching or mineral exploration, but some 50,000 acres were cultivated for the planting of cotton. Llamedo and his board of directors were eager to promote settlement on their land and to triple their cotton acreage. The Mexican Land Corporation agreed to make funds available to each prospective colonist, to loan him money to pay for his transportation expenses and to provide him with tools, water for irrigation purposes, seed, mules, fuel, housing, medicine, and some spending money.[8] Each family would receive a tract of land no smaller than 60 acres on which it would be expected to grow corn, cotton, and garden vegetables.[9] Under the terms of the contract, colonists would turn over 40 percent of their cotton and corn crop to the company and 10 percent to Ellis. The remainder of the corn and cotton and all of the produce from their garden patches would be theirs to keep.[10]

Ellis agreed to bring at least 100 families experienced in cotton cultivation to Tlahualilo by February 15, 1895. To do this he hired R. A. Williams, who for a generous fee, promised to furnish the company with 5,000 laborers within a year. Williams energetically advertised the proposed Mexican colony in Southern newspapers. Mexico was called a land of liberty, and exaggerated claims were made for the fecundity of the soil in Durango and the price of cotton in Mexico. Apparently, some blacks were led to believe that bananas, baked potatoes, and even molasses grew on trees and bushes in Mexico and were available for the picking. Opossum, deer, and other wild game, it was alleged, were plentiful.[11]

Williams was especially successful in promoting interest in colonization in Tuscaloosa and Green counties, Alabama. All but a handful of the colonists were Alabamians; the remainder came from Georgia. On January 29, 1895, the first colonists left Birmingham, Alabama, for Mexico. On February 24, 1895, five carloads of blacks bound for Williams's colony passed through Meridian, Mississippi, and several whites commented that the colonization scheme was an "indefensible outrage . . . perpetrated upon an ignorant people." They called on Negro leaders to tell the black emigrants that peonage existed in Mexico. Nonetheless, by the end of February it was estimated that there were more than 800 colonists at Mapimi.[12]

Some of the early reports indicated that the colonists were happy. Impressed with the opportunity to establish their own schools and churches and to make their own laws in what they hoped would be a land of milk and honey, they confidently expected to harvest bumper crops and become prosperous farmers. The Reverend S. F. Todd, one of three ministers in the colony, predicted that each acre of land would yield 100 to 175 bushels of corn or 1½ bales of cotton. Furthermore, he declared, colonists at Tlahualilo need not fear lynchings or racial discrimination.[13]

It quickly became apparent that Todd's rosy picture of life in Durango was most inaccurate. Poor weather conditions and a shortage of suitable agricultural tools made it difficult to plant crops. Although they had been told they would work on individual plots, the blacks were forced to work in groups under the watchful eyes of Mexican guards. Those who refused to labor on the Sabbath were not fed that day, and when some colonists complained about conditions, Ellis had them jailed. Despite some efforts on the part of the company to provide the colonists with familiar foods like cornbread, salt pork, and bacon, the settlers were unable to adjust to the diet of Mexican farmers. Worst of all, Ellis failed to have the colonists inoculated against disease, and this proved to be an inexcusable oversight. In April, a mysterious liver disease caused several deaths in the colony; soon after, smallpox and malaria epidemics erupted. At least ninety colonists died of disease within four months of their arrival in Mexico.[14]

As early as March 1895, colonists were fleeing Mapimi, telling horror stories about life in Durango. Williams, greatly disillusioned with what he had seen in the colony, completely disassociated himself from the scheme and confirmed that the colonists had suffered many privations. By the summer of 1895, all but fifty of the surviving blacks had fled the settlement. Ailing and destitute, they were soon obliged to seek assistance from U.S. consular officials in Mexico. Clothing, army rations, and money were collected for the Negroes, and the U.S. government arranged to quarantine those showing signs of smallpox or other diseases. Arrangements were made with railroads to transport the survivors to Birmingham. In 1896, Congress appropriated more than $5,600 to reimburse the railroads for the costs of bringing the Negroes back to Alabama.[15] The Mexican Land Corporation claimed that the venture cost them more than $7,000, and they were forced to bring Mexicans to the settlement to harvest what remained of the crop.[16]

Fully one-fourth of the colonists had died in this ill-fated venture. Even before the magnitude of the disaster was completely known, a few blacks had warned that not all was joy and happiness in Mexico. An Afro-American living in New Mexico Territory declared that Negroes were not really wanted in Mexico and that land there was not as bountiful as had been alleged. Some even thought that all colonization schemes were fraudulent, insisting that "those engaged in fostering [them are] . . . good examples for the State Prison or worse."[17]

Despite what had happened in Durango, a number of blacks continued to believe that Afro-Americans could be more successful in Mexico than in the South. They pointed with pride to the accomplishments of Thomas Bass, a Negro rancher living in Mexico, whose horses had won blue ribbons at state fairs in Iowa and Minnesota. There was also Dr. Jesse Mosely, who bragged that he lived in a country where "a man is a man. I am the private physician to the governor of this state [Tamaulipas]." According to Mosely, Afro-Americans in Mexico were "making money and enjoying life." Little wonder that he encouraged Negro laborers to give more consideration to settling in Mexico.[18]

Others agreed that south of the Rio Grande there were "splendid opening[s]" for ambitious blacks. Noted the *Tulsa Star*: "There are great opportunities in Mexico for young men and chances to make quick money with small investments." Boosters of colonization pointed out that Mexico was a nearby haven for those eager to escape segregation, disfranchisement, and lynchings. Typical of those expressing this viewpoint was John Prowd. To him, Mexico was "the land of freedom and opportunity—where a man breathes the atmosphere of tolerance, where his ambitions and dreams be within himself for realization and not within his COLOR."[19]

Enterprising blacks once again investigated the possibility of moving to Mexico, and in 1922, a delegation of Negro leaders met with Mexican president Alvaro Obrégon to discuss this subject with him. Obrégon cordially invited the Negroes to settle in his country and promised them that while in Mexico they need never fear racial discrimination. Thus encouraged, Afro-Americans from California and Oklahoma[20] formed the Lower California, Mexican Land and Development Company. The company sold shares of stock to hundreds of eager investors and for the sum of $39,000 purchased an 8,000-acre ranch near Ensenada on which it hoped to grow wheat and corn, raise livestock, and entertain tourists. Stockholders would be welcome to use the facilities on the ranch, and before long it was expected that colonists would be able to move to Ensenada and start their own farms.[21]

By 1935, however, there was no more talk of colonization of Mexico. Scarcely a black newspaper was willing to admit that it had ever even endorsed such a scheme. What had caused this dramatic change? There are a number of answers. First, Negroes began to doubt that they were genuinely welcome south of the Rio Grande. In 1923, the *Chicago Tribune* falsely circulated a story declaring that blacks were *persona non grata* in Mexico. This item was widely reprinted in several Afro-American journals, and not everyone realized that the story was incorrect. In 1929, the *Chicago Defender* reported that Mexican immigration officials had asked American authorities not to grant citizenship certificates to blacks seeking to cross the border. The *Defender* story, unlike the *Tribune* article, was never contradicted. Later, in 1932 and 1934, the *Los Angeles California Eagle* printed articles alleging that the Mexican government had changed its immigration laws so that it was difficult, if not impossible, for blacks to enter the country. Afro-Americans protested to Secretaries of State Henry L. Stimson and Cordell Hull, but little attention was given to their complaints.[22]

But there were other reasons to look askance at colonization schemes. The Lower California, Mexican Land and Development Company went bankrupt in 1927. Several of its promoters and its legal counsel were swindlers, and within five years their mismanagement of the company's assets had been responsible for the accumulation of debts totaling $78,000. The ranch at Ensenada had been used not for farming but rather for lavish "drinking and poker" parties. Hundreds of investors discovered that their stock was worthless, and they were not likely again to view Mexico as a land of milk and honey.[23]

A story that appeared in the May 1931 issue of *The Crisis* offered an additional reason to spurn colonization proposals. In an article about Valerio Trujano, a village populated by blacks born in Mexico, Carleton Beals described how local officials were constantly forced to send representatives to Mexico City to prevent greedy hacienda owners from taking over their meagre landholdings. Beals noted the impressive accomplishments of the blacks living in Valerio Trujano, but he concluded that "their struggle is likely to become well-nigh hopeless. The central government has turned its back on the agrarian problem. The villagers can hope for no additional lands to make life more than a barren struggle for existence."[24] If black natives could not succeed in Mexico, many wondered, how in a time of international depression could emigrants from the United States expect to do any better?

Colonization schemes had always had detractors, but few were as imaginative as the *Philadelphia Tribune*. Why, it asked, should blacks become colonists in Mexico? Instead, why not make Mexico a colony of the United States? Persuaded that the Mexican peons were lacking in "mental and physical powers," it hoped "that the day is close at hand when the United States will assume a protectionate [sic] and give Mexico, as it did Cuba and the Philippines—good government, educational facilities, and proper sanitation." Curiously enough, the *Philadelphia Tribune*, like many other Negro journals, subsequently expressed disapproval of the landing of American forces at Vera Cruz in 1914.[25]

Probably most blacks had no desire to establish colonies in Mexico or to annex its territory. To them Mexico was a "semi-civilized" land unwilling or unable to exploit its rich deposits of oil, copper, gold, and silver to help uplift its people. Although blessed with millions of acres of good farmland, the country was an undeveloped "desert" barely able to feed its tiny population, and it was reported that some of its people were forced to supplement their diet by making cakes from crushed insect eggs. According to the black press, the only plausible explanation for this sad state of affairs was that the Mexicans were a backward and uncultured people. This conclusion seemed to be reaffirmed by stories that "the most primitive methods of agriculture are still in vogue in many parts of Mexico." Even on farms near Mexico City one supposedly could see the ground being "broken by wooden plows drawn by oxen." The Mexican peon, it was said, had no interest in learning about more advanced ways of harvesting his crops. The women of Mexico were equally unaware of "modern methods" of doing their housework. "The average Mexican cook," insisted one observer, "is as primitive as the washerwoman. No matter how many times the use of a modern cooking stove [is] explained [to] her, it is probable that she would build the fire in the oven and put the bread to bake in the fire box." Moreover, Mexicans were supposed to be ignorant of the most rudimentary forms of sanitation, and thus Yankee visitors to Mexico would do well to watch what they ate and drank. Those easily susceptible to illness were advised to avoid the country entirely. "Influenza," cautioned the *Indianapolis Freeman*, "is reported unusually fatal in the City of Mexico.[26]

Why was Mexico so backward, and why were her people so miserable? A number of blacks, many of whom were fundamental Protestants, believed that Mexico's problems stemmed from the peon's ignorance of Christianity. In 1893, a visitor to the country declared that the Catholic priests in Mexico deliberately conspired to keep the common man ignorant of the Bible so that he might be more easily coerced. While in Mexico City, the Yankee stated, he had tried in vain to purchase a copy of the Roman Catholic version of the New Testament. When he asked a salesclerk in one of the city's largest bookstores for a copy of the Gospel of Christ, the bewildered employee searched every shelf of the store in a futile effort to find the elusive book. Finally, he approached his customer and asked, "Who is the author of this book, the New Testament?" Such incidents were so regularly described in black papers that the *Washington Bee* expressed no surprise when, seventeen years later, it reported that the interior of the historic church of Landin, near Saltillo, Mexico, was being "used as a corral for goats."[27]

Blacks equated this ignorance of Christianity with ignorance of morality and democracy. Therefore, it was fitting, they thought, that "in some parts of Mexico proficiency of the school children is rewarded by giving them the cigarette-smoking privilege in school." Nor was it surprising that Mexicans seemed unable to maintain a democratic form of government. "The habit of starting a revolution every time the wind blows the other way," commented the *Chicago Defender*, "is one that seems to have fixed itself on the Mexican people." So regular were reports of political turmoil, assassinations, kidnappings, and diplomatic intrigue in Mexico that in 1924, W. J. Wheaton expressed pleasure when he learned that the country had "recently inaugurated a President without the semblance of a revolution and without the shedding of one drop of blood." Perhaps, he mused, at long last "the Republic of Mexico is taking her place among the nations by showing her respect for the law."[28]

Had lurid stories about the backwardness of Mexico and its people been confined to the pens of editors eager to attract subscribers, one might dismiss these articles as unrepresentative. But Afro-American intellectuals seemed to be equally unimpressed with the Mexican people. For example, Professor Charles Alexander of Los Angeles, who visited Juárez in 1914, reported that "the Mexicans have a sullen, unfriendly look which repels even those who entertain benevolent intentions. Many of them live a lowly, depraved life."[29]

Twelve years later William Pickens, a black educator and an NAACP official, also toured Juárez, and like Alexander he too was disgusted with what he saw. In his opinion, Juárez personified "vice." He estimated that every third store in the city was either a saloon or a gambling joint. Unsavory as these spots were, they were almost pleasant when compared with the "dirty markets with flies swarming everywhere over the food" or the 300-year-old "mission church [where] beggars kneel and annoy all comers for coins." Only in "Italy below Naples" had Pickens ever before seen such conditions. Even worse, he related, the peasantry of Juárez had no sense of shame that they were living in a den of iniquity. "Women walk the streets in kitchen aprons, headclothes, and other negligee and private looking clothes, and the men dressed in dirty overalls and other working clothes—and none of them working!" Little wonder, he added, that the local jail was filled with scores of male and female drunks. In the jail, he discovered, "the women's door is not locked and generally they are lolling around, smoking, making 'eyes' and trying to 'vamp' the visitors." Pickens gladly left Juárez and returned to the United States.[30]

Picken's view of the residents of Juárez was not unlike the image of the Mexican-American that appeared in the black press from 1910 to 1935. During these years, more than 650,000 Mexicans immigrated to the United States, and some of the newcomers settled in areas populated by blacks.[31] (See Table 2.)

Table 2   Mexican and Black Population in Selected Cities, 1910–1930

CITY	Mexican (1910)	Black (1910)	Mexican (1920)	Black (1920)	Mexican (1930)	Black (1930)
Albuquerque	150	244	328	213	610	441
Austin, Tex.	516	7,478	899	6,921	5,014	9,868
Bethlehem, Pa.	N.A.	100	N.A.	344	415	715
Chicago	N.A.	44,103	1,967	109,458	19,362	233,903
Dallas, Tex.	127	18,024	2,278	24,023	5,901	38,742
Denver, Colo.	223	5,426	1,390	6,075	6,837	7,204
Detroit	N.A.	5,741	712	40,838	6,515	120,066
El Paso	12,297	1,452	30,589	1,330	58,291	1,855
Flint, Mich.	N.A.	147	82	1,701	635	5,725
Ft. Worth, Tex.	406	13,280	3,785	15,896	3,955	22,234
Galveston, Tex.	328	8,036	1,509	9,888	2,538	13,226
Gary, Ind.	N.A.	383	164	5,299	3,486	17,922
Houston	476	23,929	3,946	33,960	14,149	63,337
Kansas City, Kans.	102	9,286	2,039	14,405	2,615	19,872
Kansas City, Mo.	N.A.	23,566	1,797	30,719	2,984	38,574
Los Angeles	5,611	7,599	21,598	15,579	97,116	38,894

N.A. = Not available

SOURCE: U.S. Census Reports for 1910, 1920, and 1930.

Table 2—*Continued*

CITY	Mexican (1910)	Black (1910)	Mexican (1920)	Black (1920)	Mexican (1930)	Black (1930)
Milwaukee	N.A.	980	N.A.	2,229	1,479	7,501
New Orleans	596	89,262	1,242	100,930	717	129,632
Oakland, Calif.	249	3,055	1,026	5,489	3,200	7,503
Oklahoma City	379	6,546	788	8,241	998	14,662
Omaha	N.A.	4,426	682	10,315	940	12,123
Phoenix	792	328	2,323	1,074	7,293	2,366
Sacramento	103	486	483	675	3,374	1,086
San Antonio	9,906	10,716	28,444	14,341	82,373	17,978
San Diego	1,222	597	2,741	997	9,266	2,723
San Francisco	1,763	1,642	3,793	2,414	7,922	3,083
Topeka, Kans.	284	4,538	837	1,695	1,730	5,756
Tucson, Ariz.	2,441	222	4,261	346	10,235	1,003
Tulsa,Okla.	9	1,959	168	8,878	294	15,203
Waco, Tex.	77	6,067	437	7,726	1,692	9,370
Wichita, Kans.	337	2,457	797	3,545	1,078	5,623

Afro-Americans professed to be revolted by the crude habits of "the densely ignorant son[s] of the Astecs [sic]." According to the *Pittsburgh Courier*, they "care nothing about our civilization and are the slowest to adopt our methods, and above all, . . . simply refuse to obey American laws." Writing from San Antonio, Texas, a correspondent for the *New York Age* warned that "the American Negro has every reason to regard with grave distrust the influx of thousands of Mexican peons into the United States." He described the newcomers in rather unflattering terms:

The Mexican peon lives cheaply in shacks with scarcely any furniture. So scant is the furniture in their homes that when they decide to vacate one house to occupy another they can almost imitate the legendary Arab, who in the silence of the night folded his tent and quietly stole away. The moving of a Mexican from one house to another is but a matter of a few moments. Many of these homes do not even contain chairs—they squat on the floor as the Red Man squats in his teepee.[32]

What bothered blacks more than the newcomers' standard of living was that occasionally both competed for the same jobs and that the "grossly illiterate and greasy" Mexican worked "for almost nothing . . . [and was] taking bread from the mouths of colored people." Observers such as Carter Woodson uncomfortably noted that Mexican laborers were working on farms and railroads, as busboys, cooks, and garbagemen, toiling for factories, and for construction companies in Indiana, Oklahoma, New Mexico, Texas, Illinois, Ohio, New York, New Jersey, Colorado, California, and Pennsylvania. These jobs were previously held by blacks and whites, and so it was understandable that there was a fear that a deluge of "hordes and hordes" of Mexicans, willing to work for low wages, would promote Negro unemployment. It was noted that some cotton growers publicly declared they preferred docile Mexican workers to Negroes. Not surprisingly, Carter G. Woodson was upset that large Mexican families with "children boarded up in Fords like so many cattle" were "enroute to the cotton fields." Another commentator insisted that "it would be well . . . if 'Made by Mexican Labor' w[as] eradicated from the annals of American industry and that the black man be given preference. Certainly," he concluded, "they [sic] deserve priority over Mexican 'bootleg' labor, and, in fact, over any type of unnaturalized labor."[33]

Many whites agreed with this viewpoint. Among the most influential critics of Mexican labor was Thomas Nixon Carver, a white economics professor at Harvard University. Writing to Roscoe Conkling Simmons, an influential Afro-American editor, Carver warned that Mexican peons had already displaced significant numbers of Negroes in the Texas cottonfields. He suggested that Congress investigate the situation, and he noted that Mexico had already enacted "a law requiring every industry to employ at least 90 [p]er cent native Mexicans. Certainly she could not with a straight face object if we had a law requiring every industrial plant and every truck farm and cotton plantation to employ at least 90 per cent native Americans."[34]

Carver's prediction that unrestricted Mexican immigration would bring dire consequences was music to the ears of the *Houston Informer*. This paper had long crusaded in favor of legislation to curb the number of Mexican workers in the state. "Charity begins at home," it declared, "and all immigration should be curbed until there is more than enough work for the home folks." All too often, it concluded, "one sees Mexicans working and making wages for the support of themselves and theirs, while native citizens, black and white, are on the verge of starvation."[35]

Not all agreed that Mexican workers were that serious a threat. Charles Johnson, a black sociologist, believed that there was little real competition. In his opinion, "Mexicans [were] taking the least desirable jobs, pushing up Negroes one grade as Negroes in turn pushed up the foreign born, who in turn pushed up the native whites." Taking a different view, one newspaperman thought that the presence of Mexican laborers in the South and Southwest would prove beneficial to the blacks, for "it would provide the South with another race upon which to divide its spleen and affections." It was about time, he maintained, for Dixie to "have something new to worry about."[36]

Some concluded that the only reason for the Mexican influx was that the United States was suffering from a labor shortage. Rural areas in particular desperately needed more field hands and therefore hoped "to see as many Mexican laborers come into the country as possible." America was a "vast country," it was argued, and there was ample room for all. Besides, Negroes might learn from observing the newcomers. If Mexican bootblacks occasionally drove Negro competitors out of business, the *Los Angeles California Eagle* declared, perhaps it was because their stands were more attractive and were "embellished with mirrors and shining brass." Afro-Americans simply would have learned that the most industrious man "gets the business."[37]

George Schuyler, however, dismissed such an observation as ridiculous. "If the million Mexicans who have entered the country have not displaced Negro workers," he asked, "who[m] have they displaced?" With the onset of the Depression, more and more blacks were agreeing with Schuyler. If the Mexican really was an industrious worker, they thought, he should labor "right below the Rio Grande where there is plenty of land awaiting development. This country already has too many unemployed workers competing with each other for the right to work without bringing in more." Carter G. Woodson sarcastically disputed allegations "that Mexicans can stand the heat better than Negroes" and were "better suited for railroad work. This is mere subterfuge," Woodson claimed, "for until the Mexican came . . . with his cheaper labor, the Negro, for a similar reason, had been considered a satisfactory worker."[38]

With great alacrity, Afro-Americans enthusiastically endorsed various schemes proposed by several congressmen to bar Mexicans from the United States. "Of what use is a protective tariff," wondered the *San Francisco Western Outlook* of February 25, 1928, "if foreign labor is to be allowed to come in unrestricted to compete with American citizens, and any Republican Congressman who would vote to let down the bars should be classed as an enemy of labor."

Congress never did succeed in restricting Mexican immigration. After the start of the Depression, however, the United States no longer looked so attractive to Mexicans, and migrants were less eager to cross the border. State and local welfare agencies, eager to cut down on expenses and to trim their relief rolls, discovered that they could transport Mexicans back to Mexico for less than it cost to give them public assistance for a month. At first, voluntary repatriation was encouraged, but as time passed, officials decided to force Mexicans to "return home." With a flagrant disregard for the civil liberties of the people involved, officials during the six-year period between 1929 and 1935 rounded up over 400,000 Mexicans, packed them like cattle on railroad cars, and shipped them to destinations south of the Rio Grande. There is no evidence that blacks voiced any objections to this brutal treatment. Many merely thought that "with the repatriation of the Mexicans the labor market for colored workers will be considerably improved."[39]

That blacks in 1930 held such an opinion would have surprised some whites. It was commonly known that the Mexican government periodically denounced discrimination against Afro-Americans and that Mexican Americans "frequently s[ought] lodgings with Negroes" and occasionally even married blacks. Why was it then that relations between the two were so bad that Negroes dismissed Mexicans as a "poor people accustomed to nothing more than an adobe shack, a blanket, and a tortilla?" Why were blacks calling Mexicans immoral and "the slowest to adopt our methods?"[40] It has already been noted that in some areas Mexicans and Afro-Americans competed for the same jobs and that there was fear of wage reductions, but this does not explain all of the hostility. A very important reason for black antipathy towards Mexicans was jealousy.[41]

In the South and Southwest, the Mexican was legally classified as white. No matter how dark his skin or how untidy his appearance, one man complained, the Mexican was able to get first-class hotel and railroad accommodations and to send his children to white schools.[42] With great bitterness, the *Houston Informer* reported that local officials had set aside a 10-acre tract of city land to serve the recreational needs of Houston's Mexican community. No land had ever been given to blacks to enable them to build a park. The existing park for Afro-Americans had been purchased years before by black civic leaders, and city authorities had never appropriated any money for its upkeep. "Mexicans are aleins [sic] who swear their allegiance to a foreign power," the *Informer* observed. "But when it comes to spending a little money for recreation purposes, it seems to be all for aliens and nothing for citizens."[43]

Jealousy was also evident in the matter of lynchings. Whenever a Mexican-American was lynched, officials in Washington were quick to apologize to the Mexican government. And they immediately put pressure on state and local authorities to track down and punish those responsible for the crime. These same officials ignored the lynchings of Afro-Americans, insisting that these incidents were none of their concern. Understandably, Negroes objected to this double standard, and they occasionally took out their resentment on Mexican-Americans.[44]

All things considered, therefore, it is not difficult to comprehend why, by 1935, Negroes were unable to sympathize with the plight of their Mexican-American brothers. Consciously or unconsciously, blacks had accepted a negative image of Mexico and its people that was much like that of white Americans.[45] Whereas Mexico had once been seen as a haven for persecuted blacks, stories in the Afro-American press now invariably emphasized the backwardness of its people and government. Mexicans were supposedly skilled only at fomenting civil unrest. "Perhaps if [the]y . . . were more generally intelligent, like the people of the United States," pontificated the *Indianapolis Freeman*, they could establish a democracy. "Mexico," it concluded, "is an excellent demonstration of the fact that one kind of government is not suitable for all people."[46] It was not difficult to transfer the negative stereotype of the Mexican in Mexico to the Mexican in the United States. In fact, north of the Rio Grande, the Mexican was even more menacing than he was at home. Here he supposedly retained his low standard of living and sought to take the jobs of Negroes. In retrospect, one can note that the threat was more imagined than real, but contemporary black newspapers suggest that Negroes genuinely believed that competition from Mexicans was a very real menace.

Even worse was the matter of skin color. Color distinctions were less bothersome to Mexicans than to residents of the United States,[47] but even in Mexico a prominent citizen with obvious mulatto or African ancestry never proudly alluded to this aspect of his family heritage. His friends were careful to do likewise. As far as the U.S. government was concerned, Mexicans were Caucasians. The Immigration Act of 1924 barred entry into the United States of all persons with more than 50 percent Indian blood. At least 38 percent of all Mexicans would have fit into this proscribed category, but immigration authorities decided to classify all Mexican immigrants as white. Thus, Mexicans with darker skins than most Afro-Americans were listed on immigration forms as "whites."[48] Certainly this caused envy. Surely Negroes were jealous and resentful when they saw bronze-colored foreigners going to movies in "white" theaters and eating in restaurants open to whites only.[49]

There is no evidence that Mexicans protested Jim Crow legislation. As already noted in this chapter, stories circulated in the 1920s and 1930s that Mexico barred Afro-American tourists.[50] Therefore, Negroes saw no real reason to protest against forced repatriation of Mexicans during the Depression. It would take another generation before blacks and Mexicans recognized that they shared common problems and that they should view each other not as rivals but rather as potential partners in the fight against discrimination and prejudice.

NOTES

1. Winston Kinsey, "The Immigrant in Texas Agriculture During Reconstruction," *Agricultural History* 53 (1979): 137.
2. Rudolph Lapp, *Blacks in Gold Rush California* (New Haven, Conn., 1977), pp. 9-10, 35-36, 63-64, 88, 103.
3. Thomas Schoonover, "Misconstrued Mission: Expansionism and Black Colonization in Mexico and Central America During the Civil War," *Pacific Historical Review*, 49 (1980): 607-20. Mexico does not receive adequate attention in the best work on black colonization before the Civil War, Floyd Miller's *The Search for a Black Nationality: Black Colonization and Emigration, 1787-1863* (Urbana, Ill., 1975).
4. *Indianapolis Freeman*, August 18, 25, September 1, 8, 1888.
5. Ibid., August 26, 1893-January 26, 1895.
6. Ibid., August 26, 1893; letter from Allen, quoted in ibid., December 16, 1893.
7. Letter from Fowler, January 9, 1895, quoted in ibid., January 26, 1895.
8. *Failure of the Scheme for the Colonization of Negroes in Mexico*, 54th Congress, 1st Session, House Document 169, Serial 3420 (Washington, D.C., 1896), p. 59, hereafter cited as *Negroes in Mexico*; Alfred Reynolds, "The Alabama Negro Colony in Mexico, 1894-1896: Part I," *Alabama Review* 5 (1952): 244-46, hereafter cited as "Negro Colony: I."
9. *Negroes in Mexico*; J. Fred Rippy, "A Negro Colonization Project in Mexico, 1895," *Journal of Negro History* 6 (1921): 66-73; Reynolds, "Negro Colony: I," pp. 245-46.
10. Reynolds, "Negro Colony: I," pp. 245-47.
11. Ibid., pp. 247, 249, 256.
12. Ibid., pp. 249-51; report from Meridian, Mississippi, in *Atlanta Constitution*, March 6, 1895, quoted in *Bainbridge* (Ga.) *Democrat*, March 7, 1895.
13. Letter from Todd at Mapimi Station, Durango, Mexico, quoted in *Indianapolis Freeman*, May 4, 1895; Rippy, "Negro," *Negroes in Mexico*, pp. 11, 42; Reynolds, "Negro Colony: I," p. 265.
14. *Negroes in Mexico*; Reynolds, "Negro Colony: I," pp. 262-68 and his "The Alabama Negro Colony in Mexico, 1894-1896: Part II,"

Alabama Review 6 (1953): 31–58, hereafter cited as "Negro Colony: II."
    15. Reynolds, "Negro Colony: II," pp. 38, 55; Rayford Logan, *The Negro in American Life and Thought* (New York, 1954), pp. 137–38.
    16. Reynolds, "Negro Colony: II," pp. 41–42.
    17. Letter from J.S.H. of Santa Fe, New Mexico, quoted in *Indianapolis Freeman*, May 4, 1895; *Indianapolis Freeman*, April 27, 1895, May 9, 1903. See also W. Laird Clowes, *Black America* (London, 1891), pp. 189–90.
    18. *Indianapolis Freeman*, September 28, 1907; letter from Mosely of Tamaulipas, Mexico, quoted in *Washington Bee*, December 11, 1915.
    19. *Tulsa Star*, May 29, 1914; *Philadelphia Tribune*, July 25, 1914, May 6, 1916; *Indianapolis Freeman*, November 14, 1908, January 6, 1915; *Cleveland Gazette*, June 7, 1924; letter from Arna Bontemps, then a student at Pacific Union College, Saint Helena, California, quoted in *Los Angeles California Eagle*, March 10, 1923; John Prowd, "Big Celebration at Santa Clara Ranch, Mexico, Last Sunday," *Los Angeles California Eagle*, June 4, 1926.
    20. It is likely that colonization looked especially attractive to Oklahoma blacks. Nearly 200 Afro-Americans had been killed in the Tulsa race riot of May 30–June 1, 1921. Curiously, however, the black population of Tulsa grew significantly between 1920 and 1930 (table 2). For more on the Tulsa riot, see *Richmond Planet*, June 4, 11, 18, 1921; Lee Williams and Lee Williams II, *Anatomy of Four Race Riots* (Jackson, Miss., 1972), pp. x, 57–63.
    21. This company should not be confused with the Mexican Land and Development Company of the 1880s. *Tulsa Star*, September 18, 1920; *Los Angeles California Eagle*, July 1, 1922.
    22. *Los Angeles California Eagle*, March 3, 1923, November 18, 1932, January 26, 1934; *Norfolk* (Va.) *Journal and Guide*, March 10, October 27, 1923; *Savannah Tribune*, November 18, 1926; *Chicago Defender*, August 3, 1929, November 12, 1932; *Galveston Voice*, October 29, 1932.
    23. The failure of the Lower California, Mexican Land and Development Company is treated in great detail in *Los Angeles California Eagle*, November 26, 1926, March 4–August 19, 1927.
    24. Carleton Beals, "Valerio Trujano: Black Joy," *The Crisis* 38 (1931): 153–54, 174.
    25. *Philadelphia Tribune*, February 7, May 2, 1914. See also *Washington Bee*, April 25, 1914; *Tulsa Star*, April 25, June 20, August 1, November 14, 1914. On the other hand, reluctant approval for Wilson's Mexican policy came from the *Indianapolis Freeman*. See issues for April 26, May 2, 1914, March 25, May 6, and July 1, 15, 1916.

26. *Washington Bee*, August 9, 1902, January 4, 1908; *Philadelphia Tribune*, May 23, 1914; *Indianapolis Freeman*, April 13, 1889, March 1, 1890, January 23, 1904, June 3, 1916; *Chicago Journal*, n.d., quoted in *Indianapolis Freeman*, September 18, 1897.

27. *Indianapolis Freeman*, April 13, 1889, February 4, 1893; *Washington Bee*, January 8, 1910.

28. *Indianapolis Freeman*, February 15, 1913; *Tulsa Star*, March 7, 1914; *Washington Bee*, October 19, 1912; *Chicago Defender*, March 11, 1922, August 3, 1929; W. J. Wheaton, "Comments," *Los Angeles California Eagle*, December 5, 1924; *Galveston City Times*, March 7, September 12, 1914.

29. Article by Alexander, *Los Angeles California Eagle*, May 8, 1914.

30. William Pickens, "A Bit of Old Mexico, New Mexico and Needles," *Philadelphia Tribune*, May 15, 1926. Compare this with an article in the *Indianapolis Freeman* of April 13, 1889, discussing common law marriages in Mexico and noting that the country was populated by many "really idle people . . . who prefer to go miserably clad rather than work steadily."

31. Emory Bogardus, *The Mexican in the United States* (Los Angeles, 1934), p. 14; Leo Grebler, Joan Moore, and Ralph Guzman, *The Mexican American People* (New York, 1970), p. 64; Rodolfo Acuña, *Occupied America* (New York, 1972), p. 131.

32. *Pittsburgh Courier*, December 13, 1920, June 1, 1929, December 13, 1930; letter from San Antonio correspondent, *New York Age*, May 7, 1914; *Richmond Planet*, April 18, 1925; *Norfolk Journal and Guide*, October 17, 1925.

33. Charles B. Purvis to Francis J. Grimké, November 27, 1926 in Carter G. Woodson, ed., *The Works of Francis J. Grimké*, 4 vols. (Washington, D.C., 1942), 4: 410; Carter G. Woodson, "Economic Conditions Among Negroes in the South," *Journal of Negro History* 64 (1979): 267–70; *Galveston City Times*, October 1, 1904; *New York Age*, May 7, 1914; *Richmond Planet*, April 18, 1925; *Savannah Tribune*, September 9, 1926; *San Francisco Western Outlook*, May 5, 1928; *Pittsburgh Courier*, July 20, 1929, July 5, 1930; Vernon McCombs, *From Over the Border* (New York, 1925), p. 21; *Houston Informer*, January 23, 1932; George Schuyler, "Aframerica: Austin," *Pittsburgh Courier*, April 10, 1926; *Los Angeles California Eagle*, January 20, 1933; Lawrence DeGraaf, *Negro Migration to Los Angeles* (San Francisco, 1974), p. 25; Jay Stowell, *The Near Side of the Mexican Question* (New York, 1921), p. 43.

34. *Houston Informer*, April 9, 1932. Blacks and Mexicans also com-

peted in Texas and Oklahoma cottonfields. See *Indianapolis Freeman*, November 2, 30, 1907; *Galveston City Times*, October 1, 1904; Robert Wilson and Bill Hosokawa, *East to America* (New York, 1980), pp. 96–97.

35. *Houston Informer*, January 23, 1932.

36. Charles S. Johnson, *The Negro in American Civilization* (New York, 1930), p. 37; *New York Age*, March 10, 1928. See also *Old Hickory*, n.d., quoted in *Savannah Tribune*, November 25, 1911; *Pittsburgh Courier*, January 24, 1925; Paul Taylor, *Mexican Labor in the United States: Chicago and the Calumet Region* (Berkeley, Calif., 1932), p. 78.

37. *Chicago Defender*, May 17, 1924, January 1, 1927; *Savannah Tribune*, December 3, 1925, September 30, 1926; *Los Angeles California Eagle*, February 28, 1914; *Houston Informer*, September 27, 1930.

38. George Schuyler, "Views and Reviews," *Pittsburgh Courier*, May 26, 1928; *Pittsburgh Courier*, July 5, December 13, 1930; *Chicago Defender*, December 23, 1922. See also *Negro World* (New York), August 13, 1927; *Los Angeles California Eagle*, February 17, 1928; *Houston Informer*, October 4, 1930; *Norfolk Journal and Guide*, March 17, 1928; Woodson, "Economic Conditions," pp. 266–72.

39. For information on the repatriation of Mexicans, see Abraham Hoffman, *Unwanted Mexican Americans in the Great Depression* (Tucson, Ariz., 1974), pp. 83–132, 174–75; Neil Betten and Raymond Mohl, "From Discrimination to Repatriation, Mexican Life in Gary, Indiana During the Great Depression," *Pacific Historical Review* 42 (1973): 380–83; Carey McWilliams, *North from Mexico* (New York, reprint ed., 1961), p. 185. For the opinions of blacks on restricting Mexican immigration and repatriation, see *San Francisco Western Outlook*, December 10, 1927, February 4, 25, March 17, 1928; *Atlanta Independent*, February 16, 1928; *Norfolk Journal and Guide*, March 17, 1928; Charlotta Bass, "On the Sidewalk," *Los Angeles California Eagle*, May 16, 1930; *Houston Informer*, October 11, 1930; *Kansas City* (Kans.) *Call*, January 29, 1932. See also Matt Meier and Feliciano Rivera, *The Chicanos* (New York 1972), Chapter 9.

40. *Pittsburgh Courier*, July 20, 1929; *Houston Informer*, January 23, 1932; *Indianapolis Freeman*, June 13, 1908; *Washington Bee*, July 9, 1910; *Savannah Tribune*, November 25, 1911; Department of Welfare, Commonwealth of Pennsylvania, *Negro Survey of Pennsylvania* (Harrisburg, Pa., 1926), p. 88; Taylor, *Mexican Labor*, Chicago, pp. 252-55.

41. In Chicago, Italians unsuccessfully tried to exclude Mexicans from Hull House because they associated with blacks. Interestingly enough, some Negroes feared that associating with Mexicans would

corrupt their morals. Black papers frequently featured stories about the alleged gambling mania of Mexicans and about their supposedly bad tempers. Several Afro-Americans were shot by Mexicans. See, for example, *Chicago Whip*, September 30, 1922; *Chicago Defender*, July 27, 1929, August 15, 1931; Thomas Philpott, *The Slum and the Ghetto* (New York, 1978), p. 283.

42. For cases of blacks to pass as Mexicans in order to secure employment, see Taylor, *Mexican Labor, Chicago*, pp. 112-13. For a case of segregated breadlines during the Depression, see *Houston Informer*, May 5, 1934.

43. *Houston Informer*, May 5, 1934. For more on Negro jealousy and for information on Mexicans being considered white, see John Martinez, *Mexican Emigration to the United States, 1910-30* (San Francisco, 1971), pp. 93, 88; James Slayden, "The Mexican Immigrant," *Annals of the American Academy* 93 (1921): 124; *New York Age*, May 7, 1914; *Kansas City Call*, September 25, 1931. See also Ben Carruthers's fictional "Spick," which appeared in *Opportunity* 14 (1936): 239-40.

44. Roscoe Conkling Simmons, "The Week," *Chicago Defender*, November 25, 1922; Roy Wilkins, "Talking It Over," *Kansas City Call*, June 12, 1931; *Houston Informer*, July 18, 1931. On Mexican government protests about the lynching of Mexicans in Texas, see Lawrence Cardoso, *Mexican Emigration to the United States, 1897-1931* (Tucson, Ariz., 1980), pp. 114-15.

45. For more on this, see McWilliams, *North from Mexico*, Alphonso Pinckney, "Prejudice Toward Mexican and Negro Americans, a Comparison," *Phylon* 24 (1963): 353-59; Edward Bamford, "The Mexican Casual Problem in the Southwest," *Journal of Applied Sociology* 8 (1924): 363-71; William Albig, "Opinions Concerning Unskilled Mexican Immigration," *Sociology and Social Research* 15 (1930): 62–72.

46. *Indianapolis Freeman*, February 15, 1913.

47. Those Mexicans who lived in the United States for several generations picked up on the importance of color distinctions. If light in skin color, they often called themselves Spanish or Latin, so that they would not be considered Mexican immigrants. See Thomas Sowell, *Ethnic America: A History* (New York, 1981), Chapter 10.

48. Lapp, *Blacks in Gold Rush California*, 2: 118; Elmer Clark, *The Latin Immigrant in the South* (Nashville, Tenn., 1924), p. 35; Cardoso, *Mexican Emigration*, pp. 128-29; Robert Heizer and Alan Almquist, *The Other Californians* (Berkeley, Calif., 1971), pp. 139-41.

49. In the Southwestern states, especially Texas, and in California, Mexicans were segregated from whites. Manuel Gamio has noted that

in some areas very dark-skinned Mexicans were treated the same as Negroes, but Mexicans of medium skin color could eat in some restaurants and check into second-class hotels. Light-skinned Mexicans were typically considered whites. Blacks, however, even if seven-eighths white in ancestry, were forced to endure segregation in the South. Manuel Gamio, *Mexican Immigration to the United States* (Chicago, 1930), p. 53; Richard Burkey, *Ethnic and Racial Groups* (Menlo Park, Calif., 1978), p. 231.

50. For information on Mexicans discriminating against blacks, see Taylor, *Mexican Labor, Chicago,* p. 115, and his *Mexican Labor in the United States: Bethlehem, Pennsylvania* (Berkeley, Calif., 1931), p. 17. For the viewpoint of whites on Mexicans and vice versa, see Ozzie G. Simmons, "The Mutual Images and Expectations of Anglo-Americans and Mexican-Americans," in Nathaniel Wagner and Marsha Haug, eds., *Chicanos* (St. Louis, Mo., 1971), pp. 62-71.

4   ITALIANS IN THE SOUTH

In previous chapters, it has been noted that Afro-Americans became extremely alarmed whenever there was talk of importing foreigners to supplant black farm workers. In the case of the Chinese and especially with regards to the Mexicans and Japanese, relatively few settled in the South permanently. This chapter seeks to examine what happened when immigrants did come South. How did blacks and whites perceive Italians who came to Louisiana and Mississippi and who, in some cases, took jobs on plantations?

The Italians who settled in these two states appeared especially sinister to blacks because they came during 1880-1915, a period that has been called the nadir of Negro history. During these years, every Southern state adopted a new constitution calculated to disfranchise Afro-Americans. Simultaneously, segregation became increasingly onerous and obvious, and after the celebrated *Plessy* v. *Ferguson* decision of 1896, which sanctioned the concept of "separate but equal," Negroes realized that even the courts were blind to their grievances. Hundreds of thousands of blacks virtually lived in a state of peonage, and each year scores of allegedly "uppity" blacks were lynched, usually for trivial offenses. Truly it was time of troubles for Afro-Americans.

Some whites, however, thought that the Negroes had too easy a life. These critics expressed the fear that blacks were so inefficient they were impeding the progress of the South. When viewing the East, Midwest, and West, whites claimed to witness growing cities, prosperous farms, and contented people. When looking at Dixie, they saw underpopulated towns, vacant farmland, and disgruntled men and women. In their minds, all was not well in the land of cotton.[1]

One notable difference between Dixie and the rest of the country was the absence in the South of large numbers of European immigrants. From 1870 to 1920, millions of Europeans flocked to America, but few of them went south of the Mason-Dixon line. During the last thirty years of the nineteenth century, virtually every major Northern state doubled or tripled its foreign-born population. In the South, however, the percentage of Southerners born in Europe declined from 4 percent in 1870 to a mere 2.8 percent in 1900, and several Southern states could claim only 1 immigrant per 100 inhabitants.[2] Increasingly, suggestions were being made that what Dixie needed to attain prosperity was to have hundreds of thousands of industrious foreign-born white agriculturalists replace her allegedly shiftless, immoral, and unreliable Negro farm workers. Special attention was given to emigrants from Italy who reportedly were accomplished farmers desperately in search of land to grow crops.[3]

A number of whites were receptive to the idea of finding new sources of labor to harvest sugar cane, pick cotton, care for livestock, and plant corn and vegetables. These people believed that the South had become too dependent upon lazy Negroes. Albert Shaw, the celebrated political scientist and historian, felt that blacks had become too secure in their jobs and needed competition from Europeans. Influenced by his reading of the theories of Charles Darwin and William Graham Sumner, Shaw thought that such a rivalry would result in the survival of the fittest workers and that Dixie could only benefit from the experiment. Concurring with the point of view was the influential *Manufacturer's Record.* "The very competition of the foreign laborer with the negro," it asserted, "will stimulate the negro and be his best help towards training him to measure up to his opportunity." Similar arguments were voiced even by the *Southern Workman,* a monthly edited by the largely white staff of Virginia's Hampton Institute. "The coming of the Italian laborer," a writer in the *Southern Workman* declared, "seems . . . to be altogether desirable both for the whites and for the blacks. The whites need more labor and the blacks need competition."[4] Well before any of the above writers took up his pen in behalf of immigration, several Southern states revitalized long dormant emigrant bureaus seeking to divert some of the United States's newcomers from New York and Philadelphia to Galveston and New Orleans.

As early as 1881, the *New Orleans Louisianian*, a black weekly, considered the subject of emigration. The paper expressed no surprise that millions of Europeans were leaving their homes "to better themselves" socially and economically. After all, life in the Old World was not easy. The European laborer was "depenen[t] upon a superior who fixes his wages at the lowest rate of subsistance [*sic*] and his social condition at the most hopeless point of ignorance and dependence." Though clearly sympathetic to the plight of the European, the *Louisianian* had no desire to witness masses of white immigrants flock to the South to compete with blacks. This it did not expect, however, for it believed Negro labor to be "superior to that imported from foreign countries." Among other things, Afro-Americans understood "the ways and the speech of the American people" far better than any alien newcomer.[5]

Another black newspaper, the *Trenton Sentinel*, also editorially discussed the question of immigration in 1881. Noting that thousands of Italians were migrating from the land of their birth, it expected few of them to come to the United States. South America, the *Sentinel* assured its readers, "has proved a more attractive region for them," and it was to that continent that the sons of Italy were heading. In Argentina, Brazil, and Chile, the Italians were finding opportunities so great that the *Sentinel* predicted the day would soon come when they would be "the dominant people of the South American republic[s] as the English-speaking races are of the United States."[6]

At best, the *Sentinel* was a mediocre prophet, for if hundreds of thousands of Italians continued to migrate to South America, equally impressive numbers came to the United States. By 1900, Chicago, New York, Buffalo, Providence, San Francisco, Cleveland, New Haven, and scores of other cities boasted sizable "Little Italies." Immigration was no passing phenomenon, for in 1906 the *Baltimore Afro-American* noted with astonishment that each year as many as 14 out of every 1,000 Italians were bidding adieu to the land of their nativity and seeking their fortunes elsewhere.[7]

Prior to World War I, approximately 90 percent of America's blacks lived in the South. Afro-Americans, even those living in the North, showed great interest in what was happening in Dixie. Therefore, it was not unnatural to expect that black journals were quick to note an increase of Italian migration to the South. (See Table 3.) Among the news items reported in the Afro-American press was one concerning the expansion of the Hamburg-American Shipping Line. The company announced in 1910 that it was starting steamship service between Hamburg and New Orleans "to direct immigrants to [those] parts of this country where newcomers are urgently wanted."[8]

Blacks and others might well have wondered how "wanted" Italians really were in New Orleans. Afro-Americans had been most interested in the mass lynchings of Italians in that city about twenty years before the Hamburg-American Shipping Line began its new route to Louisiana. In October 1890, David C. Hennessey, chief of the New Orleans Police Department, was assassinated. The Italian Mafia was blamed for the crime. The native population of the Crescent City was incensed, and authorities arrested scores of Sicilians. Nine Italians were tried for Hennessey's murder; six were acquitted in March 1891, and a mistrial was declared for the other three defendants. An angry mob stormed the jail and lynched eleven Sicilians—the nine defendants and two other prisoners who were grabbed by mistake.[9]

In the South lynching was a form of punishment usually reserved for blacks. Thus, Afro-Americans paid attention when eleven white men were hanged in the streets of New Orleans. As might be expected, news of the violence engendered some sympathy for the Sicilian newcomers and modified somewhat their image as incorrigible lawbreakers. The *Richmond Planet*, unable to shake the view that Sicilians were the "scum of Italy," claimed that if the Mafia really existed, "it should be stamped out, but it can and should be done according to the forms of law." Similarly, the *Indianapolis Freeman* was disgusted with "the disloyal and fiendish acts of the unlawful element which over-rode the law in New Orleans." Hardly a friend of the alien, the *Detroit Plaindealer* favored restricting immigration but insisted that newcomers be extended the equal protection of the laws.[10]

That news of the mass lynching would temporarily promote a somewhat improved image of the Italian was not unexpected; what was surprising was that the lynching did so little to re-habilitate Sicilians in the eyes of black editors. Indeed, one Alabama Negro, the editor of the *Opelika State Alliance Banner*, argued that since the Mafia had been terrorizing the Crescent City, the eleven Italians were justly punished: "They were not killed as Italians but as proven murderers who had defrauded justice by corrupting a jury, and they would have met the same fate had they been native Americans. We do not favor lynch law as a regular method for meting out justice, but in some cases, nothing else will do it so well and so speedily."[11]

Others, like the *Cleveland Gazette*, clumsily argued that "it is a good thing for the Afro-American that the New Orleans Mafia outrage occurred." The *Gazette* was one of several newspapers predicting that the international complications resulting from the incident would promote sentiment against the lynching of blacks. Thus, Negroes did not particularly feel constrained to get upset about the murder of several Italians, whom some dismissed as gangsters, until the nation became outraged about the more frequent lynching of Negroes in Dixie, "the land of their birth."[12]

Perhaps Afro-Americans would have been more charitably disposed towards Italian victims of violence had they been aware of how opposed Sicilians were to this barbaric custom. For example, when Carlo Gardini witnessed the lynching of a black in a Texas town he was visiting, he was so horrified that he quickly boarded the railroad car on which he had a seat lest he be forced to view the mutilated cadaver. Several years later, an Italian magazine editor soundly castigated a mob for dragging a Negro from a jail call in New Albany, Mississippi, and then burning him at a stake. The editor doubted that the lynchers could be considered civilized. M. A. Pei in the 1920s favored enactment of an anti-lynching law. He noted that those who murdered blacks were the same people most insistent that prohibition laws be enforced. "To drink a glass of wine is sinful and criminal," he noted acidly, "but to deprive a human being of life without due process of law is right, proper, and one hundred percent American."[13]

As important as the lynching question was to both Italians and Afro-Americans, blacks were even more interested in Italian settlement in the South in the 1890s. Two men responsible for the growth of Italian communities in the Mississippi Delta were Captain C. H. Williams of Greenville, Mississippi, and Austin Corbin of New York City. Williams assured potential immigrants that Italian tenant farmers were in great demand on plantations near the Mississippi River. Those who settled in this region, he promised, would easily be able to get credit and would soon be given options to settle the land on which they worked.[14] Corbin, who had made a fortune in the transportation industry, shared William's enthusiasm for Italian labor, and he negotiated with the mayor of Rome to have Italian immigrants sent to Sunnyside, a colony he was forming in Chicot County, Arkansas. Initial reports from Sunnyside were quite encouraging, and it was widely noted that Italian workers there consistently picked more cotton than experienced black field hands. Within a year of its settlement, however, poor weather, inadequate drainage, depressed cotton prices, and the premature death of Corbin led most of the settlers to abandon the colony. Some of these people were resettled at Tontitown, near Springdale, Arkansas, where under the leadership of Father Pietro Bandini, they founded a successful grape-growing colony. Those few who remained at Sunnyside ultimately prospered, for within a few years of Corbin's death living conditions greatly improved.[15]

Blacks observed Italian settlement in Arkansas with alarm, fearing that it was a harbinger of a concerted effort on the part of Southerners to "be able to do entirely without the Negro." "The movement," concluded The Voice of the Negro, an Atlanta-based monthly, "has as its object to either starve the Negro or make him willing to work under any and all conditions that the white man may see fit to impose."[16] These suspicions seemed to be confirmed when news came in 1898 that Italians in Horry County, South Carolina, had established an agricultural colony to raise strawberries, lettuce, cucumbers, and potatoes. During this same decade, several hundred Italians worked at the Saint Cloud Sugar Plantation in Florida. In 1900 and 1904, blacks learned that Italian vegetable farmers were purchasing 7,000 acres of land in Washington County, Alabama, 35 miles from Mobile. Even worse were confirmed reports that 2,000 Italians had been imported from Chicago and Saint Louis to harvest sugar cane and that thousands more intended to move permanently to Louisiana. In June, 1904, Chevalier G. Donathoy told an audience in Philadelphia that "I know of no better place than the Southern part of the United States for our people." Eight months later, in February 1905, nearly seventy Italian families arrived in Kaplan, Louisiana, where they were put to work cultivating cotton, sugar cane, and rice. Soon it was alleged that immigrants from Palermo, Sicily, were rapidly crowding out the Negroes throughout the sugar district.[17] Panicky black editors began to fear that it would be quite simple to teach the foreigners to pick cotton, which had been the last exclusive field of the Negro. One Afro-American journalist ominously predicted that Southern Afro-Americans might soon be forced to "turn to some other corner of the earth to work out an existence. Bishop Turner may yet prove a prophet."[18] Another warned that "if cheap and foreign labor should take root and become well grounded in the South," the Afro-American in Dixie "would be in much the same condition as his brother in the North who cannot find work of a high character."[19]

But Afro-Americans did not intend to surrender their jobs without a struggle. They began an intensive campaign to persuade whites—and themselves—that however efficient Italians appeared in the cottonfields, it would be a mistake to import them as replacements for black workers. It was repeatedly argued that the sons of Italy possessed characteristics so repugnant that no sane man would trust them as employees or want them as neighbors.

Perhaps the most famous black to involve himself in the anti-Italian campaign was Booker T. Washington. The president of

Tuskegee Institute had voiced opposition to immigration in his famous Atlanta Exposition Address of 1895. Although the oration is best remembered for his urging his fellow Negroes to forsake political equality in return for the opportunity to make economic progress, the speech also had a message for whites:

> To those of the white race who look to the incoming of those of foreign birth and strange tongue and habits for the prosperity of the South, were I permitted, I would repeat what I say to my own race, "cast down your buckets where you are."[20]

Throughout the next twenty years, Washington would repeatedly assert that "as compared with the Italian and Irish labor[er], the Negro is far more teachable and trustworthy."[21]

Despite Washington's testimonials in behalf of the Negro worker, Southerners continued to import Italian farm workers. This perplexed the Tuskegee educator, and so in the summer of 1910 he visited Europe to acquaint himself "with the condition of the poorer and working classes in Europe from which an ever-increasing number of immigrants are coming to our country each year." After completing this trip with assistance from Robert Park, he wrote of his travels in a book provocatively entitled *The Man Farthest Down*. Plainly, the book was a work of propaganda. On one level, it sought to persuade Negroes not to complain about their lot, for, insisted Washington, the masses of laborers in Europe were infinitely worse off than American blacks. On another level, *The Man Farthest Down* had a warning for whites. It described the customs, culture, and living conditions of many Europeans in such unflattering terms that the reader was likely to question the value of allowing the degraded European to settle in the United States.[22]

In a speech he delivered in 1914, Washington stated that his trip to Sicily in 1910 taught him to think more highly of the Italian people.[23] If true, this was an incredibly devastating comment, for *The Man Farthest Down* contains a veritable catalog of alleged failings Washington ascribed to the Italians, particularly those living in Naples and Sicily. What most struck him about the Italian people was their lack of interest in sanitation.

Naples particularly depressed him. There he found himself on a street "strewn with old bottles, dirty papers and all manner of trash; at the same time it was filled with sprawling babies and with chickens, not to mention goats and other household appurtenances."[24]

Terrible as things were in the streets, they were at least as bad in the shacks and tenements in which the Italians lived. Washington observed apartments in Naples housing seven people in a single windowless room. "More than that," he noted of one dirt-floor residence he visited, "this one room, which was in the basement of a large tenement house, was not as large as the average one-room Negro cabin in the South." Such a description was hardly calculated to make the reader of *The Man Farthest Down* eager to have occupants of such dwellings as his neighbors.[25]

In similar fashion, the traits Washington ascribed to the Italians were less than flattering. In Naples, where he complained about being constantly hounded by beggars, he found more people "living in the dirt, degradation and ignorance at the bottom of society than in any other city I visited in Europe." The peasant of Italy, he discovered, was unusually superstitious and almost immune to progressive ideas. "One thing that keeps the Sicilian down," he wrote, "is the pride with which he clings to his ancient customs and ways of doing things." Frequently, he concluded, the peasant retained his hostility to new ideas in the New World. Once again the image of the Italian which Washington presented was devised to make Southern whites question whether they really wanted these people to come to Dixie.[26]

Washington's unflattering portrait of the Italian doubtless was the most famous effort on the part of an Afro-American to warn whites of the menace of importing Sicilians to the United States. In was not, however, the only such effort, for black periodicals persistently waged a campaign to alert whites to the evils of letting Italians settle in the South.

Stories about Italy in the black press invariably stressed the negative, emphasizing such things as Italy's high illiteracy rate and antipathy to cleanliness. W. S. Scarborough, a black educator who visited Italy a few years before Washington, wrote his impressions of "unwashed Naples" for the *Indianapolis Freeman*. He too was disgusted by the many beggars who crowded the "filthy streets" of the city. What most upset him "were odors unspeakable everywhere ensuing from shops and the dirty groups that gathered thick and behind." Little wonder that Afro-Americans—even those who thought they were worse off politically than Italians—feared that immigrants from such an unsanitary environment might transport infectious diseases such as cholera and yellow fever with them.[27]

In August 1905, a yellow fever epidemic struck New Orleans. Blacks were quick to note "the fact that the yellow fever originated in the Italian quarters in New Orleans and has found its chief support among the Italian population of that city." *The Voice of the Negro* was certain that "the sons of Italy are very susceptible to contagious and fatal diseases," which hardly made them desirable immigrants. More blunt was the *New York Age*, which alleged "that the dear Italian laborer is much like the dear mosquito as a possessor and distributor of yellow fever germs." This, the *Age* thought, was sure to lead to "less clamor for Italian labor for the Southern States to replace Negro labor."[28]

Besides spreading disease, Italians were blamed for the rising crime rate in the United States. Booker T. Washington insisted that "very many" of the 500,000 Italians in New York belonged to the "criminal class" and were responsible for scores of murders and other felonies. "The result," he continued, "is that the Mafia, under the name of the Black Hand, is probably as active and, perhaps, as powerful among the Italian population in New York to-day as it ever was in Italy."[29]

What had happened to New York, blacks claimed, was certain to happen to the South if "this class of scum of the Old World" poured into Dixie. Afro-Americans warned that the newcomer whom the planter was ready to welcome onto his plantation was "invariably loaded with a stiletto with which he is as handy as a Filipino with a bolo or a common Negro with a razor." Violence would be inevitable, and the "black-handed Italians" would quickly teach the South "a lesson." If wronged in any way, declared Archibald Grimké a leading black intellectual, the Sicilian would "fight and fight hard":

The Italian laborer, unlike the Negro laborer, matches violence with violence, and fronts the mob with the mob. . . . He is not afraid to kill in the open, he is not afraid to kill in the dark. If he runs away in the daytime, he comes back by night. . . . Violence, revenge are in his blood—in his blood for centuries, and he stabs a foe as naturally, as readily with knife and dagger as a snake strikes an enemy with his poisonous fang.[30]

Little wonder that Grimké, a native of South Carolina, predicted that settlement of temperamental Italians in the South would produce social convulsions more momentous than any event since the Civil War.[31]

Violence was but one of the malignant traits that Italians supposedly brought with them; another was their reputed penchant for anarchism. According to the *Nashville Globe*, the "Sicilian Mafia bandits" hated organized government and would seek "in the years to come to overturn the free institutions of this country." Dissatisfied Italian miners had rioted in Mount Carmel, Pennsylvania, and had demonstrated their expertise with dynamite. The *Richmond Planet* expected similar incidents in Dixie whenever friction developed between Americans and Sicilians. The sight of these foreigners, "their faces inflamed with passion," the *Planet* insisted, would make Southerners appreciate "the good natured, tractable, fun loving black man."[32] The black press represented Italians not only as gangsters and "the world's cast off hordes of nihilists and anarchists," but also as strikers. It was expected that shortly after their arrival "hell-generating Mafia" members would familiarize the South with their "accustomed recreation of bomb throwing and the manipulation of infernal machines." Then without any further ado they would start to organize labor unions.[33]

This nightmare, reported *The Voice of the Negro*, almost happened in Griffin, Georgia, where seventy-five Italians had been imported from New York. These immigrants, few of whom spoke English, had failed to "show up" Negro workers, but this did not prevent them from leading strikes. Failing in this endeavor, they were now ready to return to the North.[34] The behavior of these Italians was supposedly in sharp contrast with that of "the Negro laborer [who] never strikes." "We are not clear in our mind that this is a virtue," confessed *The Voice of the Negro*.

"But we are sure that the practice is wise and makes for peace of the community. [T]he [Afro-American] can be happy with half treatment." J. B. Rayner of Calvert, Texas, also advised Southern whites to shun the anarchy-loving Italians and rely instead on the humble, cheerful Negroes, "the only race the Southerner can control." Franklin Williams, a black attorney in Savannah, was positive that "after the foreigners have come over and begun their long strikes, have hurled their bombs and have smashed up cars and factories, the whites will become alarmed, will band themselves with the Negroes and begin to respect them as fellow countrymen." *The Voice of the Negro* tersely summed up Afro-American opinion when it stated, "The Negro and the white man can develop the South without the scum of Europe."[35]

Perhaps these arguments would have been more persuasive if pro-immigration whites had not anticipated them and had not prepared convincing rebuttals. Many Southerners claimed that Italians could help Dixie revitalize its agriculture by expanding the number of crops it grew. Since Italians were familiar with citrus and vine cultivation, Southerners believed, immigrants from Sicily could help Dixie expand its acreage in these marketable commodities. C. L. Buck of Independence, Louisiana, added that Italians were not only experienced farmers but also good neighbors. He strongly disagreed with the image of the Italian as a disorderly criminal. He was impressed with the frugality, modesty, and respectability of the Sicilians in his state.

> They are prompt to pay their debts at the stores, meet their paper at the banks when due and often before. I do not think there is a case on record in this parish when the State has had to prosecute them for a crime or misdemeanor. . . . I find t[hem] a great improvement and cheaper than the negro labor[er] of today.[36]

Seconding this view was Alfred Holt Stone, a Mississippi planter and an amateur—but highly respected—economist. Stone soundly castigated blacks for casting their opportunities "to the windows of improvidence" and contrasted them with the thrifty Italians. "Handicapped as they are at first, by ignorance of the language and ignorance of the cultivation of the plant they raise [cotton], still they are becoming property owners, tax-payers and citizens." From "the garden spot which the negro allows to grow up in weeds," the Mississippian asserted, the Italian will supply "his family from early spring until late fall, and also market enough largely to carry him through the winter." Thus, the Italian was not an anarchist or a disease-carrier; rather, he was the salvation of the South.[37]

Stone's opinions were shared by General J. Behan, owner of Alhambra Plantation in Iberville Parish, Louisiana. Behan, who employed both black and immigrant labor, asserted that Italians were 30 percent more productive than Negroes. A government study comparing black and white, usually Italian, laborers on Calumet Plantation in Saint Mary's Parish, Louisiana, concluded that Italians were more dependable workers, for when Afro-Americans had earned a little money, they no longer had any incentive to work. Even those who confessed a preference for Negro labor usually admitted that, unlike blacks, Italians were always ready and eager to toil in the fields.[38]

It was generally agreed that Italians were more satisfactory workers, but were they a valuable addition to the population of the South? Perhaps the most articulate proponent of the view that "Sicilians are especially desirable" immigrants for the South was Emily Fogg Meade. She considered it unfortunate that newspapers regularly printed sensational stories about drunken, ignorant, dirty Mafia members, which implied that the average Italian was likely "to stab you in the back." Meade said she had investigated matters for herself and concluded that the Sicilian was not a criminal; rather, he was temperate, patient, and hard-working. In her opinion, Italian crime in the United States resulted mainly from overcrowding in the cities of the North. The underpopulated South would find its Italian residents too busy working in the fields and planting vegetables on plots of land previously considered worthless to engage in antisocial behavior. In fact, Meade happily reported:

Italians become enthusiastic Americans. No nationality, when once it breaks its ties to the homeland, is more anxious to adopt

American ways. The children do not care to speak Italian. They
demand the freedom of American children; they adopt their dress,
their ideas and their ambitions.[39]

Others were most impressed with the thrift of the Italian. Amy
Bernardy saw no signs of anarchism among the Italians of the
South. Instead, she witnessed people who knew naturally how to
"manage and exploit with a thrift and to an extent unknown to
the colored element." They would lead the South to prosperity.[40]
This impressed LeRoy Percy of Greenville, Mississippi. Percy,
who had observed Italians working in his state, claimed that
they "make a profit of $5.00 out of a crop where the negro makes
$1.00, and yet the negro seems to be perfectly satisfied with his
returns."[41]

George Allessi, an Italian living in Independence, Louisiana,
declared in 1904 that one of his compatriots could come to
America with nothing and still become successful:

The first thing he wants to do is to buy a home. The negro rarely
owns a home or really cares for one, and spends a dollar a day
while he is only making 75 cents, and sooner or later goes to
prison, while the Italian practically lives in prison for three or four
years and spends nothing, and then buys him a home.[42]

These accounts in the press and in periodicals distressed
blacks, but they were less bothersome than published accounts
of dialogues between whites and blacks which purported to
show that the Negro enjoyed being carefree and wasteful. One
particularly offensive item appeared in the influential magazine
Charities. Adolfo Rossi, an official of the Italian Emigration
Department, who had just completed a tour of the South, professed to know why Sicilians were more efficient and frugal than
Afro-Americans. While visiting an Italian settlement in Bryan,
Texas, he claimed to have had the following conversation with a
Negro:

Rossi: How is it that the Italians on these plantations save
        money and become landowners while you colored people
        never seem to lay aside anything?

Negro: Because we don't like hard work and we love to drink
and gamble and some of us have three or even four
wives. Your people, instead, work from morning till
night and often on Sundays; they don't spend money at
the plantation stores because they get along with the
chickens, hogs, and goats they raise on their land, and
one wife is enough for them.[43]

Only slightly less objectionable was a story told by Alfred Holt
Stone about a gray-haired Negro who resolved to pick cotton as
efficiently as his Italian neighbors. The man worked hard until
one night when he and his wife were returning from church and
he saw "dat Dago en his wife en fo' chillun . . . pickin' cotton by
de moonlight." Angrily, he told Stone, "I do' no' how it looks to
you, but I calls dat er underhanded trick myse'f."[44]

Doubtless—and with good reason—many blacks thought these
two stories were apocryphal. Nonetheless, Afro-Americans
knew it was essential that they persuade Southerners either that
the efficiency and diligence of the Italian were overrated or that
these qualities were less desirable than whites imagined. *The
Colored American Magazine* was unimpressed with stories about
the reputed skills of Italian farmers and laborers, doubting that
Sicilians would "for any length of time" perform satisfactory
work. Southerners would soon discover, the magazine was sure,
that as was "pointed out recently in a newspaper article . . . the
Italian, as a laborer is unreliable and ineffective." Others
stressed that Italian immigration would lead to thousands of new
problems. It was even argued that the Afro-American was
physically superior to the Sicilian. Attention was gladly given to
a story in a Florida newspaper concerning the failure of Italian
longshoremen to outperform Negroes. Afro-Americans, it
announced, were "more docile, cheerful and rapid in their
work, and they can endure the climate and the rough work
better than the Sons of Italy."[45]

Many blacks readily conceded that Italians worked for less
money and were "satisfied with wages upon which the progressive American would starve." A. P. Nella of Newnan,
Georgia, was not surprised that Italians could make do on less
than blacks. "We see nothing strange in this," Nella, a black,
explained, for "the Italians have been taught the spirit of

accumulation for thousands of years as freemen, while Negroes have been taught just the opposite until recent years." Little wonder, exclaimed the *Richmond Planet*, that "Italians . . . live on five cents a day and there are colored men who find it difficult to live on two dollars a day."[46]

If Negroes freely admitted that their standard of living was higher than that of the Italian, they refused to concede that excessive frugality was a virtue. Several whites, particularly storekeepers, shared this opinion. Colonel John M. Gracie, a wealthy Arkansas cotton planter and merchant, complained that Italians "are money mad with no thought but for the dollar." A Southern white in Birmingham, Alabama, told William Archer, an Englishman touring the South, that he had no sympathy for the idea that Italians should supplant blacks. The Alabamian claimed that frugal Italians had already sent $400 million to their relatives in Italy. The Negroes, on the other hand, remained in Dixie and spent their earnings there, stimulating the local economy.[47]

Italians spent little in Southern stores. Some even imported their food rather than pay the high prices charged for macaroni and cheese in country grocery stores. Shopkeepers found that they profited from Negro patrons, who supposedly always were in debt. Bitter cries were heard that if an Italian "earns a dollar and a quarter, he will save the dollar; [but if the Negro] . . . earns the same amount he will spend a dollar and a half." As Professor Jean Scarpaci has pointed out, Southern businessmen equated consumerism with assimilation,[48] and they were not likely long to tolerate nonconsumers in their midst.

On the whole, the black's image of the Italian was largely negative. However, some blacks thought positive developments might arise out of Sicilian settlement in Dixie. The editor of the *Detroit Plaindealer* was certain that European newcomers "w[ould] not stand the domineering traits of the present rulers." W.E.B. Du Bois agreed. He claimed that Sicilian complaints to the Italian ambassador in Washington had resulted in a government crackdown against peonage. An unidentified writer in the *New York Age* insisted that good would result from foreign settlers moving to the South. He was eager to have immigrant laborers "guided hither by the beacon light of the Statue of Liberty" invade the South as soon as they desired. Southerners, he thought, "are too conceited and provincial. These foreigners will broaden them in many ways."[49] The *Atlanta Independent* suspected that the motley foreigners" would "make common cause with the Negro" and "put devilment in the Negro's head never dreamed of, and the white man will be the loser." Since Italians, themselves an olive-skinned people, were not known to have innate prejudice against blacks, the *Independent* was ready to welcome them to Georgia.[50] Perhaps, some Negroes imagined, "the foreigners would afford him [the Afro-American] a leadership of unscrupulous audacity."[51]

Contemporary evidence suggests that, after they came south, Italians did not immediately manifest signs of race prejudice. Sicilian women working in the fields did resent laboring for black foremen on some plantations, but, on the whole, Italians and Afro-Americans lived in adjacent cabins on farms with relatively little friction. Colgera Petruzella, whose family came from Sicily to Margaret, Alabama, a small coal mining town near Birmingham, in the 1910s, recollected recently that shortly after their arrival a black woman living nearby visited them. The Afro-American woman, seeking to be neighborly, brought them some freshly baked biscuits. On the whole however, there was little social mixing between the two groups.[52]

The occasional violence that did occur often lacked a racial motivation. These incidents frequently involved robberies, threats, or disputes over whether black customers had paid for merchandise they requested in Italian-owned businesses.[53] Enterprising Italians were less likely to view Negroes as rivals than as customers.[54] Alfred Holt Stone saw numerous Italian peddlers driving wagons in rural Southern counties. These wagons were full of soda pop, sausage, fish, fruits, and melons which the Italians sold to the blacks "for the few stray dimes that chance to remain on hand from the last trip to town." The Negro was seen as the best market for cheap goods, and so beginning Italian businessmen were particularly eager to cater to the needs of Afro-Americans. In several Alabama and Louisiana cities, Italians opened saloons that attracted a black clientele.[55]

Whites were unfavorably impressed by these developments. Whitecaps were angry that an aged Italian in Giles County, Tennessee, "had been affiliating with Negroes for several weeks and teaching them music." The vigilantes warned the man to leave the area within forty-eight hours. When he refused to move and threatened to prosecute his anonymous detractors, they shot him to death. In one Mississippi town, whites wrecked an Italian restaurant because the owner served a meal to a "nigger." The immigrant appealed to the governor of the state for compensation for his loss, but his pleas were ignored. Shortly thereafter, the Italian was forced to flee from the area. In Summerall, Mississippi, a town of 600, there was trouble in 1907, when local citizens refused to permit Italians, who represented one-sixth of the town's population, to enroll their children in the local white schools. Frank Seaglioni, a crippled shoemaker, loudly protested against school segregation for Italians. A local mob seized the cobbler and took him to a site outside the town limits, where they soundly thrashed him with a long rope and warned him not to cause any more trouble. One year earlier, several prospective candidates for governor of Mississippi were debating the relative merits of Italian immigration to the "Magnolia State." A number of the gubernatorial hopefuls criticized Sicilians for fraternizing with blacks and ominously warned that this camaraderie could ultimately lead to the birth of hundreds of mulattoes.[56]

The Mississippi politicians need not have worried, for there is no evidence that Italians were any more prone than other whites to engage in miscegenation. Furthermore, after 1910, the Italian population of Mississippi began to decline. By 1930, only three Southern states, Florida, Georgia, and Kentucky, had more Italian immigrants than in 1910, and of these three only Florida showed a steady increase in its Italian-born population. (Table 3).

In the end, Sicilian immigration did not prove to be a threat to Afro-Americans, for many, possibly most, Southern whites did not really want Italian settlers. All too common was the senti-

Table 3   Black and Foreign-Born Italian Populations in Southern States

STATE	1880 Black	1880 Italian	1890 Black	1890 Italian	1900 Black	1900 Italian
Alabama	600,103	144	678,849	322	827,307	862
Arkansas	210,666	132	309,117	187	366,856	576
Florida	126,690	77	166,180	408	230,730	1,707
Georgia	725,133	82	858,815	159	1,034,813	218
Kentucky	271,451	370	268,071	707	284,706	679
Louisiana	483,655	2,527	559,193	7,767	650,804	17,431
Mississippi	650,291	260	742,559	322	907,630	845
North Carolina	531,277	42	561,018	28	624,469	201
South Carolina	604,332	84	688,934	106	782,321	180
Tennessee	403,151	443	430,678	788	480,243	1,222
Texas	393,384	539	488,171	2,107	620,722	3,942
Virginia	631,616	281	635,438	1,219	660,722	781
Region Total	5,631,749	4,951	6,387,023	14,120	7,471,323	28,644

STATE	1910 Black	1910 Italian	1920 Black	1920 Italian	1930 Black	1930 Italian
Alabama	908,282	2,696	900,652	2,732	944,834	2,140
Arkansas	442,891	1,699	472,220	1,314	478,463	952
Florida	308,669	4,538	329,487	4,745	431,828	5,262
Georgia	1,176,987	545	1,206,365	700	1,071,125	712
Kentucky	261,656	1,316	235,938	1,932	226,040	1,589
Louisiana	713,874	20,233	700,257	16,264	776,326	13,526
Mississippi	1,009,487	2,137	935,184	1,841	1,009,718	1,613
North Carolina	697,843	521	763,407	453	918,647	438
South Carolina	835,843	316	864,719	344	793,681	188
Tennessee	473,088	2,034	451,758	2,079	477,646	1,946
Texas	690,049	7,190	741,694	8,024	854,964	6,550
Virginia	671,096	2,449	690,017	2,435	650,165	1,853
Region Total	8,189,765	45,674	8,291,698	42,863	8,633,437	36,769

SOURCE: U.S. Census Reports.

ment, "I hate a Dago worse than a nigger."[57] Jean Scarpaci has found plantation account books that listed employees in separate columns according to whether they were white, black, or "Dagoes."[58]

Evidence of hostility of Italians was evident all over the South. South Carolina, for example, which attracted some Italian settlers in Horry County who raised fruits and vegetables and others who worked on a silk farm near Summerville, only wanted immigrants from Western and Northern Europe. In 1908, the state abolished its department of immigration.[59] Virginians also expressed displeasure with emigration from Southern Europe. R. S. Parks, a member of the state senate, persuaded his colleagues to pass a resolution discouraging immigration to the commonwealth of Italians "with Mafia and Black Hand Murder Societies."[60] Congressman Adam Byrd of Mississippi was another consistent opponent of Italian immigration, and he contemptuously dismissed "Dagoes" as people who "can live almost on rats and snakes."[61] The nativist sentiments of Mississippians were most graphically expressed by the state chapter of the Farmers' Union in 1910. This chapter denounced Italians for their "Black Hand" activities, for "kidnapping our children, putting bombs under our houses, burning corncribs and stables . . . putting a sawed-off shotgun full of slugs in someone's back." The Farmers' Union had no use for "Dagoes" who lived "on a handful of sour mush and a hunk of stale bread" but had "money enough to send back to the old country for more of their kind." Even in Florida some wondered about the value of Italian farmers and cigar workers. Evangelists in the state were upset about their inability to convert Italians to Protestant sects, and others feared that the newcomers were anarchists. Most upsetting to conservative Floridians was the news that there were enough Italian socialists in Tampa for them to rent a brick house for political meetings. Such news made it understandable that T. L. Wainwright of Stonewall, Mississippi, would tell a conference on Southern industrialization in 1906 that emigrants were desirable if from Belgium, Holland, or Ireland but not if they were radicals from southern Italy.[62] So prevalent did anti-Italian feeling become that by 1915 only Louisiana, with its large Catholic population, still considered Sicilians welcome citizens.

A second reason for the failure of Italian immigration was that most Sicilians never intended to move to the South to become permanent competitors with Afro-American field hands. Despite their reputed ability to work like machines, it was not their intention to become Negroes with white skins and they did get angry whenever they were mistreated.[63] At a banquet held in his honor at New Orleans, Edmondo Mayor des Planches properly advised his Southern hosts:

Italians do not come to be the substitutes of negroes. There is room for all in the South. The black race, admitted for three centuries in this continent, has prior rights to live and to expound its proper activity. The Italian should not and does not wish to take the place which the negro occupies on the plantation. His own mission and temper[a]ment are essentially diverse. The Italian cannot come if not as an equal of the Anglo-Saxon and take the position close to that in the American community of a citizen equal to the better citizens.[64]

What des Planches failed to add was that many of the Italian immigrants coming south intended to settle in New Orleans, Birmingham, and Tampa rather than on farms. A majority of those leaving Italy associated farming with feudalism, misery and poverty. According to Joseph Lopreato, in America Sicilians often became urban dwellers to defy their old-country superiors. Besides, wages were usually better in urban areas than on plantations. The typical Italian male could save 20 percent more after eight months of construction work than he could after a full year's labor on the farm.[65]

Of those who did work in the fields, most did so only to gain capital for future investments, to support family members in Italy, or to bring over relatives to America.[66] They frequently complained to their government in Rome about poor working conditions in the South and about hostility toward Catholics from evangelical Protestants. An agent sent over from Italy to investigate their grievances told Oswald Garrison Villard, "I shall report to my government that the South does not know how to respect or treat labor, either black or white."[67] Italians in the South never considered working on Southern plantations as anything more than a transitory occupation. A few did buy farms in Arkansas, Mississippi, Texas, and Louisiana, but a much greater number opened groceries in cities such as Houston and New Orleans or left the region, settling in the North or West or returning to Italy.[68]

Around 1907, Archibald Grimké happily noted that the feared Italian influx to the South had not yet materialized. Ironically, those blacks who had been so worried about being displaced in the fields by the menacing Italians soon learned that the Sicilian in Dixie was more likely "to lurk around cities, run fruit and other easy stands" than to grow cotton or corn. "For the last two years Georgia has had more immigration than [in] all the other years since the war," commented the *Atlanta Independent* in 1907. Yet, "there never was a time when common as well as skilled laborers were as well paid as now." The *Independent* exaggerated somewhat, for black labor was not particularly well off in 1907, and there had been more immigrants in the forty years following Appomattox than the newspaper had estimated. Nonetheless, Italian immigration did not adversely affect the typical Southern Afro-American. Seldom numbering over 50,000 in Dixie, the Sicilians were in no position to displace over 8 million Negroes. The blacks finally concluded that all of the talk about "the coming foreigners" was merely "an effort to frighten the Negro. It is evident the South does not want the influx of foreigners."[69]

NOTES

1. See Rowland Berthoff, "Southern Attitudes Towards Immigration, 1865-1914," *Journal of Southern History* 17 (1951): 328-30; Bert James Loewenberg, "Efforts of the South to Encourage Immigration, 1865-1900," *South Atlantic Quarterly* 33 (1934): 363-85; G. Gundy Jordan, "The Southern Need for Labor," *National Civic Federation Review* 2 (1905): 15-16; William Garrott Brown, "The White Peril: The Immediate Danger of the Negro," *North American Review* 79 (1904): 825-41; James Roark, *Masters Without Slaves* (New York, 1977), pp. 166-67; Mildred Louise Pettus, "European Immigration to South Carolina, 1881-1908" (M.A. thesis, University of South Carolina, 1954); Willard Gatewood. "Strangers and the Southern Eden," in *Ethnic Minorities in Gulf Coast Society*, Jerrell Shofner and Linda Ellsworth, eds. (Pensacola, Fla., 1979), pp. 1-24.

2. Henry Booker, "Efforts of the South to Attract Immigrants" (Ph.D. dissertation, University of Virginia, 1965), pp. 19-20.

3. Walter Fleming, "Immigration to the Southern States," *National Geographic* 16 (1905): 517-19; *Springfield* (Mass.) *Republican*, May 15, 1906. The *Republican* was a white newspaper.

4. Albert Shaw, *Political Problems of American Development* (New York, 1907), pp. 65-67, 125; Philip Bruce, "The Negro Population of the South," *Conservative Review* 2 (1899): 262-80; "How Italians Can Help Negroes," *Southern Workman* 34 (1905): 202; *Manufacturer's Record* (Baltimore), n.d., quoted in *Boston Transcript*, December 1, 1906. The *Transcript* was a white newspaper.

5. *New Orleans Louisianian*, April 23, 1881.

6. *Trenton* (N.J.) *Sentinel*, September 17, 1881.

7. *Baltimore Afro-American*, May 5, 1906.

8. *Nashville Globe*, April 1, 1910.

9. Jean Scarpaci, "Italian Immigrants in Louisiana's Sugar Parishes" (Ph.D. dissertation, Rutgers University, 1972), p. 246, hereafter cited as "Sugar Parishes."

10. *Richmond Planet*, March 28, April 4, 1891; *Indianapolis Freeman*, April 11, 1891; *Detroit Plaindealer*, June 26, 1891.

11. *Opelika* (Ala.) *State Alliance Banner*, n.d., quoted in *Richmond Planet*, April 4, 1891.

12. *Cleveland Gazette*, April 18, May 16, 1891. See also *St. Paul Appeal*, August 12, 1899.

13. Andrew Rolle, *The Immigrant Upraised* (Norman, Okla., 1968), p. 138; editorial in *United America* (New York) 1 (October 3, 1925): 3; M. A. Pei, "Facts and Comments," *United America* 2 (July 3, 1926): 5.

14. *Huntsville* (Ala.) *Gazette*, April 28, 1894; Eliot Lord, John Trenor, and Samuel Barrows, *The Italian in America* (New York, 1905), pp. 146-51, hereafter cited as Lord, *Italian*. See also *Savannah Tribune*, July 29, 1905; *Boston Transcript*, July 15, 1904.

15. Robert Brandfon, *Cotton Kingdom of the New South* (Cambridge, Mass., 1967), pp. 144-46; A. W. Hadley, "The Tontitown Settlement," *Maxwell's Talisman* 5 (1905): 14-16; Rolle, *Immigrant Upraised*, pp. 77-84; Anita Moore, "Safe Ways to Get on the Soil: The Work of Father Bandini of Tontitown," *World's Work* 24 (1912): 215-19; Leslie Hewe, "Tontitown," *Economic Geography* 29 (1953): 125-43; Luciano Iorizzo and Salvatore Mondello, *The Italian-Americans* (New York, 1971), pp. 115-16.

16. *Voice of the Negro* (Atlanta) 2 (1905): 453.

17. Donathy in *Philadelphia Record*, n.d., quoted in *Charleston News and Courier*, June 16, 1904; *Atlanta Independent*, January 23, 1904;

Cleveland Gazette, November 10, 1900; Charles Shadabruch, "The Louisiana Immigration Movement," *Louisiana History* 18 (1977): 210. On other Italian settlements in the South, see Andrew Rolle, *The American Italians* (Belmont, Calif., 1972), p. 74; George Pozzetta, "Foreigners in Florida: A Study of Immigration Promotion, 1865-1910," *Florida Historical Quarterly* 53 (1974): 170-71; Rolle, *Immigrant Upraised*, p. 84; Lord, *Italian*, p. 127-28; Robert Foerster, *The Italian Emigration of Our Times* (Cambridge, Mass., 1919), pp. 367-68; Felice Ferreno, "A New St. Helena," in Wayne Moquin and Charles Van Doren, eds., *A Documentary History of the Italian Americans* (New York, 1974), pp. 82-84; *Memphis Bluff City News*, n.d., quoted in *New York Age*, November 9, 1905; *Boston Advertiser*, August 22, 1905; John Baiamonte, "Immigrants of Rural America: A Study of Italians in Tangipahoa Parish, Louisiana" (Ph.D. dissertation, Mississippi State University, 1972), pp. 14, 16, 27; Pettus, "European Immigration," pp. 20-22.

18. Bishop Henry McNeal Turner, a black, believed that Negroes would never be treated fairly in the United States. He advocated a black exodus to Africa. *Alexander's Magazine* (Boston) 2 (1906): 16-17.

19. *Colored American Magazine* (New York) 8 (1905): 240. See also *A.M.E. Church Review* (1905), quoted in David Hellwig, "Black Attitudes Toward Immigrant Labor in the South, 1865-1910," *Filson Club Historical Quarterly* 54 (1980): 158.

20. Booker T. Washington, *Up From Slavery* (New York, 1903), pp. 220-21

21. Victoria Matthews, comp., *Black Belt Diamonds, Gems from the Speeches, Addresses and Talks to Students of Booker T. Washington* (New York, 1969), p. 44.

22. Washington created great controversy among pro-integration black intellectuals even before he wrote his book. When in 1910 he announced that blacks were better off than the mass of Europeans, more than thirty Afro-American leaders publicly disputed this contention. But Washington controlled a large number of black newspapers, which helps account for the very positive reviews *The Man Farthest Down* usually received. See, for example, the undated typescript of James B. Clarke's favorable review of the book in the Booker T. Washington papers, the Library of Congress, Box 59. For the role of Robert Park in helping to write the book, see Winifred Raushenbush, *Robert E. Park* (Durham, N.C., 1979), pp. 51-54. On the protest against Washington's statement, see "the Appeal to Europe," *Crisis* 1 (January 1911): 9-11. I am grateful to an unidentified reviewer of this manuscript for calling my attention to the *Crisis* article.

23. E. Davidson Washington, ed., *Selected Speeches of Booker T. Washington* (Garden City, N.Y., 1932), p. 232. See also Louis Harlan, ed., *The Booker T. Washington Papers*, 9 vols. to date (Urbana, Ill., 1971-76) 5: 216.

24. Booker T. Washington, *The Man Farthest Down* (Garden City, N.Y., 1912), pp. 159-60.

25. Ibid.

26. Ibid., pp. 110, 146, 188. See also William Toll, *The Resurgence of Race* (Philadelphia, 1979), pp. 176-79; Iorizzo and Mondello, *Italian-Americans*, p. 55.

27. W. S. Scarborough, "A Day in Naples," *Indianapolis Freeman*, December 28, 1901; *Savannah Tribune*, August 5, 1893; *Baltimore Afro-American*, April 26, 1902.

28. *Voice of the Negro* 2 (1905): 594; Scarpaci, "Sugar Parishes," p. xxi; *New York Age*, September 28, 1905. See also Brandfon, *Cotton Kingdom*, p. 154-57.

29. Washington, *The Man Farthest Down*, pp. 179-80.

30. *Nashville Globe*, March 19, 1909; *New York Age*, September 28, 1905; Franklin Williams, "How Foreign Immigration Will Ultimately Solve [the] Negro Problem," *Savannah Tribune*, April 13, 1912, hereafter cited as Williams, "Immigration",; Archibald Grimké, "Washington, D.C. Correspondence," *New York Age*, June 15, 1905; Archibald Grimké, "Some Aspects of the Southern Immigration Question," undated draft of speech 1907?, Archibald Grimké Papers, Moorland-Spingarn Research Center, Howard University, hereafter cited as Grimké, "Southern Immigration."

31. Grimké, "Southern Immigration."

32. *Nashville Globe*, March 19, 1909; *Richmond Planet*, May 5, 1906.

33. *Voice of the Negro* 2 (1905): 453. See also Edward Gaston, "A History of the Negro Wage Earner in Georgia, 1880-1940" (Ph.D. dissertation, Emory University, 1957), p. 159.

34. *Voice of the Negro* 2 (1905): 271.

35. Ibid.; Rayner, quoted in *Savannah Tribune*, September 9, 1905; Williams, "Immigration." See also *Voice of the Negro* 2 (1905): 453.

36. *Boston Transcript*, June 30, 1904; Lord, *Italian*, p. 172; Richard Gambino, *Blood of My Blood*, Anchor ed. (Garden City, N.Y., 1975), pp. 99-100; Pozzetta, "Foreigners," pp. 170-71.

37. Stone, *Studies in the America Race Problem* (New York, 1908), pp. 173n-174n, 180-97; Stone, "The Italian Cotton Grower: The Negro's Problem," *South Atlantic Quarterly* 4 (1905): 42-47; Stone, "Italian Cotton Growers in Arkansas," *American Monthly Review of Reviews* 35

(1907): 209-13, hereafter cited as Stone, "Arkansas."

38. Jean Scarpaci, "The Italian Immigrant: An Answer to Louisiana's Post War Plantation Labor Problem" (unpublished paper presented at the Citadel Conference on the New South, Charleston, S.C., April 1978), pp. 13-14.

39. Fogg, "Italian Immigration into the South," *South Atlantic Quarterly* 4 (1905): 217-24. See also *Boston Transcript*, June 30, 1904.

40. Bernardy, "Immigration to the South," *Boston Transcript*, March 28, 1908. See also Bernardy, "Italians in Our South," ibid., November 28, 1906.

41. Percy quoted in *Boston Transcript*, April 7, 1904, and in Lord, *Italian*, pp. 148-50. See also Jean Scarpaci, "Immigrants in the New South: Italians in Louisiana's Sugar Parishes, 1880-1910," *Labor History* 16 (1975): 174-75.

42. Alessi quoted in *Boston Transcript*, June 30, 1904. See also Jean Scarpaci, "A Tale of Selective Accommodation: Sicilians and Native Whites in Louisiana," *Journal of Ethnic Studies* 5 (1977): 44.

43. Gino Speranza, "Italian Farmers in the South: An Interview with Adolfo Rossi," *Charities* 15 (1906): 308.

44. Stone, "Arkansas," p. 213.

45. *Colored American Magazine* 8 (1905): 240; *Voice of the Negro* 2 (1905): 596; *Florida Standard*, n.d., quoted in *New York Age*, August 9, 1906; *Indianapolis Freeman*, December 1, 1900: See also Foerster, *Italian Emigration*, p. 361.

46. Nella, "Newnan Notes," *Atlanta Independent*, January 27, 1906; *Richmond Planet*, February 19, 1909. See also Rolle, *Immigrant Upraised*, p. 82.

47. Gracie quoted in *New York Age*, March 3, 1910, and in *Baltimore Afro-American*, September 24, 1910; William Archer, *Through Afro-America, and English Reading of the Race Problem* (New York, 1910), p. 133.

48. *Voice of the Negro* 2 (1905): *Boston Transcript*, April 23, 1904; Scarpaci, "Sugar Parishes," pp. iv, 258; Rolle, *Immigrant Upraised*, p. 85; *Cleveland Gazette*, August 7, 1909; *New York Age*, April 4, 1899; Iorizzo and Mondello, *Italian-Americans*, p. 136.

49. *Detroit Plaindealer*, April 21, 1893; *New York Age*, June 29, 1905; Du Bois cited in *Horizon* (Alexandria, Va.) 3 (January, 1908): 4 and 3 (August, 1908): 7.

50. *Atlanta Independent*, March 23, 1907. This editorial was repeated in ibid., September 17, 1910.

51. *New York Age*, June 29, 1905.

52. Florette Henri, *Black Migration* (Garden City, N.Y., 1975), p. 73;

Baiamonte, "Italians," p. 27. Pozzetta, "Foreigners," p. 179; Rolle, *Italian-Americans*, p. 82. Colgera Petruzella Oral History Inverview, November 30, 1980, Cassette recording in Winthrop College Archives.

53. *Nashville Globe*, December 20, 1907; *Memphis Commercial Appeal, Little Rock Arkansas Gazette*, and *Charleston News and Courier*, all January 29, 1912; *Galveston Sentinel*, April 21, 1934. *The Commercial Appeal, News and Courier*, and *Arkansas Gazette* are white newspapers.

54. *Boston Transcript*, April 30, 1904; Scarpaci, "Sugar Parishes," pp. ix, 146–49, 173; Scarpaci, "Immigrants in the New South," p. 176; Lord, *Italian*, p. 184.

55. Stone, *Studies in the American Race Problem*, p. 190; Scarpaci, "Sugar Parishes," p. 211.

56. The Mississippi gubernatorial election mentioned in the *Age* on November 8, 1906, was not to be held until 1907. *New York Age*, November 8, 1906, October 10, 1907, March 3, 1910; *Indianapolis World*, August 14, 1897; Gino Speranza, "A Mission of Peace," *Outlook* 78 (1904): 129–30; Henri, *Black Migration*, p. 73.

57. Albert Bushnell Hart, "Through the Heart of the South," *Boston Transcript*, February 9, 1908. See also Gambino, *Blood of My Blood*, p. 78; Gaston, "Wage Earner," p. 157; Pettus, "European Immigration," p. 27.

58. Scarpaci, "Selective Accommodation," p. 38.

59. *New York Age*, April 4, 1891, May 25, 1905; *St. Paul Appeal*, January 5, 1907; *Nashville Globe*, March 9, 1907; *Boston Transcript*, February 19, 1908; *Manufacturer's Record*, January 21, 1909; Lord, *Italian*, p. 117; Pettus, "European Immigration," pp. 20–23, 55.

60. Copy of Parks's bill in Prescott Hall's Imigration Clippings, Vol. 9, Widener Library, Harvard University (Widener Call Number: U.S. 10587.29); *Boston Transcript*, February 26, 1908.

61. *Savannah Tribune*, January 25, 1908. See also Brandfon, *Cotton Kingdom*, p. 162; Albert Kirwan, *Revolt of the Rednecks* (Gloucester, Mass., 1964), pp. 185–86.

62. Pozetta, "Foreigners," pp. 177–78; Theodore Saloutos, *Farmer Movements in the South, 1865–1933* (Berkeley, Calif., 1960), p. 208; Wainwright quoted in *Proceedings of the Sixth Annual Convention of the Georgia Industrial Association Held at Warm Springs* (Atlanta, 1906), p. 31.

63. *Boston Transcript*, November 28, 1906; Bernardy, "Italians in Our South," ibid.; Brandfon, *Cotton Kingdom*, p. 163; Scarpaci, "Sugar Parishes," p. 222.

64. Des Planches quoted in Scarpaci, "Sugar Parishes," 221.

65. Ibid., p. 233; Joseph Lopreato, *Italian Americans* (New York, 1970), p. 38; Foerster, *Italian Emigration*, pp. 369, 380.

66. This was not always true, for Italians involved in the strawberry

industry of Louisiana did remain on the land well into the twentieth century. Baiamonte, "Italians"; Scarpaci, "Sugar Parishes," pp. xx, 191-92, 232.

67. Pozzetta, "Foreigner," p. 177; John Moore, *The South To-day* (New York, 1916), p. 72; Villard quoted in *The Influence of Immigration on American Culture* (New York, 1929), pp. 8–9. Examples of the peonage to which Italians in the South were subjected are readily available. Giuseppe D'Angelo was lured to a Florida labor camp in the 1910s. For eight months, the white owners of the camp had blacks guard him and prevent his escape. Giovanni Crapi found conditions in a Mississippi cottonfield so bad that he and a fellow Italian found it necessary to escape from the guards who had virtually imprisoned them. Andrew Rolle, *Italian Americans, Troubled Roots* (New York, 1980), p. 64; Patrick Gallo, *Old Bread, New Wine, a Portrait of the Italian-Americans* (Chicago, 1981), Chapter 3; Maxine Seller, *To Seek America* (Englewood, N.J., 1977), p. 109.

68. By the early 1900s, Italians operated a majority of the ice factories, groceries, and laundries in New Orleans. Gallo, *Old Bread*, Chapter 6.

69. Grimké, "Southern Immigration"; *Atlanta Independent*, March 17, 1907; Williams, "Immigration"; see also Roscoe Conkling Simmons quoted in Hellwig, "Black Attitudes Toward Immigrant Labor," pp. 163-63.

5

SOUTHERN JEWS

Relations between blacks and Jews have long been a topic of interest to sociologists, social workers, and psychologists. Of the historians who have written about blacks and Jews,[1] only one has focused on Southern Afro-Americans, and his research mainly concerns the single city of Atlanta.[2] Before 1935 most blacks lived in Dixie, and their views on Jews merit more attention than they have been given.

Dixie's Jewish population has never been large (see Tables 4 and 5), but blacks and Jews have frequently come into contact with one another in the region. After the Civil War, Jews virtually monopolized peddling and controlled the dry-goods stores of the South to a remarkable extent. Rural blacks thought of Jewish peddlers visiting their cabins as "rolling store" men, for they carried packs of exotic goods and useful household items unavailable at the local country stores. Peddling was a difficult and occasionally dangerous occupation,[3] and so, when possible, peddlers gave up their pack and purchased or leased a small store on the main street of a Southern town and began to sell notions, farm equipment, clothing, and groceries to the local population. In 1913, Timothy Thomas Fortune, who grew up in Florida during Reconstruction, recalled that after the Civil War "the Jews invaded the Southern States . . . with their merchandise in packs on their backs and began to open stores in the cities, towns, and crossroads as fast as their wholesale Jewish merchant connections in Baltimore, Philadelphia, and New York could ship the goods they ordered."[4] So completely did Jews appear to dominate the Southern retail trade that a sociologist studying Indianola, Mississippi, during the 1930s alleged that

Table 4   Estimated Number of Jews in Southern States and the
          District of Columbia

STATE	1907	1917	1927
Alabama	7,000	11,086	12,891
Arkansas	3,085	5,012	8,850
District of Columbia	5,100	10,000	16,000
Florida	3,000	6,451	13,402
Georgia	9,300	22,414	23,179
Kentucky	10,000	13,362	19,533
Louisiana	12,000	12,723	16,432
Mississippi	3,300	3,881	6,420
North Carolina	1,500	4,915	8,252
South Carolina	2,500	4,816	6,851
Tennessee	10,000	14,034	22,532
Texas	16,000	30,839	46,648
Virginia	10,000	15,403	25,656
West Virginia	1,500	5,129	7,471

SOURCE: *American Jewish Yearbook* (Philadelphia, 1928) 30: 178–79.

Table 5   Estimated Jewish Population of Selected Southern Cities, 1927

STATE/CITY	POPULATION	STATE/CITY	POPULATION
Alabama		District of Columbia	
Birmingham	4,000	Washington	16,000
Mobile	950		
Montgomery	3,000		
Arkansas		Florida	
Fort Smith	420	Jacksonville	4,000
Helena	400	Miami	2,650
Little Rock	3,000	Pensacola	1,200
North Little Rock	500	Tampa	2,000
Pine Bluff	400	West Palm Beach	600

SOURCE: *American Jewish Yearbook* (Philadelphia, 1928) 30: 182–96.

Table 5—*Continued*

STATE/CITY	POPULATION	STATE/CITY	POPULATION
Georgia		Tennessee	
Atlanta	11,000	Chattanooga	3,385
Augusta	970	Knoxville	1,250
Columbus	700	Memphis	10,000
Macon	650	Nashville	4,000
Savannah	3,800	Texas	
Kentucky		Austin	490
Covington	500	Beaumont	1,150
Lexington	750	Dallas	7,500
Louisville	12,000	El Paso	2,400
Newport	600	Fort Worth	2,100
Paducah	800	Galveston	1,940
		Houston	11,000
Louisiana		San Antonio	8,000
Alexandria	560	Tyler	500
Baton Rouge	750	Waco	1,500
Monroe	500	Wichita Falls	505
New Orleans	9,000	Virginia	
Shreveport	2,000	Lynchburg	425
Mississippi		Newport News	1,750
Meridan	575	Norfolk	7,800
Vicksburg	467	Petersburg	2,180
		Portsmouth	2,180
North Carolina		Richmond	8,000
Asheville	700	Roanoke	455
Charlotte	400	West Virginia	
Greensboro	400	Charleston	1,200
South Carolina		Huntington	1,125
Charleston	2,150	Wheeling	750
Columbia	590		

one could not purchase a pair of socks locally on a Jewish holiday.[5] In similar vein, a Texas Afro-American journal observed in 1914 that on the Jewish New Year "in Galveston about four-fifths of all retail business houses were closed during the day."[6]

A South African touring the South around 1915 noted the large number of Jewish-owned stores he passed. What particularly impressed him was that these businesses "were crammed with Negroes." More information on Jewish businesses in the South came from Bell Wiley, the late eminent Southern historian. Wiley grew up in Halls, Tennessee, during the 1910s, and the town's leading dry-goods store was operated by Joe Levy. Levy, Wiley noted, "got most of the black trade because he treated Negroes as human beings and was kindly to them, taking time to joke, inquire about their families and otherwise manifest interest in them." Mina Tropp, the talented artist who grew up in Aiken, South Carolina, in the early years of the twentieth century, recollected that Hiram Surasky, her father, never treated a black customer differently from a white. Ruth Scheinberg, who recently completed a study of Jewish peddlers in Dixie and interviewed descendants of these peddlers, uncovered considerable evidence to support Mrs. Tropp's assertion. Even John Dollard, the celebrated sociologist, made a similar observation in 1937. He attributed the success of Jewish merchants in Indianola to their ability to win the Negro trade. Whereas Gentile whites greeted blacks brusquely with "well, boy, what do you want?," Jews were wont to address Negroes as "Mr." or "Mrs." and to ask, "What can I do for you?" The Jews, Dollard noted, put business before caste principles. Moreover, he declared, Jews did not "follow a strict one-price-policy;" rather, "they bargain with the Negroes and the Negroes like this."[7]

But did they? What did blacks actually think about Jews? Prior to Appomattox, many blacks had never seen a Jew. A few Negroes had been the slaves of Jews, and urban slaves in Charleston, Mobile, Savannah, Richmond, Norfolk, Louisville, Macon, and New Orleans doubtless encountered Jewish merchants from time to time. Plantation slaves, on the other hand, probably seldom came in contact with Jews. But even those slaves who did not personally see Jews knew something about the Children of Israel. Negroes were told about the Bible, and many, like Booker T. Washington, found "the most fascinating portion of that book . . . the story of the manner in which

Moses led the Children of Israel out of the house of bondage, through the wilderness, into the promised land." According to Washington, "The Negro slaves were always looking forward to a time when a Moses should arise from somewhere who would lead them as he led the ancient Hebrews out of the house of bondage."[8]

Even after emancipation, blacks continued to show a great interest in the Jews of ancient times. The famed educator Horace Mann Bond grew up in Alabama and Georgia. The only talk about Jews in his home was "about biblical Jews; and what with prayers before each meal and Scripture reading morning and night, and three church services on Sunday and daily chapel at school, one did hear a great deal about the People of Israel." As late as 1935, Kelly Miller, a Negro Howard University professor writing in a Virginia newspaper, argued that "the Negro takes to the Hebrew Scriptures as [a] duck to water." No part of the Bible was more interesting to him than some of the stories of the Old Testament. "Noah and the Ark, Daniel in the Lion's Den, the Hebrew Children in the Fiery Furnace, Jonah and the Whale," Miller concluded, "are absorbed and relished as if they were an indigenous part of Negro folklore."[9]

Over and over again, the freedmen would be told to liken their status to that of the Jews. Addressing a rally of Negroes in Mississippi in 1876, Pinckney B.S. Pinchback, who had briefly served as governor of Louisiana, told his audience that whenever they were discouraged, they should think of the Jews. "Like you they were once slaves," he reminded his listeners, "and after they were emancipated they met with persecutions." Generation after generation they fought their oppressors, and "backed by principles they believed were right," they finally emerged victorious. Once despised, they were now "leaders of education and princes of the commercial world," and one of their number, Benjamin Disraeli, had become prime minister of England. "What an example for you, my people, whose advantages are so great," Pinchback optimistically concluded. These sentiments were hardly unique. During the dark days following the end of Reconstruction, many blacks sought solace in the Holy Scriptures. "Colored people should not become discouraged," mused the *Richmond Planet*. "Read your Bibles and you will see that the plight of the Children of Israel at one time was much worse than ours seem[s] to be."[10] After all, one black minister observed, when freed from slavery in Egypt, the ancient Israelites were as degraded and ignorant as the ex-slaves in 1865. It had taken forty years before the Hebrews were ready for settlement in the Holy Land, and now they were acknowledged world leaders. Therefore, the preacher concluded, blacks too might hope eventually to become respected citizens.[11]

Eastern European Jews doubtless would have argued that they had never achieved the status of respected citizens in their homelands, and after 1880 they flocked to the United States in great numbers. Some Americans objected to this influx of Jewish refugees, but almost without exception, Southern blacks welcomed the Jews. Typical was the opinion of the editor of the *Galveston City Times*, who declared on May 8, 1915, that the entrance of two million more Jewish immigrants to the United States would help promote the country's development.

Booker T. Washington, who rarely had a good word for European immigrants, was careful to differentiate Jews from Gentiles. When he traveled through Europe, he dismissed many would-be European immigrants as beggars, anarchists, or superstitious peasants. Jews, on the other hand, were admired for their ability to withstand the "wear and tear of centuries of persecution" and rise "up to a position of power and preeminence" in Western civilization. Once in the United States, Washington stated, the Jew retained many of his customs, but he made an earnest effort to learn English and to adjust to the "manners of the new country of which he is soon to become, if he is not already, a citizen."[12]

It was understandable to blacks that Jews would want to flock to the United States, the golden land of opportunity. Still, they were amazed to learn that in parts of Europe and North Africa, the Children of Israel had fewer opportunities and were economically worse off than American Negroes. "African people everywhere have trouble-a-plenty," declared the *Norfolk Journal and*

Guide, "but the Jews seem to be the trouble bearers of Christendom."[13] That the Hebrews were often able to dominate business affairs and the professions in the very countries that most severly presecuted them persuaded blacks that "they must be the children of the Lord." The Jews knew, Booker T. Washington enviously declared, "how to make their disadvantages their opportunities, and so get the best of the rest of the world, no matter how things are arranged."[14]

Blacks were convinced that, whatever their status elsewhere, the Israelites were thriving in the South.[15] For proof of the success of the Jews in the business world, a black needed only to read advertisements in Afro-American journals. Virtually every issue of all Negro newspapers featured ads from firms clearly owned by Jews. In Little Rock, Arkansas, Negroes were wooed by M. Stern Dry Goods, Kaufman's Cheap Store, Cohn Dry Goods and Clothing, Stern's Ladies Wear, Ottenheimer's Dry Goods, and Gershenes' Whiskey and Cigars. In Richmond, leading advertisers over the years included Isaac Straus Liquor and Tobacco Company, Salomon's Wine and Liquors, G. Kaplan, Optician, and Julius Meyer's Dry Goods. Carolina blacks were urged to patronize Rosenbaum Dry Goods in New Bern, North Carolina, H. Kaminski Dry Goods in Georgetown, South Carolina, and I. S. Leevey Clothing and J. F. Eisemann's tailor shop in Columbia, South Carolina. Galveston blacks were courted by N. Saltzman, Meyer Jewelry, B. Ganter and Son, Ullman, Stern, and Kraus Company, the Fellman Dry Goods Store, F. C. Lobenstein's, I. Schornstein's, E.. Samuels Company, M. N. Bleich, and Heyman's Notions. Atlantans could shop for wearning apparel at Rich's, Louis Stern's, Eiseman Brothers, Hirsch's, Kaplan and Shimoff's, or Clearn's. For groceries they could go to B. Hirsowitz or I. L. Goldstein, and all of their pharmaceutical needs could be met either at Jacobs' Drug Stores or at Cronheim Pharmacy. Should they need a rifle, Greenblatt Brothers advertised first-quality weapons for as little as $3.90. Nowhere were Jewish firms more eager to win the black trade than in Savannah. Rarely did an issue of a Negro paper appear in that city with fewer than six or eight Jewish advertisers; usually, the number was consistently higher, Jewish merchants may have been less numerous in Norfolk than in Savannah, but they often disguised this by taking out full-page ads in the *Journal and Guide*.[16] If one adds to the above advertisements from less obviously Jewish firms, one can readily understand why the *Columbia* (S.C.) *Southern Indicator* encouraged Negro readers to "follow the Jew [and] do 'beezness.' "[17]

Enterprising Negroes watched the success of individual Jewish merchants with awe and amazement. Booker T. Washington knew of a Jewish emigrant from Europe who had passed through Alabama in 1890 with all of his possessions in a single satchel. About 16 miles from Tuskegee, he noted an absence of stores in what seemed to him a prosperous cotton-growing region. He rented land, built a store, and within four years he owned a lucrative business grossing $50,000 per year, and he also had acquired hundreds of acres of land. Washington and other Negro leaders agreed with the editor of the *Savannah Tribune* that members of their race should emulate "the saving and economical qualities of the Jews."[18]

It was commonly believed that if Negroes properly observed the Jewish merchants of the South, they too could learn how to prosper in business. "Those of us that have tried," boasted the owner of Wood's Haberdashery in Columbia, South Carolina, "have made the Jews sit up and take notice." What Woods had learned from the Jewish merchants was not to give up easily. On occasion Jewish business ventures failed, but the merchants did not let this discourage them or persuade them to lose faith in themselves. Rather, they opened a new store in a different location and hoped for better luck.[19]

The Jew was also thrifty. "The average colored man complains that he does not have capital enough to run his business," one black editor noted, but "the average Jew starts his business on the money the Negro throws away." According to a popular joke of the 1920s, when God created the first men, He asked each what he wanted. When He approached the Negro, the black man said he wanted a million dollars. Then God came to the Jew, who merely requested "the address of the Negro you gave the million dollars."[20]

Joking aside, blacks were told that they should learn from the parsimonious habits of the Jew, keep their overhead low, and undersell the competition. According to the *Atlanta Independent*, Negro consumers, learning that "the Jew store sells for two or three cents less, . . . will go to the Jew store because he can get the same thing for less money." If the Negro merchant allowed "his goods to drop in quality and use[d] inferior help," added D. A. Hart, editor of the *Nashville Globe*, he would have no one but himself to blame if "his customers . . . go to the Jew."[21]

To the Negro merchant who complained that he could not profitably sell his goods as cheaply as the Jew, the *Savannah Tribune* offered some advice. It would be best, the *Tribune* suggested, if every member of the black merchant's family worked in the business. The Jew, his wife, and his children all worked together and were thus able to keep their store open as long as there were potential customers. According to one typical story about Jewish tradesmen, a Jewish woman once noticed black customers approach her store just after she had closed for the day. Coatless, she ran after the potential patrons and "persuaded them to buy." This she could do, for Jews were not too proud to live in a black neighborhood. Negro entrepreneurs, the *Tribune* complained, insisted upon living in a good house in another section of town and wasted much of their profit on transportation and mortgage payments. Moreover, when he made a few dollars, a black bought his wife a new dress and treated his children to a box of candy; the Jew dressed plainly and put his profits into his children's bank accounts.[22]

Even when prices were the same, Jews continued to outsell their Negro rivals. This was because, in the words of the *Savannah Tribune* "so long as you are doing business from [the]m, the Hebrews would go to any length to satisfy a customer." Thus, though often "unlearned and almost unlettered," they catered to the most sophisticated Negroes. In Washington, D.C., Kelly Miller, who wrote for black newspapers in the South, daily saw evidence that "the Negro professional classes, the graduates of Howard University, and of the city high schools are perfectly satisfied to be catered by these Jewish merchants and dealers."

These storeowners seemed to welcome criticism from patrons. Negro businessmen, on the other hand, supposedly resented suggestions from their clientele.[23]

The Jacobs Drugstore chain of Atlanta demonstrated how Jews sought to meet the needs of their Negro customers. The Jacobs stores pledged "courteous treatment to ALL," but it was impossible to serve Negroes at soda fountains in stores patronized by both races. Jacobs attempted to solve this problem by opening a drugstore in a black neighborhood that would cater exclusively to Negroes. At this store, blacks were the only ones allowed to sit at the soda fountain. Admittedly, this was a slight gesture, racist by modern standards, but it was all that Jacobs could do in a segregated society. Atlanta Negroes were aware of this, and many gladly purchased their drugs at the Jacobs pharmacies.[24]

Serving blacks at soda fountains was one way to meet the needs of Negroes. Another was to allow black patrons to examine ready-made clothing without forcing them, as Gentiles did, to purchase every garment they tried on. Jewish merchants quickly learned that "respectable" whites in Dixie would never purchase goods that might have been worn by blacks. Hebrew peddlers in rural areas, mindful of local prejudices, were careful to sell ready-made goods only to blacks. Thus, white farmers had no basis for objecting to blacks trying on dresses or suits that the peddler carried in his wagon. In urban areas, those Jews who sold clothing to Negroes normally sacrificed their white clientele. This was certainly appreciated by blacks, who were understandably annoyed at having to purchase, but not being able to return, clothing that did not fit.[25]

A more important way to help blacks was to provide them with jobs and to teach them skills needed to open their own businesses. As early as the 1900s, when few white shopkeepers employed Negroes, black help was visible in such Jewish stores as Louis Adler's Shoe Store and at Kaufman's Clothes Store in Lexington, Kentucky. In 1906, Fellman's Dry Goods Company, the largest store in Galveston, hired black men as delivery men and elevator operators and "colored women in the waiting rooms." B. M. Surasky, a Russian immigrant living in Aiken, South Carolina, employed as a helper in his dry-goods store a a young black man, "Eb" Watson. Surasky, who patronized a black pharmacist and employed an Afro-American lawyer for minor, noncourtroom, legal work, helped pay for the education of "Eb's" children at a local private Negro academy. Mandle Surasky eventually inherited his father's business and retained "Eb." Years later, when Mandle retired and sold the business, one of the conditions of the sale was that the purchaser agree to keep on "Eb" as an employee. W. S. Madden, a Negro educated at Tuskegee, told a black gathering how a Jew had helped him when he arrived jobless in Oklahoma in 1907. Work was virtually impossible to get, for times were bad. A Jewish tailor agreed to hire Madden as a journeyman and to pay him the then impressive salary of $12 per week. Unemployed whites angrily demanded that the Jew fire his black employee and replace him with a white. The tailor refused, responding that Madden was a competent, efficient, punctual, and reliable man; moreover, he did not drink. The grateful employee remained at the job for three months and, when economic conditions improved, was able to go into business for himself.[26]

Such incidents were not uncommon. Even Kelly Miller, who had ambivalent feelings about Jewish businessmen, admitted that if Negroes ever became their "own merchant[s]," it would be due to "Jewish tutelage." Working for a Jew as a clerical helper, Miller insisted, was better training than studying for years at a business school or working for a white Christian, who would never give "such intimate instruction." He also noted that Jewish businessmen and entrepreneurs had promoted the cultural renaissance of Harlem. In New York and elsewhere, "the Jew who controls the theaters, amusements, and largely the channels of literary publication of the nation, had given the Negro his chance."[27]

It was never suggested that Jews hired Negroes solely for altruistic reasons. The black salesman in the Jewish-owned store, a Savannah weekly acknowledged, was expected to be "a great drawing card for Negro trade." Thus, it is not surprising that black leaders were upset when confronted with evidence that black clerks did not necessarily attract black customers. In 1928, a Jewish merchant named Bernstein opened a department store,

The Fair, in Washington, D.C., which catered to the city's Negro community and employed seventy-five black salesladies. Although Bernstein stocked the store with quality merchandise, he went bankrupt in 1931, and the Negro women were jobless. To be sure, the Great Depression was partially responsible for the store's failure, but according to Ben Davis, a Negro editor in Atlanta, Washington blacks avoided the store, not because they thought its goods were shoddy or its prices were too high, but because they preferred to shop at places where whites would wait on them. "Th[is] enterprising Jew is . . . bankrupt because he tried to help a race of people who would not help themselves." The lesson was clear: Jews would employ blacks only if Negroes demanded that it be done and if blacks then patronized those stores.[28]

But if Jewish merchants were seen as potential employers and teachers of enterprising blacks, they were also portrayed as crafty exploiters and sharp traders.[29] They were the type of people who might sell a Negro some property on the installment plan, pocket the money, flee, and force the luckless black to toil on his land as a sharecropper or tenant.[30] Kelly Miller might praise Jews for their willingness to train blacks, but he still thought that they looked "upon the Negro as an easy field" for their "cheap, shoddy goods, which by artistic arrangement and handling," they made "look attractive." Miller wondered if the Jewish talent for business was "inborn or acquired." He suspected that in ancient times "Jewish servant women borrowed earrings and finger rings of their Egyptian mistresses, presumably to set up their husbands in the jewelry business." Over the centuries Jews have learned how to conduct business affairs

"more successfully than any other variety of the human family . . . the Jew seems to deem it his mission to cater to Christian needs and necessities. They violate their own Sabbath,[31] gathering shekels, to supply Christians with their requirements for Sunday. Christmas and Easter furnish their superlative opportunity. When the Jews take a holiday, the Gentiles suffer for lack of their accustomed supply of creature comforts."[32]

The *Atlanta Independent* echoed Miller's statement that some Jews kept their businesses open on both Saturday and Sunday.

Particularly offensive was the fact that "the cheap Jew" operated dance halls, movie theaters, and other entertainment emporiums on Sunday. Why, the paper asked, should the Hebrew "desecrate our Sabbath and insult our religion by conducting places of amusement that interfere with the sanctity of our Sabbath?" These places of amusement allegedly catered "to the Negro underworld" and promoted the "foolishness of social equality." Two decades earlier Roy Stannard Baker, a prominent white social critic, had noted that in Atlanta "many of the saloons for Negroes were kept by foreigners, usually Jews."[33]

Operating saloons and dance halls was considered disreputable, and Southern blacks criticized Jews for engaging in such enterprises. In similar fashion, blacks were quick to denounce Jewish businessmen whenever they mistreated or exploited them. As early as 1881, a New Orleans black editor had castigated the "despicable" Jewish vendors at Spanish Fort, a fashionable Louisiana lake resort, for refusing to sell refreshments to Negroes: "The Jews, of all other people, should be the last to discriminate." Those who were prejudiced against blacks merited nothing but scorn. Two decades later, another black newspaper happily reported the fate of a Jewish peddler in Brunswick, Georgia, who had dismissed Negroes "as being a worthless set." Upon hearing reports of these comments, Brunswick blacks staged a meeting, denounced their detractor, and refused to purchase his wares. "This," exulted the *Baltimore Afro-American*, "is the right way to treat our enemies. Make them feel our power." Southern Negroes paid close attention to the way Jews treated them, and black newspapers occasionally printed stories about Jews falsely accusing blacks of shoplifting, evicting black tenants when white neighbors protested, and even physically assaulting Negro customers.[34] Although Negroes did not boycott Jewish department stores in Savannah or Atlanta, as had occurred in Harlem during the 1930s, Southern Negro newspapers dutifully reported what was going on in the North.

Despite frequent contacts between blacks and Jews in the South, stories about Jews mistreating blacks were infrequent.[35] When it was pointed out that Jews charged high prices for poor quality goods, blacks readily indicated that this practice was not uniquely Jewish. Jews were favorably compared with Greek, Italian, and German storekeepers. "Not only Jewish people thrive from [unfair] . . . practice[s]," a Chicago paper—approvingly quoted in the *Savannah Tribune*—admitted, "Gentiles [als]o mercilessly grind human flesh through their money-making machines [to] reap full harvests." Even Kelly Miller concluded "that the Jewish merchant is a blessing rather than a bane to the gullible Negro purchaser. If he were withdrawn, the white Gentile dealer would exploit him no less ruthlessly and with much less geniality."[36]

This view of the Jewish businessman helped soften the image of the Jew as an unprincipled merchant. More important was the recognition that "some of our truest and staunchest friends are numbered among the members of the Hebrew race." In the North, Joel and Arthur Spingarn, Julius Rosenwald, Henry Moskowitz, Lillian Wald, Abraham Flexner, and Jacob Billikopf donated their time, talent, and fortunes to improve the quality of medical care and education available to Southern blacks.[37] Rabbi Stephen S. Wise, whose daughter Justine married a South Carolinian, and Rabbis Joseph Silverman of New York and Emil Hirsch of Chicago were quick to condemn lynchings and other manifestations of racial discimination. In 1927, the Social Justice Commission of the Central Conference of American Rabbis passed resolutions supporting the rights of Pullman porters to organize and insisting that labor conditions be compatible with good health. One year later, the Association of Jewish Charities and Settlement Workers boycotted the annual meeting of the National Conference on Social Work which was being held in Memphis. The reason for the boycott was that black delegates would be forced to endure segregated facilities. In 1921, the Workman's Circle refused to become chartered in several Southern states because incorporation laws required that membership be limited to whites. The Workman's Circle did not expect blacks to apply for membership, but it believed that incorporation would imply sanctioning racism.[38]

In the South, some Jews were willing to speak out for black rights. A black newspaper in 1927 lauded Rabbi George Solomon of

Savannah's Congregation Mickve Israel for being "one of the most liberal minded clergy of the city and [one] deeply concerned in civic affairs." Other rabbis who championed Afro-Americans included Ben Goldstein-Lowell and Bernard Ehrenreich, both of Alabama, and David Marx of Atlanta. Marx, the most prominent rabbi in Georgia, was active in the Commission of Interracial Cooperation (CIC), a pioneer civil rights group in the South. Also active in the CIC were Rhoda Kaufman and Dr. Josiah Morse, a professor at the University of South Carolina who taught race relations courses in the 1910s. William Lovenstein of Richmond served as president of that city's school board, and while serving in the Virginia state senate, he worked hard to improve educational opportunities for Negroes.[39]

The role of Southern Jewish women in combatting injustice is best shown by the activities of the National Council of Jewish Women (NCJW). In Montgomery, Alabama, in 1931, under the leadership of Rebecca Gershon of Atlanta, the Southern Interstate Conference of the NCJW publicly condemned the practice of lynching. Four years later, at the NCJW national meeting held in New Orleans, the NCJW unanimously adopted a resolution in favor of a federal anti-lynching law. Southern delegates took a prominent role in supporting the resolution. Moreover, Mrs. Gershon, Mrs. Joseph Friend of New Orleans, Mrs. I. L. Kaplan of Jacksonville, Florida, and Hattie Weinberg of Greensboro, North Carolina, were quite active in the Association of Southern Women for the Prevention of Lynching.[40]

Shad Polier devoted his life to promoting justice for all and for working to improve the status of blacks. Several years before his death in 1976, Polier, a native of Aiken, South Carolina, recollected that his birthplace was a gorgeous town, not a "tobacco road community." Yet, before he completed his studies at the University of South Carolina, there had been three lynchings in his hometown. He resolved then to work to rid the world of injustice. Following one of these lynchings, a druggist came into Hiram Surasky's store and told Mina, the merchant's daughter, that they had just lynched a young Negro "boy" for raping a white girl. Mina, who was Shad Polier's cousin, was incensed and demanded of the pharmacist, "How can you talk like that?"

Some months later another man confessed to the crime, but there was no remorse over the lynching. Most people felt it was no big deal to kill an innocent Negro. Mina Tropp, however, never forgot the incident.[41] There was good reason for Booker T. Washington to state that Jews consistently demonstrated "a sympathy and support . . . for the work I have had to do with my own people."[42]

This support was very much appreciated, and during the 1930s, when Northern blacks were becoming increasingly critical of Jews, their Southern counterparts insisted that "there is no Jew hated among us. . . . there are many things we must hate before we get to so lovable a people as the Jew." An Alabama black who had lived in eight states claimed that "the anti-Jewish feeling that exists among my people is small and insignificant." When the black-owned American Mutual Savings Bank contributed to a Jewish charity drive in 1926, the *Louisville News* lavished praise on the bank and doubted that "American Mutual ever made a better investment." Similar praise had come twice before when Afro-Americans contributed to Jewish causes. In December 1905, students and faculty at Hampton Institute in Virginia raised $52.10 at a Sunday evening service to assist victims of tsarist anti-Semitism. Fourteen years later, Galveston, Texas, blacks collected in excess of $112 for a Jewish charity to assist victims of World War I.[43]

Only one article has been found that called Jews "despicable" and people with "obnoxious habits," and this was published on July 23, 1881. Far more common were newspaper editorials that praised Jews as good, gentle, and law-abiding.[44] In their sermons and editorials, Negro preachers and editors frequently contrasted the alleged shortcomings of blacks with the supposed virtues of Jews. Most important was the fact that Jews were proud of their heritage and were always willing to stick together whenever one of their number was in need, unlike blacks, who were "ashamed of being black." "The most exalted Jew," claimed newspaper columnist Frank Crosswaith, "will gladly unite with his less fortunate kinsman to oppose injustice of any sort aimed at Jews." When trouble struck, a Norfolk editor added, "Jews d[id] not disown and run away from Jews."

Rather, they came together and "assist[ed] one another in all reasonable ways."[45]

The B'nai B'rith was often cited as an example of the way Jews helped each other. This popular Jewish fraternal order fostered business cooperation, provided insurance benefits and other assistance to Jewish widows, sponsored the construction and maintenance of orphanages, dispensed sick benefits, and collected funds to help immigrants. What blacks needed, insisted one editor, was to establish their own counterparts to B'nai B'rith. In unity there was strength, and the *Savannah Tribune* admired the way American Jews had learned the value of "group protection [in] . . . combatting collectively attacks which are heaped upon them."[46]

Credit for the "race pride" of the Jew belonged to the Jewish religion, which "idealizes marriage and the home." Jewish children "grow up in an atmosphere of reverence and respect for parents, teachers, rabbis, and all proper authority." They were taught to revere their heritage. By teaching that "Jewish history" represented "the highest possibilities of the human family," the Jew made certain that his child would never be ashamed of his origin.[47] T. Thomas Fortune marveled at how the Jewish child was encouraged to learn and to chase after honors in scholarship. In the Jewish home, "education is considered the handmaid of religion." "They want to know everything there is to be known on a given subject," commented an envious black writer for the *Savannah Tribune*. "They often work hard all day and study half the night, while the colored man frolics."[48]

Education inspired Jews to be hard workers and to reject idleness.[49] "You have never heard of Jews begging anybody for anything," declared B. C. Baskerville. "They have sense enough to invest their money productively." Jews were not drunkards or beggars or residents of almshouses, added the *Richmond Reformer*. "Success seems to attend their pathway . . . [they] are our most progressive citizens." Blacks should emulate the Jew. "What he has done we can do. . . . When we add money, character, intelligence, and industry to our stock in trade, we will have friends to come to our assistance." Reverend T. Jefferson Goodall, minister of Savannah's First African Baptist

Church, similarly traced the success of the Jews to their good habits. They abided not only by "the common law but the laws of health and nature also . . . They furnish a fitting example for life along these lines."[50]

Another reason why blacks viewed Jews sympathetically was the continuous existence of anti-Semitism. "The Jew, our faithful ally," quoted one clergyman, "has come in for his share of humiliation too." Hotels denied admission to potential guests with Jewish surnames, colleges imposed quotas on Jewish applicants, employment agencies often turned away Jewish job-seekers, and even the army once was accused of failing to promote Jewish soldiers. All of this was duly noted in the black press.[51] A Virginia editor who accepted the stereotype of the Jew as a shrewd businessman noted that, even though Southern Jews could vote and move about freely, they were not fully accepted by their neighbors. "In many of our Southern States . . . the Jews are considered undesirable citizens, mainly because of their racial clannishness and their ability to overreach every other kind of trader." In 1889, the *New Orleans Weekly Pelican* reported the pillaging of Jewish stores in in Delhi, Louisiana, "by an armed mob." "The cause of the 'disturbance," the *Pelican* concluded, "has been traced to business rivalry." A more subtle form of anti-Semitism was encountered by the famed black writer Charles Waddell Chesnutt, when he grew up in North Carolina. In 1880, he began the study of German and French with a private tutor, Professor E. M. Neufeld, who had attended classes at Oxford and at the University of Paris. Whites in Fayette-ville, North Carolina, were unimpressed with Neufeld's erudition; they were prejudiced against him because he was Jewish and a foreigner. So moved was Chesnutt by this bigotry that he hoped his professor would some day be able to hurt those who had mistreated him.[52]

Even Booker T. Washington, a frequent beneficiary of Jewish philanthropy, had to deal with the popular prejudice against Jews. Edward Attwell, a white man, wrote him in 1909 that more prominent—and presumably wealthy—whites would attend commencement ceremonies at Tuskegee if the number of Jews present was reduced. Washington's response was as follows:

"Of course I do not want to keep the Jews away, but I think it would be a good plan to increase the number of Gentiles if possible."[53] It cannot be determined how many, if any, Jews were kept away from Tuskegee commencements.

Some Jews experienced even more serious manifestations of Southern hostility, which caught the attention of black editors. The most famous incident was the lynching of Leo M. Frank for the alleged murder of Mary Phagan, one of his employees. Ten years after Frank was murdered, Joseph Needleman, a young Jewish traveling salesman, was mutilated by a mob in Martin County, North Carolina, for supposedly mistreating a young girl. "Relatives of the girl and others took him from the jail," sympathetically related the *Chicago Defender*, "and subjected him to horrible treatment [castration]. The youth lingered between life and death for some days." Needleman survived, however, and later instituted an unsuccessful suit in federal court against members of the mob.[54]

Of greatest interest to blacks, however, was the mistreatment of David Weinberg, a forty-four-year-old tailor in Miami. Weinberg was considered a "dangerous" radical by his neighbors, since it was alleged that he was a communist and that he was associating with Negroes. One night three men enticed him to leave his house, beat and gagged him, disrobed him and then tarred and feathered him. Then "they tied him in a white hooded garment and tossed him from an automobile at a downtown street intersection." Weinberg was treated at a local hospital, but his ordeal was not yet over. He "was removed to the city jail on the charge that he had been too friendly with Negroes of the town." The tailor "denied the charges and was later released after his attorney had filed habeas corpus proceedings."[55]

But to be pernicious, discrimination need not take so violent a form. In rural Bryan County, Georgia, Jews were regularly eliminated from grand and petit juries. Even in the more cosmopolitan Richmond, Virginia, the local YMCA accepted Jews as members but not as lodgers. This prompted the *Richmond Planet* to comment, "It may not be too much to say that in some sections of the country the antipathy to Jews in the hotels is almost as marked as it is to Negroes." J. A. Rogers, a syndicated columnist in black newspapers, concluded that Jews "have certainly not been admitted to the sacred circles of Aryan or Caucasian or whatever term it is that the 'pale faces' have used to designate themselves."[56] Echoing Rogers' sentiments, another columnist, Frank Crosswaith, noted that "Jews, like the Negroes fac[e] a more or less hostile majority except that the Negroes meet this hostility in a more naked and brutal form since because of his color, he is unable to escape as easily as the Jew."[57]

Blacks could not change their color to avoid prejudice, but they could emulate the Jew by making use of the courts and economic pressure. For example, one Negro paper noted, the Jews of Bryan County, Georgia, had not tolerated second-class citizenship. They took their case to court and persuaded the state supreme court to rule that they were entitled to serve on juries. The *Savannah Tribune* welcomed the decision and hoped it would spur Negroes to sue for their rights as well. A Richmond, Virginia, journal once offended that city's Jews, "and they of right withdrew their patronage from the paper" until it changed its editorial policy. The same paper "delight[ed] in attacking the Negro," and the *Richmond Reformer* suggested that if anything should be learned from the Jews, it was that "we must have manhood to retaliate." Retaliation could tumble even the mightiest; Jews had forced as powerful a man as Henry Ford to apologize for his "attacks upon their race." "When someone injures a Jew, observed the writer of "Colorful News Movies," a syndicated black news column, "he's going to look right square into the muzzle of a gun loaded with serious consequences. It wouldn't hurt if we were more like the Jews."[58]

On occasion, Jews and blacks cooperated to fight a common foe; blacks welcomed and expected such assistance. "We want their sympathy and it is their duty to give it," declared Dr. H. R. Butler, a Negro minister. "They should line up . . . always to lighten the burdens of the oppressed." Working together, marveled the *Norfolk Journal and Guide*, "it is quite remarkable how much success the Jew and Negro and the foreign-born have forced from the reluctant grasp of restraining laws and hostile public opinion." But eternal vigilance was necessary, the *Journal and Guide* added, and if men and women "had to fight for what they have got, . . . [so too will] they have to fight to hold on to it."[59]

Blacks recognized that Jews were not acting out of pure altruism in allying with them, for by helping the blacks, the Jew fought his own battle for justice. When Jewish groups joined the NAACP in protesting efforts to force a black woman to sell a house in a white neighborhood, the *Savannah Tribune* suspected that the Jews were interested in the matter "because of the effect the case will have on similar" lawsuits involving Jews. The *Norfolk Journal and Guide* analyzed Jewish assistance: "in many ways he [the Jew] sympathizes with and helps us. He gets his pound of flesh for doing it, but that is his due and the due of everyone who takes as well as gives." Less charitable was the *Atlanta Independent*, which insisted that "the Jew never gives his time and talent for his health," that rich Jews owned, directed, and controlled the major civil rights organizations, and that the NAACP was really affiliated with the Democrats and sought to defeat the Republican party at the polls.[60]

Other than the *Independent*, no paper has been located that cast suspicions on the motivation of the NAACP. Several journals, however, did object that to many people oppression of Jews seemed more important than persecution of Negroes. Black writers were outraged that tens of thousands would assemble to weep for Jewish victims of pogroms or Nazi outrages but that these same people remained indifferent to the persecution of Southern blacks. Hitler, cautioned a Texas paper, "might tell us to wash our own dirty linen before telling him that his is soiled." There was also resentment that politicians avidly courted Jews but invariably ignored Negroes. Harry Byrd, for example, denounced those Virginia hotels that barred Jews, while he did nothing for blacks and was, in fact, in the words of a Richmond editor, "one of the chief exponents of racial prejudice and discrimination against the Negro citizens of Virginia, whom he also represents in the Senate of the U.S."[61]

Perhaps the prevailing sentiment of Southern blacks was best expressed by the *Norfolk Journal and Guide* on September 30, 1916: "The Jews are victims of petty prejudices in this country and in that account deserve sympathy, and they have ours. They certainly deserve more tolerant treatment at the hands of Christian Americans. But the real sufferers from race prejudice are the tens of millions of black[s]."

Not surprisingly, nothing upset blacks more than to discover that some Jews in the South had adopted the same "philosophies pursued by other white groups" and that "to curry favor with the ruling classes," they had joined the Negro haters.[62] In *Black Boy*, Richard Wright recalls that when he worked for an optical company in Memphis, one of the employees, a Jew named Don, expressed a "frantic desire to demonstrate racial solidarity with the whites against Negroes." Similarly, Isador Raynor and Isaac Strauss in Maryland promoted the disfranchisement of blacks during the early years of the twentieth century. This may explain why in 1931 Joseph Berman, a Jewish alderman in Atlanta, introduced a segregation ordinance before the Atlanta City Council, which provided that "persons of different races shall not live within a radius of fifteen blocks of a school for either white persons or Negroes." Curiously, Berman's district was largely populated by blacks.[63]

Apparently there was justification for believing that some Southern Jews had accepted the prejudices of their neighbors. Samuel Rosenberg, who lived in Virginia, admitted that Southern Jews from rabbis to merchants regard the Negro "as a second or third class being . . . treat Negroes as inferiors and are raising their children to do the same." While studying race relations in Indianola, Mississippi, during the 1930s, the distinguished anthropologist Hortense Powdermaker, who was Jewish, met with the sisterhood of the Reform temple of Greenville, the town nearest Indianola with a Jewish congregation. Greenville was a typical Mississippi Delta community. Professor Powdermaker distributed questionnaires to those who were present at a sisterhood luncheon to determine attitudes on the race question.

The data from the questionnaire confirmed my impression of no difference between the attitudes of Jews and Protestants towards Negroes. Conversations with a few Jews who had moved from the North to Greenville indicated that some had become more Southern than the Southerners . . . in order to be accepted by the community."[64]

Similar findings were reported by Charles Rubin, a Polish immigrant growing up in Georgia, and Baruch Charney Vladeck, an editor for the *Jewish Daily Forward* in New York City and a labor leader. Rubin was shocked to see white youths throwing rocks at blacks. In Atlanta, he recalled: "I heard the term 'nigger' used by Jewish sons of immigrant parents with the same venom and contempt as the term 'Zhid' was used in the old country." Vladeck, traveling through the South, saw whites in Norfolk mistreat blacks. A group of Russian-Jewish immigrants silently viewed the scene. Stunned at the passivity of the Jews, Vladeck berated them, shouting, "How can you stand watching such outrages without trying to protect the innocent people? Why this is exactly what you fled from only a few years since."[65]

Blacks also remembered such incidents. In 1916, Horace Mann Bond and his parents moved to Atlanta. Shortly after their arrival, young Bond passed by a small grocery store, and the young son of the owner began to chant, "nigger, nigger, nigger, nigger." Bond, himself but twelve years old at the time, had never before been called "nigger," and without any further ado, he retorted, "You Christ killer." Upon hearing this the Jewish boy burst into tears, and Bond left the scene, ashamed of what he had said. Nearly fifty years after the incident took place, Bond recollected:

We moved to Atlanta one year after the lynching [of Leo Frank]. I now think that, somehow, the word I used hung immanent in the Atlanta air; and, somehow, it had entered my mind, and remained there like a knife, waiting only for opportunity for release. But of course the thought that Christ had been killed, and by the Jews, and that this little boy was such a one, may have had a more ancient basis in my twelve-year-old mind that I can now bring myself to admit.[66]

Bond was correct, for many Negroes were taught that Jews had had a role in the death of Jesus. One of the slave spirituals included the following lines:

> The Jews killed poor Jesus, an' laid him in a tomb.
> He 'rose, he 'rose, and 'went to heaven in a cloud.

Another spiritual spoke about how "de Jews and de Romans had him [Jesus] hung." Decades after emancipation, Jews continued to be represented as the betrayers and slayers of Jesus. Richard Wright remembered that, during the 1910s, when he was growing up in Elaine, Arkansas, "All of us black people who lived in the neighborhood hated Jews . . . because we had been taught at home and in Sunday School that Jews were 'Christ killers.' With the Jews thus singled out for us, we made them fair game for ridicule." Among the chants local children learned was the following:

> Bloody Christ killers
> Never trust a Jew
> Bloody Christ killers
> What won't a Jew do?[67]

There is little available in print to verify the accuracy of Wright's contention that black ministers taught their congregations to blame Jews for the crucifixion of Jesus. Some Negro clergymen did apparently believe that the Jews had a role in His death. Dr. J. H. Butler thought that "some of their people [had a part] in the crucifixion." He softened this statement somewhat by reminding people "that not all of the Jews of that day took part in that awful tragedy." The Reverend S. N. Vass of Raleigh, North Carolina, was silent on the role of Jews in the death of Jesus, but he believed that descendants of the old Hebrew Nation "are scattered over the earth to-day because they ceased to hold the whole Bible as their platform and chart."[68]

Charles Johnson and E. Franklin Frazier advised Hortense Powdermaker "not to reveal [her] Jewish background to Negroes or whites in a Bible Belt Community." The two black sociologists

explained that to both groups "the Jews were still 'Christ killers,' "
and they suggested that Powdermaker temporarily become a
Christian. She followed this advice, and for the duration of her
stay in Indianola, she pretended to be a Methodist.[69]

Blacks did consider Jews to be different from other whites.[70]
Socially, Jews and Christian whites seldom mixed, and
according to a writer for *The Voice of the Negro*, "Only now and
then does a Jew cross the line and marry into another race." Miscegenation was uncommon among Jewish storekeepers living
"right in the middle of a strictly colored neighborhood." Richard
Bowling, a black Baptist minister in Virginia, commented about
the Jewish businessman:

He will run his store on the first floor, live on the second floor
himself, and in some cases rent out a possible third floor to some
family of Negroes. Six days out of seven he, his wife, and his
children will see more of colored people than . . . even their
fellow Jews. Howbeit, they all remain Jews. Neither does colored
blood filter into their family nor does any of the Jewish blood filter
into the veins of Negroes. They are in the Negro world but not of it.

Southern blacks, declared *The Voice of the Negro*, admired a people whose actions disputed "the Anglo-Saxon's argument that
every other race is fairly crazy to marry into his race. Other races
have more self-respect than the white man imagines."[71] Jews
were admired as being too proud of their heritage and achieve-
ments to desire assimilation.

To Southern blacks, Jews had always been and would remain a people apart. This may explain why from 1880 to 1935
they were so fascinated with the Children of Israel. Every aspect
of Jewish life interested Negroes. None, however, was more
carefully studied than the way Jews earned their livelihood.
Influenced by Booker T. Washington, Southern Negroes to an
extraordinary degree admired the Hebrew shopkeeper and
peddler. However menial peddling may have been to white
Southerners, blacks respected the man with the pack on his
back, for he escaped what Barry Supple has called the *"real*
degradation of toiling for others."* If he owned a store, however

small, he was the boss. If he chose, he would close his shop to observe his holidays. To blacks—who were very conscious of the necessity of sending their wives and teenage children out to work to supplement the family income—there was a certain dignity to the Jewish family. When Jewish women and children worked, they did so in the family store, not in the kitchens or laundry rooms of rich white folks.[72]

Blacks and Jews seldom competed for jobs, for as already noted, relatively few blacks became businessmen and virtually no Jews in the South were farm laborers or menial workers. "To put a Jew in the field cultivating [sugar] cane and corn along-side of a negro or a common white man, I don't believe in doing," asserted Joseph Weill of New Iberia, Louisiana. "There is no chance for a Jew in that capacity," he cautioned, "to improv[e] himself or his condition."[73] Unsuccessful experiments of Jewish agriculturalists in Virginia, Louisiana, South Carolina, and elsewhere provided ample testimony as to the wisdom of Weill's words. Little wonder that the *Jewish Daily Forward* of November 23, 1907, declared that "a region where sold slavery still rules cannot offer for Jewish masses a better outlook than a region where we have a worker's movement."[74]

Nor were the Jews' opportunities to work as common laborers in Southern cities any better. Visiting Atlanta, David M. Bressler, secretary of the Jewish Immigrants' Information Bureau, noted that Negroes, paid only $0.75 to $1.00 a day, monopolized this work. "There is no earthly chance to compete with them," he wrote in 1906, "even if they [the Jews] were so inclined."[75] Clearly, Jews were not "so inclined." A group of un-successful Jewish farmers was forced to abandon a farming colony near Newberry, South Carolina, in 1906. According to one of them, they then "decided to go to work on the docks, but who can compete with the Negroes, who work for 50 and 60 cents a day?"[76] In 1910, a well-intentioned Christian lady from Rome, Georgia, Annie Johnson, wrote Jacob Schiff that she would be able to find employment for six to eight orthodox Jewish families from Russia to work in her family's woolen mill and trouser factory. Her offer was rejected, probably because there was no desire to promote settlement of Jewish factory help that might some day compete with Afro-Americans.[77] As already shown in this book, competition for jobs was a major factor in explaining black prejudice toward the Chinese, Italians, Japanese, Irish, and Mexicans. It seems reasonable to conclude that the absence of this competition helps account for the more favorable stereotype blacks had of Southern Jews.

Thus, the Southern black's image of Jews was reasonably positive. To be sure, Jews were occasionally criticized for their alleged greed, obnoxious habits, and indifference to the problems of Negroes. And there were those who still blamed the Jews for killing the Messiah or for "getting Negro money while the Negro church is getting Jew religion."[78] More commonly, however, praise was expressed for the "patience, perseverance, pluck, education and wealth" of the Jew.[79] The Jew was the merchant who said "mister," the Northern philanthropist who built schools and hospitals, the fellow sufferer in a society whose highest rungs were reserved for white Gentiles. As T. Thomas Fortune declared, the Jew was the man on the make, the one who "has not lost faith in himself," the person to imitate. Even though there were obstacles in the Jew's path, Southern blacks were certain he would eventually rise to the top, and when he made it, it would somehow be easier for Negroes to advance. Blacks watched and applauded the Jew's progress, hoping they too could develop what the *Atlanta Independent* described as "a racial consciousness, a cohesion that binds them together."[80] By no means did Jews and Southern blacks have a model relationship, but life in the South during those years was hardly ideal.[81]

NOTES

1. Philip S. Foner, "Black-Jewish Relations in the Opening Years of the Twentieth Century," *Phylon* 36 (1975): 359-76 and Foner, *American Socialism and Black Americans* (Westport, Conn., 1977); Eugene Levy, "Is the Jew a White Man?: Press Reaction to the Leo Frank Case, 1913-1915," *Phylon* 35 (1974): 212-22; Lawrence Levine, *Black Culture and Black Consciousness* (New York, 1977); Oscar Williams, "Historical Impressions of Black-Jewish Relations Prior to World War II," *Negro History Bulletin* 40 (1977): 728-31; Morris U. Schappes, "Historical

Impressions of Black-Jewish Relations Prior to World War II, Another Comment," *Negro History Bulletin* 40 (1977): 890-92; David Hellwig, "The Afro-American and the Immigrant, 1880-1930" (Ph.D. dissertation, Syracuse University, 1973), Chapter 7; Steven Hertzberg, "The Jews of Atlanta, 1865-1915" (Ph.D. dissertation, University of Chicago, 1975), Steven Hertzberg, *Strangers Within the Gate City* (Philadelphia, 1978).

2. Hertzberg, "Jews"; Hertzberg, *Strangers*.

3. Murders of peddlers have been documented. In 1912, two blacks killed and robbed Harry Swaitz near Round Lake, Mississippi. About a decade earlier near Aiken, South Carolina, a white murdered Abraham Surasky. His brother, Benedict (B. M.) Surasky barely escaped from a family who offered him shelter but hoped to kill him when he was asleep. *Memphis Commercial Appeal*, February 8, 1912; *New Orleans Daily Picayune*, February 8, 1912; *Baton Rouge New Advocate-State-Times*, February 9, 1912; Mina Tropp, "Memoirs Mostly About a South Carolina Childhood," *Jewish Currents* 34 (February, 1980): 29; Esther Surasky Pinck, "Rememberance of Things Past" (memoir for a Bethesda, Md., synagogue bulletin, 1979), copy in Pinck Papers, Winthrop College. See also "A Socialist View of the Jews of the South: The Observations of Baruch Charney Vladeck," *Southern Jewish Historical Society Newsletter* 3 (Winter, 1981): 2-4, hereafter cited as "Socialist View"; Louis Schmier, "Helloo! Peddler Man! Helloo!," in *Ethnic Minorities in Gulf Coast Society*, Jerrell Shofner and Linda Ellsworth, eds. Pensacola, Fla., 1979), pp. 75-88.

4. Eli Evans, "Southern Jewish History," in Nathan Kaganoff and Melvin Urofsky, eds., *Turn to the South* (Charlottesville, Va., 1979), p. 161; T. Thomas Fortune, unsigned editorial note, *New York Age*, August 21, 1913. See also Thomas Clark, *Pills, Petticoats, and Plows: The Southern Country Store* (Norman, Okla., 1964), pp. 6-7; Clark, "The Post-Civil War Economy in the South," in Leonard Dinnerstein and Mary Dale Palsson, eds., *Jews in the South* (Baton Rouge, La., 1973), pp. 159-69.

5. John Dollard, *Caste and Class in a Southern Town* (New Haven, Conn., 1937), p. 129. See also William Ivy Hair, *Bourbonism and Agrarian Protest: Louisiana Politics, 1887-1900* (Baton Rouge, La., 1969), pp. 158-60; Allison Davis, Burleigh Gardner, and Mary Gardner, *Deep South* (Chicago, 1941), p. 264; David Tucker, *Memphis Since Crump* (Knoxville, Tenn., 1980), p. 15.

6. *Galveston City Times*, September 26, 1914.

7. Maurice Evans, *Black and White in the Southern States* (London, 1915), pp. 56-58; Steven Hertzberg, "Southern Jews and Their En-

counters with Blacks: Atlanta, 1850–1915," *Atlanta Historical Journal* 23 (1979): 10; Hortense Powdermaker, *After Freedom* (New York, 1939), p. 9; Wiley to writer, December 19, 1979 and January 11, 1980; Tropp, "Memories"; Ruth Scheinberg, "The Pekl: Folk Histories of Jewish Peddlers in the South" (unpublished paper and cassette tape recordings, Emory University, 1979–1980), pp. 35, 43, 61–62 (Mrs. Scheinberg has deposited this material at the Emory University Special Collections); Dollard, *Caste and Class*, pp. 4, 129–30. Dollard does not imply that by bargaining with blacks, Jews cheated or overcharged their Negro patrons. In Natchez, Mississippi, "When a few Jewish merchants in a Negro shopping area broke . . . caste rules [and called Negroes 'Mr.' and 'Mrs.], they were roundly condemned by other white merchants." See Davis, Gardner, and Gardner, *Deep South*, p. 459. See also Harry Golden, *Forgotten Pioneer* (Cleveland, 1963), pp. 33, 40; Hertzberg, "Jews of Atlanta," pp. 286–88; David Davis, "Recollections of Atlanta," *Jewish Currents* 32 (September, 1978): 14–18.

8. Booker T. Washington, *The Man Farthest Down* (Garden City, N.Y., 1912), pp. 240–41; Eli Shepperd, *Plantation Songs* (New York, 1901), pp. 135–36; J. Mason Brewer, *American Negro Folklore* (New York, 1968), pp. 147–59; Charles Nichols, *Many Thousand Gone: The Ex-Slaves' Account of Their Bondage and Freedom* (Bloomington, Ind., 1969), pp. 96–97; Henry Feingold, *Zion in America* (New York, 1974), pp. 59–60. See also William Wells Brown, *My Southern Home* (New York, 1969), pp. 86–87; Kate Picard, ed., *The Kidnapped and the Ransomed: The Narrative of Peter and Vina Still* (Philadelphia, 1970), especially the introduction by Maxwell Whiteman; Levine, *Black Culture and Black Consciousness*, pp. 23, 43, 50; Albert Raboteau, *Slave Religion* (New York, 1978), pp. 311–12.

9. Horace Mann Bond, "Negro Attitudes Towards Jews," in Meir Ben-Horin, comp., *Negro-Jewish Relations in the United States* (New York, 1966), p. 4; Kelly Miller, "The Cultural Kingship [sic] of Negro and Jew," *Richmond Planet*, April 20, 1935, hereafter cited as "Cultural Kinship." See also Benjamin Mays, *The Negro's God* (New York, 1968), pp. 25–28; James Weldon Johnson, *The Book of American Negro Spirituals* (New York, 1925), pp. 20–25.

10. Pinchback, quoted in *Alexandria* (Va.) *People's Advocate*, April 29, 1876; *Richmond Planet*, September 29, 1900; *Richmond Reformer*, n.d., quoted in *Savannah Tribune*, July 8, 1911. See also Raymond Gavins, *The Perils and Prospects of Southern Black Leadership: Gordon Blaine Hancock, 1884–1970* (Durham, N.C., 1977), p. 89.

11. Unidentified clergyman cited in speech of Booker T. Washington,

in Louis Harlan, ed., *The Booker T. Washington Papers*, 9 vols. to date (Urbana, Ill., 1971-), 2: 446. See also Hertzberg, "Jews of Atlanta," p. 305.

12. Washington, *The Man Farthest Down*, pp. 241, 257. See also "The Hebrew Race in America," *Voice of the Negro* (Atlanta) 3 (January 1906): 20; *Galveston City Times*, February 26, 1916.

13. *Norfolk Journal and Guide*, January 14 and November 25, 1922, September 22, 1923.

14. Washington, *The Man Farthest Down*, p. 382. See also *Savannah Tribune*, May 4, 1912; *Atlanta Independent*, September 21, 1907; Booker T. Washington, *Putting the Most into Life* (New York, 1906), p. 33; *Indianapolis Leader*, n.d., quoted in *Alexandria* (Va.) *People's Advocate*, March 27, 1880; *New Orleans Louisianian*, August 6, 1881.

15. See, for example, C. E. Chapman's article on Memphis. "The Gristmill," *Kansas City* (Kans.) *Call*, December 27, 1935.

16. The advertisements mentioned above came from issues of the *Arkansas Mansion* (Little Rock) (1883-1884); *Richmond Southern News* (1893); *Richmond Planet* (1913-1915); *Galveston City Times* (1914-1916); *Georgetown* (S.C.) *Planet* (1873); *Raleigh Gazette* (1894, for Rosenbaum's of New Bern, N.C.); *Columbia* (S.C.) *Southern Indicator* (1921); *Atlanta Independent* (1906-1907); *Savannah Echo* (1883-1884); *Savannah Tribune* (various years); *Norfolk Journal and Guide* (1916-1923). Other cities in which Jews were prominent advertisers in black journals include Nashville, Tulsa, and Lexington, Kentucky.

17. *Columbia* (S.C.) *Southern Indicator*, August 6, 1921. There is no simple way to determine the religion of the owners of firms bearing such names as Peachtree Tailor Shop, Ace Jewelry, Sam's Drugs, or Queen City Clothing.

18. Harlan, ed., *Booker T. Washington Papers* 3: 408-409; *Savannah Tribune*, September 26, 1914. See also Hellwig, "Afro-American and the Immigrant," p. 146.

19. *Columbia* (S.C.) *Southern Indicator*, October 15, 1921. See also *Norfolk Journal and Guide*, March 5, 1921; T. Thomas Fortune, "The Passing Show," *Norfolk Journal and Guide*, February 11, 1928.

20. Richard Bowling, "Jews and Discipline," *Norfolk Journal and Guide*, December 15, 1928; William Pickens, *American Aesop* (Boston, 1926), pp. 113-15; Daryl Dance, *Shuckin' and Jivin'* (Bloomington, Ind., 1978), pp. 153-54. See also *Richmond Planet*, April 13, 1935; *Atlanta Independent*, October 22, 1931, February 25, 1932.

21. *Atlanta Independent*, July 8, 1926; D. A. Hart, quoted in *Nashville Globe*, December 2, 1910. See also unidentified newspaper quoted in

Savannah Tribune, December 13, 1923; *Chicago Whip*, n.d., quoted in
Savannah Tribune, October 22, 1931; Kelly Miller, "The Negro and the
Jew in Business," *Richmond Planet*, April 13, 1935, hereafter cited as
"Jew in Business"; *Houston Informer and Texas Freeman*, September 19,
1931.

22. *Savannah Tribune*, December 13, 1923. See also Hertzberg, "The
Jews of Atlanta," p. 287; "Socialist View," p. 2.

23. *Savannah Tribune*, December 13, 1923; Miller, "Jew in Business."

24. See *Atlanta Independent*, October 7, 1926; January 20, 1927, and
scattered issues for 1929.

25. Golden, *Forgotten Pioneer*, pp. 70–73, and Golden, *Jewish Roots in
the Carolinas* (Charlotte, N.C., 1955), p. 47. See also Hertzberg, "Jews of
Atlanta," pp. 285–86.

26. *Galveston City Times*, March 31, 1906; personal interview with
Esther Surasky Pinck, November 13, 1979 (casette recording of
interview in Winthrop College Archives); Lorenzo Greene and Carter G.
Woodson, *The Negro Wage Earner* (New York, 1969), p. 120; statement of
Madden in *Report of the Fifteenth Annual Convention, National Negro
Business League* (Nashville, Tenn., 1915), pp. 164–65. Things had not
always been so good for blacks and their Jewish employers. In Franklin,
Tennessee, in 1868, the Ku Klux Klan lynched a liberal Jewish merchant and his Negro employee. See Morris U. Schappes, ed., *A Documentary History of the Jews in the United States, 1654–1875* (New York,
1952), pp. 515–17. On the lynching of Samuel Fleishman, who urged
blacks to retaliate against the Ku Klux Klan, see Jessie Fortune, "Among
the Children of the East Side Jews (1905)," *Jewish Currents* 29 (February
1975): 4.

27. Miller, "Cultural Kinship" and "Jew in Business."

28. *Savannah Tribune*, August 7, 1924; "What Ben Davis Says,"
Atlanta Independent, March 5, 1931; Gordon Hancock, "Between the
Lines," *Norfolk Journal and Guide*, October 11, 1930, February 14, 1931.

29. Blacks often told stories and jokes about the alleged Jewish love
for money and their supposed willingness to set fires to collect
insurance. Daryl Dance observes, "Every anti-Jewish joke that I collected
came from urban, rather than rural areas. The jokes usually depict the
Jew as a dishonest, unscrupulous but successful businessman." Dance,
Shuckin' and Jivin', p. 151–58.

30. W.E.B. Du Bois tells of a Russian Jew who cheated a rural Georgia
black of his land and fled the scene, forcing the man to work on "his"
own land for thirty cents a day. This is no worse, however, than H. G.
Wells, the Englishman, complaining about "the dirty fortunes of the

Russian Jews who prey upon color in the Carolinas." Du Bois, *The Souls of Black Folk* (Chicago, 1931), pp. 133, 170; Wells, *The Future in America* (New York: reprint ed., 1974), p. 191. Jacob Schiff, Stephen Wise, and Morris Schappes called Du Bois's attention to the fact that some readers might see anti-Semitic implications in his unfavorable references to Russian Jews. Du Bois admitted that he was unsure the exploiter was either Russian or Jewish. After 1952, editions of *The Souls of Black Folk* omitted remarks that could mistakenly be considered anti-Jewish. Herbert Aptheker, "The Souls of Black Folk: A Comparison of the 1903 and 1952 Editions," *Negro History Bulletin* 34 (January 1971): 15–17; Aptheker, ed., *The Correspondence of W.E.B. Du Bois*, 3 vols. (Amherst, Mass., 1978), 3: 343; Morris Schappes to Philip Foner, February 11, 1976 (copy in my possession); Schappes to writer, June 27, 1976. For other Negro images of Jews as money grubbers, see Levine, *Black Culture and Black Consciousness*, p. 305; Hertzberg, "Jews of Atlanta," Chapter 8.

31. Because he worked on Saturdays, Sarah Ann Surasky would not let her husband Benedict slaughter chickens in the ritual fashion for the family. Rather, she had the chickens killed by an observant Jew who kept the Sabbath. Personal interview with Esther Pinck, November 13, 1979.

32. Miller, "Jew in Business." See also *Norfolk Journal and Guide*, April 28, 1917; *Chicago Whip*, n.d., quoted in *Savannah Tribune*, May 25, 1922; Dr. H. R. Butler, "He Came to His Own, and His Own Received Him Not," *Atlanta Independent*, December 30, 1926, hereafter cited as "He Came"; S. B. Williams, "Cimbee's Rambles," *Houston Informer and Texas Freeman*, July 22, 1933.

33. *Atlanta Independent*, June 23, 1927; caption under pictures of Cohen's Saloon (whites only) and Abelsky's Saloon (Colored only), in Ray Stannard Baker, *Following the Color Line* (New York, 1908), between pages 34 and 35. See also Hertzberg, "Jews of Atlanta," p. 287; Hertzberg, "Southern Jews," pp. 12–13. On Jewish-owned saloons in Savannah, see "Socialist View," p. 3.

34. *New Orleans Louisianian*, July 23, 1881, account of Brunswick incident in *Baltimore Afro-American*, October 18, 1902. *Tulsa Star*, December 12, 1914; *Savannah Tribune*, September 6, 1934; *Houston Informer and Texas Freeman*, August 18, 1934.

35. The only stories the writer ever found about a Jew killing a black in the South was not even reported in Negro newspapers. It involved Mier Schwartz, a demented nineteen-year-old Jewish youth, in Natchez, Mississippi, who killed two blacks and wounded another. *Memphis Commercial Appeal*, December 11, 21, 1911.

36. *Chicago Whip*, n.d., quoted in *Savannah Tribune*, May 25, 1922; Kelly Miller, "Jew in Business," and Miller, "Cultural Kinship." See also Dr. H. R. Butler, "The High Cost of Prejudice," *Atlanta Independent*, June 14, 1928; letter from Jackson McHenry of Atlanta, quoted in *Atlanta Independent*, October 31, 1914. It is the writer's impression that blacks were more willing to denounce Jewish businessmen than Gentiles for unfair treatment of Negro customers.

37. Editorial on Jews as the friend of blacks in *Savannah Tribune*, November 15, 1913. The topic of Jews helping blacks is well treated in Hasia Diner, "In the Almost Promised Land: Jewish Leaders and Blacks, 1915-1935" (Ph.D. dissertation, University of Illinois at Chicago Circle, 1975), Chapters 2, 3, hereafter cited as "Promised Land." See also *Galveston City Times*, July 25, 1914, February 5, 12, 1916.

38. Diner, "Promised Land," pp. 148-49, 164-65, 180, 196. For Melech Epstein's shortlived protest against segregated streetcar seating in Montgomery, Alabama, in the 1910s, see Epstein, *Pages from a Colorful Life* (Miami Beach, Fla., 1971), p. 56.

39. Miss Kaufman was active in the CIC and the Urban League. *Savannah Tribune*, February 17, October 27, 1927, November 15, 1931; *Richmond Planet*, May 13, 1899; *Norfolk Journal and Guide*, March 5, 1921, November 25, 1922; S. B. Williams, "Cimbee's Rambles," *Houston Informer and Texas Freeman*, April 8, 1933; Byron Sherwin, "Portrait of a Romantic Rebel, Bernard Ehrenreich," in Kaganoff and Urofsky, eds., *Turn to the South*, p. 8; Marion Wright, "Two Southerners Who Made a Difference," *Jewish Currents* 31 (February 1977): 22-26; Marion Wright, *Human Rights Odyssey* (Durham, N.C., 1978), pp. 4-6, 24-25; Myron Berman, *Richmond's Jewry* (Charlottesville, Va., 1979), p. 235; Ann Ellis, "The Commission on Interracial Cooperation" (Ph.D. dissertation, Georgia State University, 1975); Herman Pollack, "A Forgotten Fighter for Justice: Ben Goldstein-Lowell," *Jewish Currents* 30 (June 1976): 14-18; Mark Bauman, "Centripetal and Centrifugal Forces Facing the People of Many Communities: Atlanta Jewry from the Frank Case to the Great Depression," *Atlanta Historical Journal* 23 (1979): 46-47.

40. Julius Dudley, "A History of the Association of Southern Women for the Prevention of Lynching" (Ph.D. dissertation, University of Cincinnati, 1979), pp. 182-183, 252, 329.

41. Polier quoted in *New York Times*, July 1, 1976; Tropp, "Memoirs."

42. Washington, *Man Farthest Down*, p. 255. In their efforts to be helpful, Jewish philanthropists even brought Aaron Aaronsohn, director

of the Jewish Agricultural Experimental Station in Palestine, to talk about farming to Tuskegee students. Diner, "Promised Land," pp. 148–49.

43. Letter from Leon Miller of Welch, West Virginia, to *Crisis* 43 (1936): 122; letter to J. E. Malone of Mobile, ibid. (1936): 801; *Louisville News*, n.d., quoted in *Cleveland Gazette*, May 1, 1926; *Southern Workman* 25 (1906): 56; *Galveston City Times*, April 26, 1919.

44. Editorial entitled "Our Lake Resorts," *New Orleans Louisianian*, July 23, 1881. The *Louisianian* was the only paper located that regularly portrayed Jews in an unfavorable light. The editor and correspondents to the paper seemed persuaded that Jews were among the Negro's foremost opponents. Rolla, the newspaper's Washington correspondent, alleged, "It is a melancholy fact that the Jews in order to curry favor with the ruling classes, are, except in a few sections, classed with the negro haters." Letter from Rolla, Washington, D.C., September 20, 1879, quoted in the *Louisianian*, October 4, 1879. See also letter from James Kennedy, sent November 10, 1879, while traveling through Delta and Water Proof, La., ibid., November 15, 1879, and item printed in ibid., June 25, 1881, p. 2.

45. Crosswaith, "Contrast Worth Noting," in both *Atlanta Independent*, September 25, 1930, and *Savannah Tribune*, October 2, 1930; *Norfolk Journal and Guide*, April 28, 1917. See also Butler, "He Came"; Booker T. Washington, *The Future of the American Negro* (New York, 1969), p. 183; Washington, *Putting the Most into Life*, pp. 30–31; address of Washington at Hampton Institute, May 1905, quoted in *Southern Workman* (Hampton, Va.) 34 (1905): 405; Washington, *Man Farthest Down*, 263; *Voice of the Negro* 3 (1906): 20; *Savannah Tribune*, August 19, 1899, July 14, 1927.

46. *Savannah Tribune*, July 14, 1927. Blacks seemed unaware that many B'nai B'rith lodges barred Russian Jews from membership before the 1930s. See unidentified black newspaper quoted in *Alexandria* (Va.) *People's Advocate*, March 27, 1880; *Savannah Tribune*, November 15, 1913; *Houston Informer and Texas Freeman*, September 19, 1931, and May 27, 1933.

47. Article on a sermon by a rabbi on the way Judaism idealizes marriage, reported in *Houston Informer and Texas Freeman*, March 21, 1931; editorial comment on Jewish history in *Atlanta Independent*, February 7, 1914.

48. T. Thomas Fortune, "The Passing Show," *Norfolk Journal and Guide*, February 11, 1928; *Savannah Tribune*, December 13, 1923. Clearly, blacks underrated tensions between parents and children on

such questions as education, assimilation, and pride in one's heritage. See also *Savannah Tribune*, October 12, 1889; *Norfolk Journal and Guide*, December 3, 1921; Booker T. Washington, *The Man Farthest Down*, p. 263; Eugene Hayne, "The African in America," *Voice of the Negro* 3 (1906): 565.

49. David Hellwig has perceptively noted the illogical nature of some of the praise for Jews and education. Booker T. Washington, for example, asked Negroes to emulate the Jews but proposed that they, unlike Jews, get industrial and agricultural education. In addition, Washington wanted blacks to remain a rural people, but Jews were largely urbanized. David Hellwig, "Building a Black Nation: The Role of Immigrants in the Thought and Rhetoric of Booker T. Washington," *Mississippi Quarterly* 31 (1978): 547.

50. Baskerville, "Too Many Churches," *Atlanta Independent*, October 9, 1930; *Richmond Reformer*, n.d., quoted in *Savannah Tribune*, July 8, 1911; Goodall's sermon quoted in *Savannah Tribune*, October 23, 1915.

51. The Reverend Ernest Hall, "Hall's Review," *Atlanta Independent*, June 17, 1926. *Savannah Tribune*, April 20, 1918, November 2, 1920, and October 22, 1931; *Richmond Planet*, November 10, 1934.

52. *Norfolk Journal and Guide*, January 14, 1922; *New Orleans Weekly Pelican*, November 2, 1889; Helen Chesnutt, *Charles Waddell Chesnutt* (Chapel Hill, N.C., 1952), pp. 22–23. See also Hair, *Bourbonism and Agrarian Protest*, pp. 158–60; William F. Holmes, "Whitecapping: Anti-Semitism in the Populist Era," *American Jewish Historical Quarterly* 64 (1974): 245–61.

53. Donald Spivey, *Schooling for the New Slavery: Black Industrial Education, 1868–1915* (Westport, Conn., 1978), p. 63.

54. *California Eagle* (Los Angeles), May 8, 1925; *Chicago Defender*, July 7, 1928. For information on Negro reaction to the Frank lynching, see Levy, "Is the Jew a White Man?," and Levy, *James Weldon Johnson* (Chicago, 1973), pp. 158–59; *Martinsburg* (W. Va.) *Pioneer Press*, August 28, 1915. For more on Needleman, see *New York Times*, March 30, 1925.

55. *Houston Informer and Texas Freeman*, October 4, 1930.

56. *Savannah Tribune*, April 11, 1929; *Richmond Planet*, May 14, 1910; J. A. Roberts, "News Commentators Ignorant of the Psychology of American Color Complex," *Savannah Tribune*, July 4, 1935. See also Hall, "Hall's Review," *Atlanta Independent*, June 17, 1926.

57. Crosswaith, "Contrast Worth Noting," *Savannah Tribune*, October 2, 1930. In 1912, when a dark-complexioned Russian Jew and a light-skinned white woman entered a fashionable cafe in Arkansas, the man was mistaken for a Negro. Local whites were incensed, and had the Jew

not been a rapid runner, he would probably have been lynched. *Pine Bluff* (Ark.) *Herald*, n.d., quoted in *Pittsburgh Courier*, February 24, 1912.

58. *Savannah Tribune*, November 15, 1913, April 11, 1929; "Colorful News Movies," *Savannah Tribune*, March 24, 1927; *Richmond Reformer*, January 27, 1900; *Norfolk Journal and Guide*, July 16, 1927. See also *Richmond Planet*, June 27, 1936.

59. Butler, "He Came"; *Norfolk Journal and Guide*, June 12, 1926.

60. *Savannah Tribune*, January 14, 1932; *Norfolk Journal and Guide*, May 22, 1926; *Atlanta Independent*, October 22, 1931.

61. *Houston Informer and Texas Freeman*, April 8, 1933; *Richmond Planet*, November 10, 1934. Similar comments can be found in *Richmond Planet*, March 24, 1934; *Norfolk Journal and Guide*, September 30, 1916; *Savannah Tribune*, May 30 and July 11, 18, 1903, August 26, 1905. See also Foner, "Black Jewish Relations," and Foner, *American Socialism and Black Americans*, pp. 107–108.

62. J. Waties Waring, the famous white South Carolina judge, who was not Jewish, believed that when he grew up in Charleston at the turn of the century, the Jews would have liked to have been more liberal on civil rights, but they were a timid minority in the South. Therefore, many were silent on injustices endured by blacks, and their neighbors may have assumed that the Jews had no special sympathy for Negroes. Interview of Judge J. Waties Waring, Columbia University Oral History Collection, p. 383.

63. Letter from Rolla, Washington, D.C., September 20, 1879, on Jews as "Negro haters," quoted in the *New Orleans Louisianian*, October 4, 1879; Richard Wright, *Black Boy* (New York, 1945), p. 215; "The Cameraman," *Richmond Planet*, January 31, 1925; Foner, "Black-Jewish Relations," pp. 365–66; Hertzberg, "Jews of Atlanta," p. 308. *Kansas City* (Kans.) *Call*, April 3, 1931.

64. Letter from Samuel Rosenberg, *The Crisis* 43 (1936): 122; Hortense Powdermaker, *Stranger and Friend* (New York, 1966), p. 195. Golden, *Jewish Roots in the Carolinas*, p. 47; Hertzberg, "Jews of Atlanta," pp. 297–98. See also Hertzberg, "Southern Jews," pp. 14–15.

65. Vladeck also complained when he learned that Bernard Cone, a Jewish textile-mill owner in North Carolina, had fired some black workers for joining a union. Diner, "Promised Land," pp. 409–10; Charles Rubin, *The Log of Rubin the Sailor* (New York, 1973), p. 15; Foner, *American Socialism and Black Americans*, p. 239; "Socialist View," p. 2. See also Hertzberg, "Jews of Atlanta," pp. 296–97.

66. Bond, "Negro Attitudes Towards Jews," pp. 3–4; *New York Times*,

May 4, 1964. See also Hertzberg, "Jews of Atlanta," pp. 300–301; spiritual on the death of Jesus quoted in Brewer, *American Negro Folklore*, p. 161.

67. Another taunt went:

> Jew, Jew
> Two for five
> That's what keeps
> Jew alive. (Wright, *Black Boy*, p. 53)

Spiritual on Jews killing Jesus placing him in a tomb quoted in the Reverend H. H. Proctor, "The Theology of the Songs of the Southern Slave," *Southern Workman* 36 (1907): 587; spiritual on Jews and Romans hanging Jesus, from Thomas Wentworth Higginson, "Negro Spirituals," *Atlantic Monthly* 19 (1867): 685-95; quoted in Bruce Jackson, ed., *The Negro and His Folklore* (Austin, Tex., 1967), p. 90; Wright, *Black Boy*, pp. 53–54.

68. Butler, "He Came"; letter from Vass in *Richmond Planet*, April 29, 1899. The *Savannah Tribune* favored the "rehabilitation of Palestine by the Jews" in its September 5, 1929, issue.

69. Powdermaker, *Stranger and Friend*, pp. 145.

70. This is especially evident in black jokes that feature a Negro, a white man, and a Jew. See Dance, *Shuckin' and Jivin'*, pp. 31–32, 96, 191–93, 201.

71. "The Hebrew Race in America," *Voice of the Negro* 3 (January 1906): 20; Bowling, "Jews and Discipline," *Norfolk Journal and Guide*, December 15, 1928. See also *New York Age*, August 21, 1913; 1864 black newspaper quoted in Leon Litwack, *Been in the Storm So Long: The Aftermath of Slavery* (New York, 1979), p. 532.

72. Barry Supple, "A Business Elite: German Jewish Financiers in Nineteenth Century New York," *Business History Review* 31 (1957): 151. Oscar and Mary Flug Handlin, *A Century of Jewish Immigration to the United States* (New York, 1949), p. 16.

73. Joseph Weill to Morris Waldman, December 16, 1907 [copy], Papers Relating to the Galveston Immigration Plan and the Industrial Removal Office, American Jewish Historical Society, Waltham, Mass. See also "Socialist View," p. 3.

74. *Forward* quoted in Bernard Marinbach, "The Galveston Movement" (Ph.D. dissertation, Jewish Theological Seminary of America, 1976), p. 63; Arnold Shankman, "Happyville, the Forgotten

Colony," *American Jewish Archives* 30 (1978): 3-19; Louis Ginsberg, "The Jewish Colony at Waterview," *Virginia Magazine of History and Biography* 66 (1958): 459-62.

75. David Bressler to Morris Waldman, October 15, 1906, Papers Relating to the Galveston Immigration Plan; Marinbach, "Galveston Movement," p. 15.

76. "Russian Jews Made Unhappy in South Carolina," *Di Varheit* (New York), August 21, 1906 (translated courtesy of Morris Schappes).

77. Arnold Shankman, "The Galveston Movement," *Atlanta Historical Journal* 23 (1979): 77-83.

78. B. C. Baskerville, "Too Many Churches," *Atlanta Independent,* October 9, 1930.

79. *Savannah Tribune,* May 13, 1893. See also *Norfolk Journal and Guide,* May 22, 1926.

80. T. Thomas Fortune, "The Passing Show," *Norfolk Journal and Guide,* February 11, 1928; *Atlanta Independent,* January 3, 1914. See also *Norfolk Journal and Guide,* May 22, 1926, July 16, 1927; S. B. Williams, "Cimbee's Rambles," *Houston Informer and Texas Freeman,* April 8, 1933.

81. For a perceptive view on black-Jewish relations, see the poem of I. J. Schwartz quoted in Hertzberg, *Strangers,* p. 186.

BLACKS AND
6 IMMIGRANTS

In 1887, a black newspaperman accurately predicted that millions of emigrants from Europe and elsewhere would soon flock to the United States. The prospect of so many new aliens coming to live in America did not seem to alarm this writer for the *New Orleans Pelican*, who was sure that the foreigners would bring with them not only their families but also their personal wealth. Evidently, he thought this wealth was extensive, and he believed that in the United States "there is room for both the men and the money." Whereas Europe had an average population of 160 per square mile, America barely had one-eighth that figure. Thus, in his view, America was under-populated. "Only a fifth of our arable land is yet in cultivation; half of that is little better than half tilled. We have only opened the edges of our iron and coal mines. We are only in the youth of our manufacturing system."[1]

Slightly more than forty years after the above was written, another Afro-American editor turned his attention to the question of immigration, but he came up with rather different conclusions. According to the owner of the *Western Outlook*, a black journal published in San Francisco, immigration had greatly overpopulated the United States. In his opinion those who had flocked to America from Mexico, Asia, and Europe had not added to the nation's wealth. On the contrary, he insisted, these newcomers of "divided interests and allegiances," a veritable "conglomeration of citizens of different languages and nationalities," had contributed to the nation's unemployment and had lowered wages paid working men and thereby reduced the laborer's standard of living. To him it was a national calamity that "can best be avoided by restrictive immigration and a sufficient personnel to see that the immigration laws are strictly enforced." Why was there such a radical change of opinion between the 1887 and 1928 editorials? The answer, declared the *Norfolk Journal and Guide*, was that blacks had "learned through bitter experiences that foreign labor, though it may be crude, illiterate, and hopelessly unsympathetic with American institutions and ideals, is used to press us further down the economic ladder . . . in spite of our proved loyalty to America."[2]

In accounting for the generally unfavorable image that blacks came to have of most immigrant groups, one first must consider what life was like for Negroes between 1880 and 1935. This was a period of great disappointment for Afro-Americans, most of whom lived in the South. The rights, privileges, hopes, dreams, and expectations associated with the Reconstruction era were quickly dashed after Dixie was "redeemed." Negro voters, Afro-American jurors, and most certainly elected black public officials were increasingly rare. By 1890, blacks were being disfranchised by new state constitutions, eight box laws, poll taxes, literacy tests, and grandfather clauses. Scarcely a month passed at the turn of the century that was not marred by half a dozen or more lynchings. These lawless incidents came about not because, as whites liked to claim, black males were raping white females but rather because individual Negroes were judged to be making too much money, to be acting too haughty and "uppity," or in other ways to be threatening the Southern caste system. Blacks were never allowed to forget their "place."

The "place" reserved for Afro-Americans was at the very bottom of the economic pyramid. At a time when the nation was rapidly industrializing and when the population of the North and Middle West was steadily growing, most blacks were still living in rural sections of Dixie[3] and occupying unskilled jobs that were rapidly becoming superfluous. As August Meier has perceptively noted, this was an era during which blacks increasingly viewed wealth as proof of success.[4] But no matter where they lived, be it north of south of the Mason-Dixon line, most Negroes either remained fixed in their economic status or actually experienced downward mobility. As mechanization made the jobs of many farm hands unneeded and as low prices for agricultural products insured that these rural laborers would live at the subsistence level, large numbers of blacks continued to pick cotton, sort tobacco leaves, and harvest sugar cane. As late as 1910, fully 55 percent of all black workers, compared with 33.2 percent of all American laborers, were engaged in agricultural occupations. By 1930, only 21.4 percent of the nation's workers but 36.1 percent of all blacks remained on the farm.[5] During this same half century, use of electric sweepers, ringer washing machines, steam laundries, and razor blades lessened the need for cleaning ladies, washerwomen, and barbers. As families decreased in size, as apartments became more fashionable, and as bakeries and prepared foods grew in popularity, there was less demand for maids, butlers, and yardmen. Yet, blacks remained concentrated in these very occupations. In 1900, about 33 percent of all blacks were employed in jobs categorized as domestic or personal service in nature. Thirty years later, 28.6 percent of all Negro workers still held such occupations; this was nearly three times the percentage of all American laborers so employed.[6] On the other hand, blacks were greatly underrepresented in those jobs with a promising future. In 1930, a paltry 2.5 percent of all Negroes were professionals, only 3.3 percent were engaged in trade, and a mere 0.7 percent held clerical jobs.[7] In short, blacks were expected to be the invisible Americans: maids, butlers, porters, cotton pickers, or janitors, but not bankers, secretaries, lawyers, merchants, or doctors. The likelihood that blacks would remain at the bottom of the economic ladder and not experience significant upward mobility was as true in New York as in Georgia, Massachusetts, Colorado, Ohio, or Tennessee.[8]

During this half century, millions of immigrants from Europe, Asia, and Hispanic America flocked to the United States. Blacks carefully watched these newcomers, observing their customs and noticing what jobs they took and how they were being treated in America. The comments Afro-Americans made about the immigrants often told as much about their own status and aspirations as about the activities of foreigners in the United States.

With the exception of the Jews, especially those living in the South for whom blacks felt a special friendship, the Negroes' image of immigrants was relatively negative. A variety of factors help to account for this unfavorable image. Ethnocentrism, xenophobia, religious bias, jealousy, and economic competition all had a part in accounting for why blacks sometimes regarded immigrants unsympathetically. Often Negroes mirrored white attitudes. In his brilliant book *Black Culture and Black Consciousness*, Lawrence Levine gives one reason why Negroes shared white stereotypes about aliens. Echoing commonly held prejudices, Levine notes, "allowed Negroes to join the white majority in looking down upon and feeling superior to the strange folkways of an alien group. For once black Americans could feel part of the mainstream as they ridiculed the awkward actions of unassimilated immigrants." Blacks could "identify with and shared the superior feelings of the groups at the center of American society."[9]

Nearly all black Americans were fundamentalist Protestants. They usually regarded with suspicion any theology that deviated from their beliefs. They often dismissed as paganism the religious and cultural practices of non-Protestants, especially those of the Chinese. Opium smoking, idol worship, fan tan gambling, pimping, and incense burning were but a few of the alleged transgressions of the Chinese. Especially repugnant to blacks was the Chinese custom of transporting the bones of their deceased to China. This practice came about because of the Chinese belief that they were mere sojourners in America and that if they died while in the United States, their remains should eventually be shipped back to their native province. Blacks found this a repulsive and bothersome custom and took a dislike to a people who hoped to make money and return home rich. Negroes readily argued that there was no real political or moral reason to thrust privileges on people who had no real desire to assimilate. According to one San Francisco black newspaper, it was "useless to encumber our statute book with laws in favor of those whose customs and traditions render them migratory."[10]

Japanese religious practices and cultural modes were also criticized. Shinto temples were no more welcome to an Afro-American than Chinese houses of worship with their joss sticks. Some blacks accused emigrants from Japan of using their religion to promote emperor worship and maintained that Japanese cultural schools fostered loyalty to a foreign nation with which the United States at best had an uneasy diplomatic relationship. "Their religion is not our religion," a Chicago black newspaper argued, adding, "Our civilization and culture [are] . . . not theirs."[11]

Mexicans and Italians, to be sure, were Christians, but Afro-Americans, like most Southerners and like some whites in other parts of the country, had a limited appreciation of Roman Catholicism. The anti-Catholic American Protective Association had some support in the black community,[12] and Negroes tended to criticize Catholics for being superstitious and for displaying excessive veneration of—and even worship of—saints. This lack of sympathy for Catholicism can partially be explained by the fact that in several states barely 3 out of 1,000 blacks were Roman Catholics. The Negro press was quick to note that as late as the 1930s there were only six Negro priests in the whole country. "The Catholic Church is about as eager to get Negro priests," claimed George Schuyler, the black Negro intellectual newspaper columnist, "as the U.S. Army is to get Negro officers." Black Catholics, it was observed, were usually required to attend segregated churches and masses, and they seldom were permitted to send their children to parochial schools. Blacks evidently were unaware that Irish priests and nuns, who dominated the American Catholic church, also greatly discriminated against Mexicans and Italians.[13]

Jews, on the other hand, were more acceptable to blacks. Negro spirituals, hymns, and sermons were full of accounts of the various trials and tribulations of the Children of Israel, who, like blacks, once had been slaves. Even if some Afro-Americans could not rid themselves of the notion that Jews were guilty of deicide, they still found much of value in the Hebrew religion. Observant Jews were praised for their morality, scholarship, and ability to triumph over persecution. Not to be overlooked was that several nationally known Jewish religious leaders were regarded as allies against bigotry. Nothing seemed more to please a black editor than to be able to quote from a speech of an erudite rabbi which condemned race prejudice. Although Afro-Americans did not seem to be aware of the intensity of Italian hostility to lynching, they were well informed about the forthright appeal of the Union of American Hebrew Congregations in behalf of federal legislation against this crime. Rabbi Julius Mack's speech to the Tennessee Interracial Committee in Nashville in which he condemned as false the belief that one race was superior to another was reprinted in part in a New York black journal. Rabbi Stephen Wise's protest that the celebrated motion picture, *The Birth of a Nation*, was "an indefensible libel against a race" was well known in the black community. In similar fashion, the black press noted that Rabbi Emil Hirsch of Chicago publicly declared that Negroes "are just as good as whites. I would rather have a good black neighbor than a poor white one." The *New York Age* praised this "very sound and sensible reply coming from the representative of a race that has endured centuries of oppression and yet risen above it."[14]

Blacks had not yet risen above "centuries of oppression," and they were upset that relatively few voices were ever raised in their behalf. Thus, they appreciated it when rabbis spoke out in their defense. But there were few spokesmen defending blacks, and Afro-Americans found it extremely distressing that most foreigners were given greater consideration than blacks when they were mistreated. An alien, even if he were an anarchist, socialist, or criminal, could complain to his native government and seek assistance, and the United States would listen. The murder of Italians in Louisiana or Mississippi, of Chinese in Wyoming, or of Mexicans in Texas, or the assault of Japanese visitors in California normally brought forth investigations, apologies, and, in some cases, even indemnities, but the slaying of innocent blacks yielded no similar response. Instead, some racist politicians in the South encouraged, if not personally incited, antiblack mobs, and law enforcement officials typically made only half-hearted attempts to protect their Negro prisoners from vigilantes. Surely this state of affairs promoted jealousy and resentment of foreigners. After two Italians had been lynched in Erwin, Mississippi, in 1901, many Americans and Italians called on Theodore Roosevelt to send a message to Congress condemning the outrage. Booker T. Washington asked the president to issue a statement attacking all cases of mob law. Roosevelt did not send a message to Capitol Hill on this occasion, but his views on the subject of lynching would hardly have pleased the president of Tuskegee Institute. Whereas he saw international implications in the killing of Italians, Roosevelt was aware of no serious political consequences if he failed to demand justice for blacks. Lynching was bad, Roosevelt believed, but so too was the crime that inspired it. The president shared the common misapprehension that rape was the cause of nearly all lynchings. He even argued that Negroes should "take the lead" in hunting for and in apprehending blacks who attacked white women.[15] Roosevelt, like other American presidents before and after him, was sensitive to affairs in Tokyo and Rome but easily ignored blacks who had no clout in Baton Rouge or Montgomery.

In similar vein, the blacks noted, Negroes had been subjected to peonage for decades without evoking any real protest from whites. In contrast, when some Italians and Greeks suffered the same fate, they complained to their nation's ambassadors in Washington. The outcry from these diplomats compelled "Theodore the Perfect," as W.E.B. Du Bois sarcastically called President Roosevelt, to send investigators to the South to ferret out these post-Emancipation "slaveholders." More than a dozen whites were arrested and jailed as a result of the investigation. Blacks bitterly observed how the government's efforts to protect aliens had led to the freeing of several Negroes, who had been involuntarily held on farms.[16]

The black community was well aware that olive-skinned Italians and Orientals could ride in "white-only" streetcars and trains, attend colleges in Dixie closed to blacks, patronize first-class theaters without being required to sit in the balcony, and secure rooms in quality hotels. Even in the nation's capital, such eminent blacks as Dr. Charles Wesley, the distinguished historian, were denied these rights.[17] Immigrants with as low a status as the Chinese nonetheless had privileges that were not accorded Afro-Americans. For example, when Orientals living in Mississippi were barred from attending white schools and were asked to enroll in black public schools, that state's Chinese residents became incensed. They would not consider sending their offspring to the same schools as Negroes. In the end, they were able to force Mississippi to establish separate schools for the few hundred Oriental youngsters living in the state.[18] Such incidents were very bitter pills for Afro-Americans to swallow. It was hard for blacks to accept the fact that aliens were more esteemed than native-born Negroes who had lived in the United States since 1619.[19]

As upsetting as it was for blacks to learn that aliens were given considerations denied blacks, things were made worse when Negroes and foreigners competed for the same jobs. Chinese laundries and restaurants were serious threats to black washerwomen and cooks, Japanese butlers and yardmen jeopardized the jobs of Afro-American servants and gardeners, Mexican field hands and factory workers menaced the livelihoods of black cotton pickers and steel workers, and Italian farm laborers and barbers competed with and sometimes took jobs from their black counterparts.

The Afro-American's realization that the immigrant might deprive his children of bread and clothing was probably the single most important reason for his having a negative image of the alien. It was difficult for blacks to accept the reality that American racism was so pervasive that immigrants would often be given job preference over Negroes. Even the "talented tenth" of the black community might find themselves "submerged by . . . the wave of immigration." "Negro labor is native labor," insisted the *Washington Colored American*, "and should be preferred to that of the offscourings of Europe and Asia. Let America take care of its own." "The American Negro is the only citizen of this country," added the *Tulsa Star*, "who does not point with boastful pride to his foreign ancestry. He alone is the only laborer who is not sending the bulk of his savings to the mother country."[20]

The more blacks discovered that immigrants jeopardized their jobs, the more they began to list reasons why these newcomers were undesirable. Aliens were criticized for their illiteracy, their alleged un-American political ideology, their standard of living, and their supposed love of strikes and labor turmoil. According to the *Topeka Weekly Call* of June 16, 1894, the United States was being "flooded with a foreign element to whom peace is a total stranger and who knows no satisfaction no matter how favorable the wages nor how short the duration of time of labor." Immigrants, the *Weekly Call* thought, had been sent to the United States by the devil "for the purpose of bringing about national disturbance."

One of the most detailed accounts of the alleged menace of immigration to appear in a black magazine was written by John Waller, Jr. Entitled the "Evils of European Emigration," this piece appeared in *The Colored American Magazine* in 1904. Waller argued that the immigrant was a serious threat to labor "because of his liability to be swayed by revolting passions." He represented "a restless element" who brought with him "the spirit of anarchy" and the love of industrial disorder. The "natural results" of this, Waller maintained, were "reductions in wages, strikes, riots and bloodshed."

Most ominous to Waller was that thousands of these immigrants were joining the United States Army and Navy. No nation, he warned, had as many foreigners "mingled in its national affairs as the United States. Is this condition of affairs safe to our future welfare?" Would there not be an unmitigated disaster if the United States ever went to war with a European nation? Thus, immigration threatened not only the industrial peace but also the very military security of the nation.

To Waller the solution to this problem was simple:

By restricting emigration . . . and giving preference to native sons whenever there is work to do . . . serious trouble to the government and . . . inconvenience to commerce . . . would soon decrease to the minimum. The Chinese who are restricted in entering the country are no more dangerous to its welfare than the anarchist from Europe. The one is peaceful and law-abiding, the other fiery and violent. If the restriction upon the one is justified to protect the nation, why would it not be equally just to restrict the other for the same, if not for more, vital reasons.[21]

Waller's assessment of the immigration problem paralleled that of the *Washington Colored American*. This newspaper blamed pauper immigrants for the nation's labor problems and for offering "the bitterest competition for the domestic service which the Negro once controlled." These "untutored aliens" cared nothing for the "deep principles" or "lofty ideals" which inspired American democracy, and their dangerous political philosophies threatened those freedoms Americans held most dear. "Bear in mind," the newspaper insisted, "the Negro is not a striker, an anarchist or a beggar. He simply wishes a chance to work and the quiet enjoyment of his rights as a citizen."[22]

Even worse than the threat to Negro domestics was the possibility that aliens would replace Afro-Americans on the farm. From 1890 to 1910, the spectre of Italians, Greeks, and others employed on Southern plantations haunted black leaders. Negroes paid attention when white Southerners argued that their region had a pressing need for new, more reliable labor.

In the words of William Holcombe Thomas, a white Alabamian, the immigrants would supposedly compete "with the Negro, stimulating a laudable contest between them to take hold of the opportunities presented each." Several officials of the federal government encouraged such sentiments, for they too hoped to promote pro-immigrant sentiment in the South. Such sentiment could help disperse foreigners to all parts of the nation, which many government authorities considered desirable. For example, Mary Grace Quackenbos, who worked for the U.S. attorney general, was interested in reports that Southerners believed that "the colored people cannot supply enough labor to secure the best development of that section of the country." She felt sure that immigrants could assist in this "development" and would themselves benefit in the process. "The chances are better," she declared, "that the immigrant will become a better citizen and learn American ideas in a shorter time if he and his family begin life in a plantation cabin in Louisiana rather than in an unhealthy tenement in New York or Boston."[23]

As stories mounted in white newspapers of Belgian laborers being brought to Charleston for domestic and factory positions, of Delta planters hiring Mexicans and Italians to pick cotton, and of Mississippi lumber companies offering work to Japanese, worried blacks launched a campaign to protect their interests.[24] As David Hellwig has correctly noted, Afro-Americans exploited white nativism by greatly exaggerating the dangers inherent in the presence of strangers in the xenophobic South.[25] Negroes pointed out the negative aspects of even those traits which whites typically considered laudable in immigrants. Southerners consistently observed that Italians were frugal and contrasted this quality with the alleged wastefulness of blacks. Negroes dissented from this viewpoint but simultaneously observed that it would not be good to encourage the settlement of people from Southern Europe willing to "live on as simple and scanty a diet as any Oriental." Those willing to be satisfied with pauper wages upon which "progressive Americans would starve" would soon learn better and before long would be conducting strikes. "Every white man brought into the South with the hope of displacing the Negro," warned the *Wichita Searchlight*, "will someday turn upon the hand that brought him there." "If the South wants the anarchist, the nihilist, and the mafia with their murderers, strikes, robberies, and crimes innumerable let them come, but the South will rue it."[26]

Although nearly all black leaders found the threat of immigrants in the South to be quite bothersome, a few Negro intellectuals thought some good might result from the influx. Even Booker T. Washington, who did so much to promote a negative image of emigrants, once admitted that the presence of a thousand immigrants in each Southern county might well promote increased black efficiency and worthwhile competition. Washington's nemesis, W.E.B. Du Bois, noted in *Horizon* that mistreatment of Greeks and Italians in the South had compelled the federal government to outlaw peonage. Timothy Thomas Fortune thought that foreigners could help destroy the conservative character of the South. Since the aliens had not owned slaves and since they had not been involved in fighting the Civil War, they would probably have less innate racial prejudice than most Southerners.[27] Moreover, even if Negroes lost farm jobs and had to move to the North and West, not all would be lost. If blacks scattered themselves all over the United States, race prejudice, Fortune thought, would lessen and Negroes would find employment opportunities in new occupations.[28]

Among Southern newspapers, the *Richmond Planet* professed not to be uneasy about immigrants and even claimed to welcome their entry into the Southern labor market. "It will be a question of survival of the fittest," the *Planet* believed. "If we cannot stand alone and walk upright in competition with these lower strata of humanity, then let us go down and from a racial standpoint, we deserve to fall, to rise no more." The *Kentucky Standard* agreed. If immigrants succeeded in displacing blacks, color would not be the only factor. The main reason, it suspected, would be that blacks had failed to keep up "with the improved way of doing things." Unless Negroes learned to do better work than others, they would inevitably lose "what we have" and have nothing to leave to their children.[29]

The battle anticipated by the *Planet* and feared by the *Kentucky Standard* did not take place. In the end, relatively few immigrants came to the South, and those who did seldom competed with blacks for agricultural jobs or for positions as domestics. White farmers' unions and other groups expressed so much opposition to Southern and Eastern European, Asian, and Mexican aliens that Dixie did not appear to be a hospitable home for them. Of the aliens who did come to the South, a large percentage lived in urban areas and opened small businesses such as fruit stands, restaurants, bakeries, hotels, and barbershops.[30]

It was as a businessman that the immigrant won praise in the Afro-American community. Booker T. Washington, Timothy Thomas Fortune, Kelly Miller, and scores of other black leaders routinely urged Negroes to establish their own commercial enterprises. The Italian, Greek, Chinese, Japanese, or Jew who opened a store, however modest in scope it might be, won the envy and admiration of his Afro-American customers and of black editors and community leaders. Repeatedly, Negroes were told to emulate the thrifty foreigner who came to the country impoverished, worked hard, peddled until he could raise enough money to buy a business, and ultimately found himself on "easy street." Through success in commerce the alien, and the Negro as well, could rise in the estimation of his neighbors.[31]

Franklin Williams, a black attorney in Savannah, observed the progress of the Greeks in his city, but what he wrote about them he considered equally applicable to other foreigners. The silent but persistent Greek, Williams declared, saved his money and devoted all his attention to starting a business. Before long, he owned attractive tracts of real estate and even organized his own banks, thereby forcing Southerners to take notice of him. What the Greek had done the black also could do. "Afro-Americans can compel the white races to recognize them when they prove their real worth and their practical ability by acquiring personal and real estate and by establishing banks and other enterprises." The *Atlanta Independent* agreed that Negroes had to get into commerce, for "no race can expect to exert the proper amount of influence and receive the proper recognition in the community who does not figure conspicuously in its business." As a perfect example, it pointed to the Jews. "The reason why the Jews' rights are respected," the *Independent* was sure, "is because they constitute such a large factor of the business and financial interest of the community in which they live."[32]

Blacks could learn additional positive lessons from immigrant entrepreneurs. One was not to waste money on fancy wearing apparel, lavish entertainment, or alcoholic beverages. Too many Negroes, alleged the *Savannah Tribune*, spent the bulk of their earnings on "good times." These same Negroes were wont to patronize alien businessmen rather than struggling black entrepreneurs. "The Greek, the Italian, and the Chinaman," complained the *Chicago Whip*, "have shown a surprising facility to come into our districts and conduct business with splendid success." It was a mistake for the blacks to ignore their own. Rather, they should learn some "useful" things from the "race loving Greeks." Whenever possible the Greeks employed only Greeks, and they patronized Greek ice dealers, fruit wholesale suppliers, bakeries, and barbers. The Chinese, Japanese, and Italians showed a similar inclination to hire and purchase from their own. While they hired their own, they sold to all. The

California Eagle doubted that Jews and Japanese would be able to bank any money if they catered only to the 4 million Jews or 100,000 Japanese in the country. Instead, they worked hard and sought to satisfy all their customers. In many cities, it was argued, even such numerically small immigrant groups as the Chinese owned six to eight times as many businesses serving the general public as did blacks.[33]

But as much as blacks might be able to discover from watching the Japanese or Chinese, even more could be learned from the Jews. The case of the Jews, whom blacks sometimes called "a nonwhite people,"[34] was said to be "almost parallel" to that of the Negroes. Were it not for the Jews' ability to accumulate money, it was argued, they and Afro-Americans would "be lying side by side, groveling in the same pit." The Jew, stated Roy Wilkins, a black newspaperman who later became head of the NAACP, quickly realized that in America "money would be boss for many generations to come . . . money is the thing. So Jews get money." As the industrious Hebrew acquired wealth, religious and social prejudice against him declined. Charles Purvis wrote Francis Grimké that by the 1920s Jews with money were able to get accommodations in the fanciest of hotels. "As money is the American God and as the Jew has it, he is received." Added Elson Higginbotham of Lynchburg, Virginia, "We laugh at the Jew as being a race scheming to get the dollar. We should do well if we imitated the Jew."[35]

How had the Jews succeeded? First and foremost, they learned how to cater to their patrons' every need. They bargained, ran sales, put eye-catching displays in windows, stocked the latest merchandise, and advertised. So much did they dominate trade in many Negro neighborhoods that a black woman in Baltimore who ran a grocery store told an Afro-American newspaperman, "I wish every Saturday and Sunday was Rosh Hashonah."[36]

To a degree unmatched by other immigrant groups, Jews were admired in the black community for more than their business success. They were also viewed as models for Negroes seeking to learn how to combat prejudice. Unlike the Mexicans or Chinese, Jews would not tolerate second-class status. In contrast with the Italians and Japanese, however, Jews had no foreign government to whom they could register protests about mistreatment. In this regard they were like blacks. How then did the Jews fight their enemies? First, they learned to "stick together like Siamese twins." They knew that the best way to get results was to unite and to realize that "an insult to one Jew is an insult to all Jews." Next, they formed organizations to look after their general welfare, to fight discrimination, to lend money to their needy, and to promote pride in their heritage. Negroes were urged to form similar organizations and to take pride in the accomplishments of the race. Just as Hebrew free loan societies furnished capital and advice to young, ambitious Jews, so too could black organizations assist Negroes with ability.[37] Jews learned that to get ahead they had to be better than the competition. Success was their goal, and their desire to achieve despite social handicaps caused them to make "eminent contributions" to society. Blacks, observed Herbert A. Miller of the Columbus (Ohio) Urban League, could do the same. Gordon B. Hancock, a black Virginia college professor and newspaper columnist, agreed and hoped that members of his race would spend more time working on self-improvement as Jews did rather than on blaming whites for all of their problems.[38]

Blacks not only had a positive view of the Jewish religion, but they also admired the personal habits of the Hebrew family. Jewish men were invariably portrayed as devoted to their wives and children, Jewish women were seen as virtuous wives and model mothers, and Jewish children were praised for their industry, energy, and desire to bring honor to their parents. In short, Jewish families demonstrated "faith in their own people" and showed "that they possess the essential elements for the development of a great race."[39] To blacks this seemed a perfect blueprint for success and one that the Negro family would do well to copy.

Most of all, however, Jews were admired for their helpfulness to blacks. Whereas Italian,[40] Mexican, Japanese, and Chinese philanthropists and civil rights advocates were unknown in the black community, educated Negroes had heard of Joel Spingarn,

Louis Marshall, Felix Warburg, Samuel Fels, Jacob Billikopf, and Herbert Lehman. That Samuel Leibowitz, the attorney defending the Scottsboro Nine, was Jewish was more important to some blacks and promoted more positive attitudes towards Jews than a dozen interfaith brotherhood meetings could ever hope to achieve.[41]

Above all, the name of Julius Rosenwald was revered in black homes because of the millions of dollars he contributed to charity. It was noted that when he gave assistance to Southern libraries it was with the provision that library service be made available to blacks. The money he spent on rural schools for Afro-Americans similarly was planned to generate local support and made Negro schools, especially in areas where there had been virtually no education available for blacks, a "fixed part of the educational system."[42] Kelly Miller, who sometimes was critical of Rosenwald, was forced to admit that the Chicagoan's philanthropy would provide "fundamental and lasting good." In 1931, one black editor even proposed making August 12, Rosenwald's birthday, a national holiday since his philanthropic "gifts have done more than those of any other single individual to lighten our burdens."[43] In 1932, when Rosenwald died, fully 25 percent of all black children in the United States were being taught in schools whose construction he had helped pay for. Even after his death, the fund Rosenwald established continued to dispense funds until 1948, and during the last years of its existence, it increasingly provided money for interracial purposes.[44]

Rosenwald, of course, was wealthy. But one need not be a millionaire to help Negroes. Southern Jewish bankers and merchants were viewed positively in the black press for their willingness to employ Negroes and even to lend them money. Timothy Thomas Fortune and Walter White were but two black leaders who as youngsters obtained their first jobs working for Southern Jewish storekeepers. Since Southern Afro-Americans and Jews seldom competed for jobs, blacks almost never complained about the presence of Jews in Dixie. Whereas there were hundreds of articles and editorials in the Negro press on the menace of immigrant settlement in the South, these items tended to refer to Italians, Greeks, Bohemians, Belgians, Orientals, or Mexicans. There was no real reason to fear Jews displacing black farmers, domestics, or barbers.[45]

If it had been possible to exclude all immigrants from Asia, Latin America, and Europe except for the Jews, at least a few Afro-Americans would probably have favored such a course of action. That, however, was not feasible. Sentiment among white Americans for immigrant restriction steadily grew during the early years of the twentieth century. After World War I and the Red Scare, everyone realized that Congress would soon limit the number of aliens who could come to America. Legislation passed in 1921 and in 1924 greatly reduced immigration, and, on the whole, blacks welcomed the new laws.[46] Five years after the passage of the 1921 law, a black writer credited restrictive immigration with increased economic opportunity and better wages for Negro workers. The *Philadelphia Tribune* was even more blunt in its assessment of the matter: "The TRIBUNE believes that restricted immigration is fundamentally sound and will help keep the workers with full dinner pails. The laws were not even passed to help Negroes but that they benefit from them no reasonable person can deny.[47]

The Depression would soon empty those full dinner pails. With millions of workers, both white and black, out of jobs, there was no sentiment for reopening the gates at Ellis Island. With only minor modifications, the restrictionist legislation of the 1920s remained on the statute books until 1965, when President Lyndon Johnson signed Public Law 89–236, which limited immigration but abolished the racist quotas of the national origins immigration laws.[48]

NOTES

1. *New Orleans Pelican*, January 22, 1887. See also quotations from other black newspapers in the 1860s and 1870s quoted in David Hellwig, "Black Attitudes Toward Immigrant Labor in the South, 1865-1910," *Filson Club Historical Quarterly* 54 (1980): 155.

2. *Western Outlook* (San Francisco) and *Norfolk Journal and Guide*, both March 17, 1928.

3. As late as 1900, more than 77 percent of blacks lived in areas with less than 2,500 people, and 89 percent of all Afro-Americans resided in the South Atlantic or South Central states. Walter Wilcox, *The Negro Population* (Washington, D.C., 1904), pp. 11–12.

4. August Meier, *Negro Thought in America, 1880–1915* (Ann Arbor, Mich., 1963), p. 23.

5. National Urban League, *500,000 Jobs: The Negro at Work in the United States* (New York, 1933), p. 13.

6. Ibid.; Wilcox, *Negro Population*, pp. 58–59; Rayford Logan, *The Negro in American Life and Thought* (New York, 1954). See also Elizabeth Pleck, *Black Migration and Poverty: Boston, 1865–1900* (New York, 1979), pp. 40, 104, 125, 139.

7. National Urban League, *500,000 Jobs*, p. 13.

8. A recent study of Denver shows that blacks in the late nineteenth century were twice as likely to be holding unskilled or semiskilled jobs as immigrants. With the passage of time, 32 percent of the immigrants experienced upward occupational mobility. Blacks were the only segment of Denver's population not to rise in economic status. Robert Trask, "Mobility and Occupational Structure on the Late Nineteenth Century Urban Frontier: The Case of Denver, Colorado," *Pacific Historical Review* 47 (1978): 191, 198–200. See also Pleck, *Black Migration*, pp. 128, 145.

9. Levine, *Black Culture and Black Consciousness* (New York, 1977), p. 302.

10. *San Francisco Elevator*, February 8, 1870. See also ibid., February 21, 1868.

11. *Chicago Defender*, September 17, 1921.

12. Examples of anti-Catholic sentiment from blacks active in the American Protective Association can be found in "Slumbering America, Awake!" (May 20, 1892) and "The Duty of the Hour" (n.d.), speeches of R. C. Barnes, in Barnes Papers, Michigan Historical Collections, Bentley Library, University of Michigan. Hostility towards Catholics is also quite evident in *Washington New National Era*, December 22, 1870, and in letters from J. B. Turner on May 11, 1893, and from M. L. Windiate, August 13, 1893, in the Frederick Douglass Papers, Library of Congress.

13. *Baltimore Afro-American*, August 21, 1921; *Pittsburgh Courier*, May 26, 1927, January 21, 1933; Schuyler, "Views and Reviews," *Pittsburgh Courier*, June 28, 1930; Linda Bresette, *Mexicans in the United States* (Washington, D.C., 1929), pp. 41–42; Thomas Sowell, *Ethnic America: A History* (New York, 1981), Chapter 5.

14. *Baltimore Afro-American*, January 12, 1923; *Philadelphia Tribune*,

February 14, 1925; Wise quoted in *Crisis* 11 (February 1916): 174; Mack cited in *New York Amsterdam News*, February 5, 1930; Hirsch quoted in *New York Age*, January 10, 1920; *Crisis* 41 (August, 1934): 244.

15. The U.S. government eventually paid Italy a $5,000 indemnity in this case. Louis Harlan, ed., *The Booker T. Washington Papers*, 9 vols. to date (Urbana, Ill., 1971-1977), 6: 371-73; Luciano Iorizzo, "The Padrone and Immigrant Distribution," in S. M. Tomasi and M. H. Engel eds., *The Italian Experience in the United States* (New York, 1970), pp. 50-51; Thomas Dyer, *Theodore Roosevelt and the Idea of Race* (Baton Rouge, La., 1980), pp. 113-14.

16. *Horizon* (Alexandria, Va.) 3 (January, 1908): 4; ibid. 4 (August, 1908): 7.

17. *Richmond Planet*, March 24, 1934.

18. James Loewen, *The Mississippi Chinese: Between Black and White* (Cambridge, Mass., 1971), pp. 66-67; *San Francisco Elevator*, May 12, 1865. See also Douglas Daniels, *Pioneer Urbanites: A Social and Cultural History of Black San Francisco* (Philadelphia, 1980), pp. 32-35.

19. *Voice of the Negro* 2 (September, 1905): 594.

20. *Baltimore Ledger*, May 6, 1899; *Colored American Magazine* 11 (September, 1906): 149; *Washington Colored American*, July 26, 1902; *Tulsa Star* April 7, 1917; *Norfolk Journal and Guide*, March 17, 1928.

21. Waller, "Evils of European Emigration," *Colored American Magazine* 7 (September, 1904): 595-97.

22. *Washington Colored American*, August 9, 16, 23, 1902.

23. Thomas, *The New South—An Inside View, an Address Delivered Before the Congregational Club, Kingsley Hall, Boston, March 22, 1908* (Montgomery, Ala., 1908), p. 18; Quackenbos quoted in *Charleston News and Courier*, February 9, 1908, and in *Boston Morning Herald*, February 12, 1908; *Edgefield* (S.C.) *Advertiser*, n.d., quoted in *Columbia State*, March 13, 1908.

24. *Boston Transcript*, November 1, 1904, September 25, 1906.

25. Hellwig, "Black Attitudes," p. 168.

26. *Washington Bee*, September 30, 1905; *Washington Colored American*, August 16, 1902; *Wichita Searchlight*, May 26, 1906; *Reformer*, n.d., quoted in *Wichita Searchlight*, December 7, 1907; *Voice of the Negro* 2 (September, 1905): 596; Hellwig, "Black Attitudes," p. 160.

27. This, in fact, happened. Bohemian farmers in Virginia caused consternation when they first moved to the state. They ate in the same places as blacks, shook hands with Negroes, and called Afro-American men "Mr." Later, however, the Bohemians had little contact with blacks. Nels Anderson, "Petersburg: A Study of a Colony of Czech-

Slovakian Farmers in Virginia," in Edmund Brunner, ed., *Immigrant Farmers and Their Children* (Garden City, N.Y., 1929), pp. 209-10.

28. Hellwig, "Black Attitudes," p. 153; David Hellwig, "Building a Black Nation: The Role of Immigrants in the Thought and Rhetoric of Booker T. Washington," *Mississippi Quarterly* 31 (1978): hereafter cited as "Black Nation"; *Horizon* 3 (January, 1908): 4 and 4 (August, 1908): 7.

29. *Richmond Planet*, November 20, 1909; *Kentucky Standard*, n.d., quoted in *Baltimore Ledger*, August 27, 1898.

30. See, for example, Thomas Burgess, *Greeks in America* (New York, reprint ed., 1970), pp. 171-74; Theodore Saloutos, *Farmer Movements in the South, 1865-1933* (Berkeley, Calif., 1960), pp. 207-208.

31. *Savannah Tribune*, July 30, 1910.

32. Williams quoted in ibid., April 13, 1912; *Atlanta Independent*, July 10, 1915.

33. *Savannah Tribune*, February 12, 1910, October 19, 1912; *Chicago Whip*, n.d., quoted in *Kansas City Call*, October 16, 1931; *Los Angeles California Eagle*, August 22, 1924; *Pittsburgh Courier*, April 7, 1928.

34. See, for example, Roscoe Simmons, "The Week," *Chicago Defender*, September 30, 1922.

35. Purvis greatly underestimated the amount of prejudice against Jews when they sought hotel accommodations. Meier, *Negro Thought*, p. 57; *Kansas City Call*, November 16, 1934; Roy Wilkins, "Talking It Over," *Kansas City Call*, April 29, 1927; Purvis to Grimké, January 14, 1921, quoted in Carter G. Woodson, ed., *The Works of Francis J. Grimké*, 4 vols. (Washington, D.C., 1942), 4: 297; *Philadelphia Tribune*, n.d. quoted in *Kansas City Call*, September 13, 1929; Higginbotham to editor, *Norfolk Journal and Guide*, August 24, 1929.

36. On Rosh Hashonah, the Jewish New Year, nearly all Jewish-owned businesses were closed. *Chicago Whip*, n.d., quoted in *Kansas City Call*, October 16, 1931; *The Half-Century Magazine* 9 (August-September, 1920): 3; C. A. Franklin, "Observations by the Way," *Kansas City Call*, October 4, 1929; George Lee, "Beale Street," in Hollis Lynch, ed., *The Black Urban Condition* (New York, 1973), p. 212; William Jones, "Day by Day," *Baltimore Afro-American*, October 12, 1929.

37. *Pittsburgh Courier*, June 20, 1931; *Negro World*, July 3, 1926; *Philadelphia Tribune*, April 6, 1918.

38. Miller, "Race Relations," in Charles S. Johnson, comp., *The Negro in American Civilization* (New York, 1930), p. 478; Raymond Gavins, *The Perils and Prospects of Southern Black Leadership: Gordon Blaine Hancock, 1884-1970* (Durham, N.C., 1977), p. 89.

39. *Chicago Defender*, October 20, 1923, July 8, 1933.

40. Blacks seemed unaware of the Italians' efforts to combat prejudice. One of the few articles on this subject to appear in a black newspaper was an account of Luigi de Pasquale, a legislator from Rhode Island, to get his state's legislature to pass a civil rights bill. In a speech to his fellow solons, de Pasquale said that it was reprehensible that, regardless of their ability and achievement, blacks were disliked and discriminated against merely because of their skin color. *Cleveland Advocate*, April 26, 1919.

41. *One Year's Work in Race Relations: The Twenty-First Annual Report on the NAACP* (for 1930) (New York, 1931), p. 55; *Cleveland Gazette*, September 21, 1929; Adam Clayton Powell, *Marching Blacks* (New York, rev. ed., 1973), pp. 64–65; *Chicago Defender*, February 11, 1928.

42. W.E.B. Du Bois, who considered Rosenwald "a subtle, stinging critic of American democracy," noted that the Chicago merchant realized the white South had no intention of building "decent school houses for most colored children." Therefore, he hoped to promote progress by offering to help pay for schools for blacks, provided they were modern facilities. Du Bois concluded,

The South accepted his gift effusively, and never, even to this day, has apparently grasped the failure of democracy which permitted an individual of a despised race to do for the sovereign states of a great nation that which they had neither the decency nor justice to do for themselves.
Du Bois, "Postscript," *The Crisis* 39 (February, 1932): 58.

43. *Cleveland Gazette*, September 21, 1929; *Kansas City Call*, September 20, 1920; James Weldon Johnson to Alfred Stern, January 7, 1931 [1932? intended], and Johnson to Edwin Embree, January 7, 1931 [1932? intended], James Weldon Johnson Papers, Yale University; Kelly Miller quoted in *Philadelphia Tribune*, January 21, 1932; *Galveston City Times*, July 25, 1914; *Los Angeles California Eagle*, June 12, August 7, 1931, January 8, 1932; Alfred Jarrette, *Julius Rosenwald, Benefactor of Mankind* (Greenville, S.C., 1975).

44. John Kirby, *Black Americans in the Roosevelt Era* (Knoxville, Tenn., 1980), pp. 13–14; Sowell, *Ethnic America*, Chapter 8.

45. *Washington Bee*, January 8, 1916, June 2, 1917, April 5, 1919; *Philadelphia Tribune*, February 12, 1916; Walter White, *A Man Called White* (New York, 1948), p. 23.

46. *The Crisis*, the organ of the NAACP, was one of the few black periodicals to criticize the new laws and note that "The insult to

Japanese, Jews, and southern Europeans in the [immigration laws] . . . is a logical deduction from the American pastime of Negro baiting." *The Crisis* 29 (March 1925): 201. See also David Hellwig, "Black Leaders and United States Immigration Policy, 1917-1929" *Journal of Negro History* 66 (1981): 110-127.

47. "Colorful News Movies," *Savannah Tribune*, September 9, 1926; *Philadelphia Tribune*, October 25, 1928. During the Depression, the Savannah newspaper favored a bill to deport all aliens. See the July 4, 1935, issue of the *Savannah Tribune*.

48. Maxine Seller, *To Seek America* (Englewood, N.J., 1977), p. 270.

BIBLIOGRAPHY

NEWSPAPERS AND PERIODICALS

Afro-American Newspapers

Alexandria (Va.) *People's Advocate*
Atlanta Independent
Baltimore Afro-American
Baltimore Ledger
Baxter Springs (Kans.) *Southern Argus*
Boston Colored Citizen
Boston Guardian
Chicago Broad Ax
Chicago Defender
Chicago Whip
Cleveland Advocate
Cleveland Gazette
Colored American (New York)
Columbia (S.C.) *Southern Indicator*
Des Moines Iowa Bystander
Detroit Plaindealer
Frederick Douglass' Paper (Rochester)
Galveston City Times
Galveston New Idea
Galveston Sentinel
Galveston Voice
Georgetown (S.C.) *Planet*
Harrisburg State Journal
Houston Informer and Texas Freeman
Huntsville (Ala.) *Gazette*
Indianapolis Freeman

Indianapolis World
Kansas City (Kans.) *Call*
Lawrence (Kans.) *Historic Times*
Leavenworth Advocate
Little Rock Arkansas Freeman
Little Rock Arkansas Mansion
Los Angeles California Eagle
Martinsburg (W. Va.) *Pioneer Press*
Milwaukee Wisconsin Weekly Advocate
Nashville Globe
Negro World (New York)
New Orleans Louisianian
New Orleans Pelican
New York Age
New York Amsterdam News
New York Freeman
New York Globe
New York National Anti-Slavery Standard
Nicodemus (Kans.) *Western Cyclone*
Norfolk Journal and Guide
Oakland Sunshine
Omaha Progress
Parsons (Kans.) *Blade*
Philadelphia Tribune
Pittsburgh Courier
Portland (Ore.) *New Age*
Portland (Ore.) *Times*
Raleigh Gazette
Richmond Planet
St. Louis Argus
St. Louis Palladium
St. Paul Appeal
San Francisco Elevator
San Francisco Pacific Appeal
San Francisco Spokesman
San Francisco Vindicator
San Francisco Western Outlook
Savannah Echo
Savannah Tribune
Topeka Call
Topeka Kansas State Ledger

Topeka Times Observer
Topeka Tribune
Trenton Sentinel
Tulsa Star
Washington Bee
Washington Colored American
Washington New National Era
Wichita National Reflector
Wichita Tribune

White Newspapers

Atlanta Constitution (1924)
Bainbridge (Ga.) *Democrat* (1895)
Baton Rouge New Advocate State Times (1912)
Boston Advertiser (1905)
Boston Morning Herald (1908)
Boston Transcript (1903–1908)
Charleston News and Courier (1908–1912)
Columbia State (1908)
Little Rock Arkansas Gazette (1912)
Memphis Commercial Appeal (1912)
Mobile Register (1912–1913)
New Orleans Picayune (1865–1869, 1911–1913)
New York Times (various dates)
Springfield (Mass.) *Republican* (1906)

PERIODICALS

Abbott's Monthly (Chicago)
Alexander's Magazine (Boston)
The Colored American Magazine (New York)
The Competitor (Pittsburgh)
The Crisis (New York)
Douglass' Monthly (Rochester)
The Freedman (Boston)
Horizon (Alexandria, Va., and Washington, D.C.)
The Messenger (New York)
Opportunity (New York)
Southern Workman (Hampton, Va.)
The Voice of the Negro (Atlanta, later Chicago)

MANUSCRIPT COLLECTIONS

R. C. Barnes Papers, Bentley Library, University of Michigan.
John E. Bruce Papers, Schomburg Branch, New York Public Library.
Commission on Interracial Cooperation Papers, Trevor Arnett Library, Atlanta University
Galveston Movement and Industrial Removal Office Papers, American Jewish Historical Society
Archibald Grimké Papers, Moorland-Spingarn Research Center, Howard University
Prescott Hall Immigration Scrapbooks, Harvard University
James Weldon Johnson Papers, Yale University
Ruth Scheinberg Collection of Cassette Interviews and other material on Jewish Peddlers, Emory University
Surasky and Tropp Family Papers, Winthrop College
Robert Ward Immigration Clippings, Harvard University
Booker T. Washington Papers, Library of Congress

ORAL HISTORY COLLECTIONS

W.E.B. Du Bois Memoirs, Columbia University Oral History Collection.
Colgera Petruzella Interview, 1980, copy deposited at Wintrhop College.
Esther Pinck Interview, 1979, copy deposited at Winthrop College
Mina Tropp Interviews, 1978 and 1979, copies deposited at Winthrop College
J. Waties Waring Memoir, Columbia University Oral History Collection.
Marion A. Wright Interviews, 1976 and 1977, copies deposited at Winthrop College and at the University of North Carolina, Chapel Hill

BOOKS

Acuna, Rodolfo. *Occupied America*. New York: Harper and Row, 1972.
Adler, Cyrus, ed. *The Voice of America on Kishineff*. Philadelphia: The Jewish Publication Society of America, 1904.
Ander, O. F. *In Trek of the Immigrants*. Rock Island, Ill.: Augustana College Press, 1964.
Aptheker, Herbert. *The Correspondence of W.E.B. Du Bois*. 3 vols. Amherst, Mass., University of Massachusetts Press, 1978.

Archer, William. *Through Afro-America, an English Reading of the Race blem.* New York: Dutton, 1910.

Athearn, Robert. *In Search of Canaan: Black Migration to Kansas, 1879–1880.* Lawrence Kans.: Kansas University Press, 1978.

Baker, Ray Stannard. *Following the Color Line.* New York: Doubleday, Page, and Company, 1908.

Baron, Salo. *The Russian Jew Under Tsars and Soviets.* New York: Macmillan, 1964.

Barron, Milton. *Minorities in a Changing World.* New York: Knopf, 1967.

Barth, Gunter. *Bitter Strength, A History of the Chinese in the United States, 1850–1870.* Cambridge, Mass.: Harvard University Press, 1964.

BeDunnah, Gary. *A History of the Chinese in Nevada, 1855–1904.* San Francisco: R and E Publishing Company, 1973.

Ben-Horin, Meir, comp. *Negro-Jewish Relations in the United States.* New York: Citadel, 1966.

Berman, Myron. *Richmond's Jewry.* Charlottesville, Va.: University Press of Virginia, 1979.

Berwanger, Eugene. *The Frontier Against Slavery.* Urbana, Ill.: University of Illinois Press, 1967.

Bogardus, Emory. *Immigration and Race Attitudes.* Boston: Henry Holt, 1928.

_____. *The Mexican in the United States.* Los Angeles: University of Southern California Press, 1934.

Brandfon, Robert. *Cotton Kingdom of the New South.* Cambridge, Mass.: Harvard University Press, 1967.

Brazeal, Braisford. *The Brotherhood of Sleeping Car Porters.* New York: Harper, 1946.

Bressette, Linda. *Mexicans in the United States.* Washington, D.C.: National Catholic Welfare Conference, 1929.

Brewer, J. Mason. *American Negro Folklore.* New York: Quadrangle, 1968.

Brown, William Wells. *My Southern Home.* New York, reprint ed., Negro Universities Press, 1969.

Bullock, Penelope. *The Afro-American Periodical Press, 1838–1909.* Baton Rouge, La.: Louisiana State University Press, 1981.

Burgess, Thomas. *Greeks in America.* New York: reprint ed. Arno Press, 1970.

Burkey, Richard. *Ethnic and Racial Groups.* Menlo Park, Calif.: Cummings Publishing Company, 1978.

Cardoso, Lawrence. *Mexican Emigration to the United States, 1897–1931.* Tucson, Ariz.: University of Arizona Press, 1980.

Chesnutt, Helen. *Charles Waddell Chesnutt.* Chapel Hill, N.C.: University of North Carolina Press, 1952.

Chicago Commission on Race Relations. *The Negro in Chicago*. Chicago: University of Chicago Press, 1922.

Clark, Elmer. *The Latin Immigrant in the South*. Nashville, Tenn.: Cokesbury, 1924.

Clark, Thomas D. *Pills, Petticoats and Plows: The Southern Country Store*. Norman, Okla.: University of Oklahoma Press, 1964.

Clowes, W. Laird. *Black America*. London: Cassell and Company, 1891.

Conroy, Hilary, and T. Scott Miyakawa, eds. *East Across the Pacific*. Santa Barbara, Calif.: American Bibliographical Center-Clio Press, 1972.

Coulter, E. Merton. *The Confederate States of America*. Baton Rouge, La.: Louisiana State University Press, 1950.

_____. *The South During Reconstruction*. Baton Rouge, La.: Louisiana State University Press, 1947.

Dance, Daryl. *Shuckin' and Jivin'*. Bloomington, Ind.: Indiana University Press, 1978.

Daniels, Douglas. *Pioneer Urbanites: A Social and Cultural History of Black San Francisco*. Philadelphia: Temple University Press, 1980.

Daniels, Roger. *The Politics of Prejudice*. Berkeley and Los Angeles: University of California Press, 1961.

_____, and Harry Kitano. *American Racism*. Englewood Cliffs, N.J.: Prentice-Hall, 1970.

Davis, Allison, Burleigh Gardner, and Mary Gardner, *Deep South*. Chicago: University of Chicago Press, 1941.

DeGraaf, Lawrence. *Negro Migration to Los Angeles*. San Francisco: R and E Publishing Company, 1974.

Diner, Hasia. *In the Amost Promised Land*. Westport, Conn.: Greenwood Press, 1977.

Dinnerstein, Leonard. *The Leo Frank Case*. New York: Columbia University Press, 1968.

_____, and Mary Dale Palsson, eds. *Jews in the South*. Baton Rouge, La.: Louisiana State University Press, 1973.

Dobkowski, Michael. *The Tarnished Dream*. Westport, Conn.: Greenwood Press, 1979.

Dollard, John. *Caste and Class in a Southern Town*. New Haven, Conn.: Yale University Press, 1937.

Douglass, Frederick. *The Life and Times of Frederick Douglass*. New York, reprint ed., Bonanza Books, 1962.

Du Bois, W.E.B. *The Souls of Black Folk*. Chicago, reprint ed., A. C. McClurg, 1931.

Dyer, Thomas. *Theodore Roosevelt and the Idea of Race*. Baton Rouge, La.: Louisiana State University Press, 1980.

Epstein, Melech. *Pages from a Colorful Life*. Miami Beach, Fla.: I, Bloch Publishers, 1971.

Erwin, J. M. *The Participation of the Negro in the Community Life of Los Angeles*. San Francisco: R and E Publishing Company, 1973.

Evans, Eli. *The Provincials*. New York: Atheneum, 1974.

Evans, Maurice. *Black and White in the Southern States*. New York and London: Longmans Green, 1915.

Failure of the Scheme for Colonization of Negroes in Mexico. 54th Congress, 1st Session, House Document 169 (Serial 3420). Washington, D.C.: Government Printing Office, 1896.

Feingold, Henry. *Zion in America*. New York: Twayne, 1974.

Feldstein, Stanley. *The Land That I Show You*. New York: Anchor Press/ Doubleday, 1978.

Fletcher, Marvin. *The Black Soldier and Officer in the United States Army, 1891-1917*. Columbia, Mo.: The University of Missouri Press, 1974.

Foerster, Robert. *The Italian Emigration of Our Times*. Cambridge, Mass.: Harvard University Press, 1919.

Foner, Jack. *Blacks and the Military in American History*. New York: Praegar, 1974.

Foner, Philip. *American Socialism and Black Americans*. Westport, Conn.: Greenwood Press, 1977.

_____, ed. *The Life and Writings of Frederick Douglass*. 5 vols. New York: International Publishers, 1954-1975.

_____, and Ronald Lewis, eds. *The Black Worker*. 5 vols. Philadelphia: Temple Unversity Press, 1978-1980.

Franklin, John Hope. *From Slavery to Freedom*. 5th ed. New York: Knopf, 1980.

Gallo, Patrick. *Old Bread, New Wine, A Portrait of the Italian-Americans*. Chicago: Nelson Hall, 1981.

Gambino, Richard. *Blood of My Blood*. New York: Anchor Press, 1975.

Gamio, Manuel. *Mexican Immigration to the United States*. Chicago: University of Chicago Press, 1930.

Gavins, Raymond. *The Perils and Prospects of Southern Black Leadership: Gordon Blaine Hancock, 1884-1970*. Durham, N.C.: Duke University Press, 1977.

Gerber, David. *Black Ohio and the Color Line*. Urbana, Ill.: The University of Illinois Press, 1976.

Gibbs, Mifflin. *Shadow and Light*. New York, reprint ed., Arno Press, 1969.

Glanz, Rudolph. *Jew and Irish*. New York: Ktav Publishing, 1966.

Golden, Harry. *Forgotten Pioneer*. Cleveland: World, 1963.

————. *Jewish Roots in the Carolinas*. Charlotte, N.C.: Carolina Israelite Publishing Company, 1955.

Goode, Kenneth. *California's Black Pioneers*, Santa Barbara, Calif.: McNally and Loftin, 1974.

Grant, Donald. *The Anti-Lynching Movement*. San Francisco: R and E Publishing Company, 1975.

Grebler, Leo, Joan Moore, and Ralph Guzman. *The Mexican American People*. New York: Free Press, 1970.

Greenberg, Louis, *The Jews in Russia*. New Haven, Conn.: Yale University Press, 1951.

Greene, Lorenzo, and Carter G. Woodson. *The Negro Wage Earner*. New York: reprint ed., Russell and Russell, 1969.

Hair, William Ivy. *Bourbonism and Agrarian Protest: Louisiana Politics, 1877–1900*. Baton Rouge, La.: Louisiana State University Press, 1969.

Handlin, Oscar. *Boston's Immigrants*. Cambridge, Mass.: Harvard University Press, 1941.

————. *Truth in History*. Cambridge, Mass.: Harvard University Press, 1979.

————. *The Uprooted*. Boston: Little, Brown, 1951.

————, and Mary Flug Handlin. *A Century of Jewish Immigration to the United States*. New York: American Jewish Committee, 1949.

Harlan, Louis, ed. *The Booker T. Washington Papers*. 9 vols. to date. Urbana, Ill.: University of Illinois Press, 1971.

Hartley, Eugene, and Ruth Hartley. *Fundamentals of Social Psychology*. New York: Knopf, 1959.

Heizer, Robert, and Alan Almquist. *The Other Californians: Prejudice and Discrimination Under Spain, Mexico and the United States to 1920*. Berkeley, Calif.: University of California Press, 1971.

Henri, Florette. *Black Migration*. Garden City, N.Y.: Anchor/Doubleday, 1975.

Hertzberg, Steven. *Strangers Within the Gate City*, Philadelphia: Jewish Publication Society of America, 1978.

Higham, John. *Send These to Me*. New York: Atheneum, 1975.

————. *Strangers in the Land*. New Brunswick, N.J.: Rutgers University Press, 1955.

Hoffman, Abraham. *Unwanted Mexican Americans in the Great Depression*. Tucson, Ariz.: University of Arizona Press, 1974.

Horton, James and Lois Horton. *Black Bostonians*. New York: Holmes and Meier, 1979.

Hosokawa, Bill, *Nisei: The Quiet Americans*. New York: Morrow, 1969.

Huggins, Nathan. *Slave and Citizen: The Life of Frederick Douglass.* Boston: Little, Brown, 1980.

Ichihashi, Yamato. *Japanese Immigration: Its Status in California.* San Francisco: Marshall, 1915.

The Influence of Immigration on American Culture. New York: Conference on Immigration Policy, 1929.

Iorizzo, Luciano, and Salvatore Mondello. *The Italian-Americans.* New York: Twayne, 1971.

Isaacs, Harold. *Scratches on Our Minds*: New York: John Day, 1958.

Iyenaga, T., and Kenoske Sato. *Japan and the California Problem.* New York: Putnam, 1921.

Jackson, Kenneth T., and Stanley Schultz, eds. *Cities in American History.* New York: Knopf, 1972.

Jarrette, Alfred. *Julius Rosenwald, Benefactor of Mankind.* Greenville, S.C.: Southeastern University Press, 1975.

Johnson, Charles S., comp. *The Negro in American Civilization.* New York: Henry Holt and Company, 1930.

Johnson, Herbert. *Discrimination Against the Japanese in California.* Berkeley, Calif.: Courier Publishing Company, 1907.

Johnson, James Weldon. *The Book of American Negro Spirituals.* New York: Viking, 1925.

Kaganoff, Nathan, and Melvin Urofsky, eds. *Turn to the South.* Charlottesville, Va.: University Press of Virginia, 1979.

Katzman, David. *Before the Ghetto.* Urbana, Ill.: The University of Illinois Press, 1973.

_____. *Seven Days a Week.* New York: Oxford University Press, 1978.

Kirby, John. *Black Americans in the Roosevelt Era.* Knoxville, Tenn.: University of Tennessee Press, 1980.

Kirwan, Albert. *Revolt of the Rednecks.* Gloucester, Mass.: Peter Smith, 1964.

Kitano, Harry L. *Japanese Americans.* Englewood Cliffs: Prentice Hall, N.J., 1969.

Lane, Ann. *The Brownsville Affair.* Port Washington, N.Y.: Kennikat, 1971.

Lapp, Rudolph. *Blacks in Gold Rush California.* New Haven, Conn.: Yale University Press, 1977.

Lavender, Abraham. *A Coat of Many Colors.* Westport, Conn.: Greenwood Press, 1977.

Lee, Rose Hum. *The Chinese in the United States.* Hong Kong: Hong Kong University Press, 1960.

Lerner, Gerda, ed. *Black Women in White America: A Documentary History.* New York: Pantheon Books, 1972.

Levine, Lawrence. *Black Culture and Black Consciousness*. New York: Oxford University Press, 1977.

Levy, Eugene. *James Weldon Johnson*. Chicago: University of Chicago Press, 1973.

Litwack, Leon. *Been in the Storm So Long: The Aftermath of Slavery*. New York: Knopf, 1979.

————. *North of Slavery*. Chicago: University of Chicago Press, 1961.

Loewen, James. *The Mississippi Chinese: Between Black and White*. Cambridge, Mass.: Harvard University Press, 1971.

Logan, Rayford. *The Negro in American Life and Thought: The Nadir, 1877–1901*. New York: Dial Press, 1954.

Lord, Eliot, John Trenor, and Samuel Barrows. *The Italian in America*. New York: B. F. Buck, 1905.

Lortie, Francis. *San Francisco's Black Community, 1870–1890*. San Francisco: R and E Publishing Company, 1973.

Lynch, Hollis, ed. *The Black Urban Condition*. New York: Crowell, 1973.

McCombs, Vernon. *From Over the Border*. New York: Council of Women for Home Missions, 1925.

McKay, Claude. *A Long Way from Home*. New York, reprint ed.: Arno Press, 1969.

McKenzie, R. D. *Oriental Exclusion*. Chicago, University of Chicago Press, 1928.

McWilliams, Carey. *North from Mexico*. New York, reprint ed.: Monthly Review Press, 1968.

Marden, Charles. *Minorities in American Society*. New York: American Book Company, 1952.

Marden, Charles, and Gladys Meyer. *Minorities in American Society*. New York: Van Nostrand, 1973.

Martinez, John. *Mexican Emigration to the United States, 1910–30*. San Francisco: R and E Publishing Company, 1971.

Matthews, Victoria, comp. *Black Belt Diamonds, Gems from the Speeches, Addresses and Talks to Students of Booker T. Washington*. New York, reprint ed.: Negro Universities Press, 1969.

Mays, Benjamin. *The Negro's God*. New York, reprint ed.: Russell and Russell, 1968.

Meier, August. *Negro Thought in America, 1880–1915*. Ann Arbor, Mich.: The University of Michigan Press, 1963.

————, and Elliott Rudwick. *From Plantation to Ghetto*. New York: Hill and Wang, 1970.

Meier, Matt, and Feliciano Rivera. *The Chicanos*. New York: Hill and Wang, 1972.

Miller, Kelly. *The Everlasting Stain*. New York: Arno Press, reprint ed., 1968.

Miller, Stuart Creighton. *The Unwelcome Immigrant: The American Image of the Chinese, 1785-1882*. Berkeley: Calif.: The University of California Press, 1969.

Millis, H. A. *The Japanese Problem in the United States*. New York: Macmillan, 1915.

Modell, John. *The Economics and Politics of Racial Accommodation: The Japanese of Los Angeles, 1900-1942*. Urbana, Ill.: University of Illinois Press, 1977.

Moore, John. *The South To-day*. New York: Missionary Education Movement of the United States and Canada, 1916.

Moquine, Wayne, and Charles Van Doren, eds. *A Documentary History of the Italian Americans*. New York: Praegar, 1974.

National Urban League. *500,000 Jobs: The Negro at Work in the United States*. New York: National Urban League, 1933.

Newmark, Harris. *Sixty Years in Southern California*. Boston: Houghton Mifflin, 1930.

Nichols, Charles. *Many Thousand Gone: The Ex-Slaves Accounts of Their Bondage and Freedom*. Bloomington, Ind.: Indiana University Press, 1969.

Nolen, Claude. *The Negro's Image in the South: The Anatomy of White Supremacy*. Lexington, Ky.: University of Kentucky Press, 1967.

Ogawa, Dennis. *From Japs to Japanese: An Evolution of Japanese-American Stereotypes*. Berkeley, Calif.: McCutchan, 1971.

Olson, James. *The Ethnic Dimension in American History*. New York: St. Martin's, 1978.

One Year's Work in Race Relations: The 21st Annual Report of the NAACP. New York: NAACP, 1931.

Osofsky, Gilbert. *Harlem: The Making of a Ghetto*. New York: Harper and Row, 1965.

Ottley, Roi. *The Lonely Warrior: The Life and Times of Robert S. Abbott*. Chicago: Regnery, 1955.

Painter, Nell I. *Exodusters*. New York: Knopf, 1977.

Paschal, Andrew, ed. *A W.E.B. Du Bois Reader*. New York: Macmillan, 1971.

Pennsylvania Department of Welfare. *Negro Survey of Pennsylvaina*. Harrisburg, Pa.: Commonwealth of Pennsylvania, 1926.

Penrose, Eldon. *California Nativism. Organized Opposition to the Japanese 1890-1913*. San Francisco: R and E Publishing Company, 1973.

Philpott, Thomas. *The Slum and the Ghetto*. New York: Oxford University Press, 1978.

Picard, Kate, ed. *The Kidnapped and the Ransomed: The Narrative of Peter and Vina Still.* Philadelphia, reprint ed.: Jewish Publication Society of America, 1970.

Pickens, William. *American Aesop.* Boston: Jordan and More, 1926.

Pleck, Elizabeth. *Black Migration and Poverty: Boston, 1865-1900.* New York: Academic Press, 1979.

Powdermaker, Hortense. *After Freedom.* New York: Viking, 1939.

————. *Stranger and Friend.* New York: Norton, 1966.

Powell, Adam Clayton. *Marching Blacks.* New York, rev. ed.: Dial Press, 1973.

Proceedings of the California State Convention of Colored Citizens Held in Sacramento on the 25th, 26th, 27th and 28th of October 1865. San Francisco, reprint ed.: R and E Publishing Company, 1969.

Quarles, Benjamin. *Black Abolitionists.* New York: Oxford University Press, 1969.

Raboteau, Albert. *Slave Religion.* New York: Oxford University Press, 1978.

Rauschenbush, Winifred. *Robert E. Park.* Durham, N.C.: Duke University Press, 1979.

Rice, Lawrence. *The Negro in Texas, 1874-1900.* Baton Rouge, La.: Louisiana State University Press, 1971.

Rischin, Moses. *The Promised City.* Cambridge, Mass.: Harvard University Press, 1962.

Roark, James. *Masters Without Slaves.* New York: Norton, 1977.

Rolle, Andrew. *The American Italians.* Belmont, Calif.: Wadsworth, 1972.

————. *The Immigrant Upraised.* Norman, Okla.: University of Oklahoma Press, 1968.

————. *The Italian Americans, Troubled Roots.* New York: Free Press, 1980.

Rubin, Charles. *The Log of Rubin the Sailor.* New York: International Publishers, 1973.

Rusco, Elmer. *Good Time Coming.* Westport, Conn.: Greenwood Press, 1975.

Salmon, Lucy. *Domestic Service.* New York: Macmillan, 1897.

Saloutos, Theodore. *Farmer Movements in the South, 1865-1933.* Berkeley, Calif.: University of California Press, 1960.

Savage, W. Sherman. *Blacks in the West.* Westport, Conn.: Greenwood Press, 1976.

Saxton, Alexander. *The Indispensable Enemy: Labor and the Anti-Chinese Movement in California.* Berkeley, Calif.: University of California Press, 1971.

Schappes, Morris U., ed. *A Documentary History of the Jews in the United States, 1654-1875.* New York: Citadel, 1952.

Scheiner, Seth. *Negro Mecca: A History of the Negro in New York City, 1865-1920.* New York: New York University Press, 1965.

Scottron, Samuel. *Chinese vs. Negroes as Americans.* New York?: n.p., 1899?

Seller, Maxine. *To Seek America.* Englewood, N.J.: Jerome Ozer, 1977.

Seward, George. *Chinese Immigration in Its Social and Economic Aspects.* New York: Scribner's, 1881.

Shaw, Albert. *Political Problems of American Development.* New York: Columbia University Press, 1907.

Shepperd, Eli. *Plantation Songs.* New York: Russell, 1901.

Shofner, Jerrell H., and Linda V. Ellsworth, eds. *Ethnic Minorities in Gulf Coast Society,* Pensacola, Fla.: Gulf Coast History and Humanities Conference, 1979.

Smith, Bradford. *Americans from Japan.* Philadelphia: Lippincott, 1948.

Sowell, Thomas. *Ethnic America: A History.* New York: Basic Books, 1981.

Spero, Sterling, and Abraham Harris. *The Black Worker.* Port Washington, N.Y., reprint ed.: Kennikat, 1966.

Spivey, Donald. *Schooling for the New Slavery: Black Industrial Education, 1868-1915.* Westport, Conn.: Greenwood Press, 1978.

Stone, Alfred. *Studies in the American Race Problem.* New York, rev. and reprint ed.: Negro Universities Press, 1969.

Sung, Betty. *Mountain of Gold: The Chinese in America.* New York: Macmillan, 1967.

Szajkowski, Soza. *Jews, Wars and Communism.* 2 vols. New York: Ktav, 1972.

Takaki, Ronald. *Iron Cages.* New York: Knopf, 1979.

Taylor, Joe Gray. *Louisiana Reconstructed.* Baton Rouge, La.: Louisiana State University Press, 1975.

Taylor, Paul. *Mexican Labor in the United States: Bethlehem, Pennsylvania.* Berkeley, Calif.: University of California Press, 1931.

————. *Mexican Labor in the United States: Chicago and the Calumet Region.* Berkeley, Calif.: University of California Press, 1932.

Toll, William. *The Resurgence of Race.* Philadelphia: Temple University Press, 1979.

Tomasi, S. M., and M. H. Engel, eds. *The Italian Experience in the United States.* New York: Center for Migration Studies, 1970.

Tucker, David. *Memphis Since Crump.* Knoxville, Tenn.: University of Tennessee Press, 1980.

184   BIBLIOGRAPHY

Vecoli, Rudolph. *The People of New Jersey*. Princeton, N.J.: Van Nostrand, 1965.

Wagner, Nathaniel, and Marsha Haug, eds. *Chicanos*. St. Louis, Mo.: Mosby, 1971.

Warner, Robert. *New Haven Negroes*. New Haven, Conn.: Yale University Press, 1940.

Washington, Booker T. *The Future of the American Negro*. New York, reprint ed.: Negro Universities Press, 1969.

_____. *Putting the Most into Life*. New York: Crowell, 1906.

_____. *Up from Slavery*. New York: Doubleday, Page and Company, 1903.

_____, and Robert Park. *The Man Farthest Down*. Garden City, N.Y.: Doubleday, Page and Company, 1912.

Washington, E. Davidson, ed. *Selected Speeches of Booker T. Washington*. Garden City, N.Y.: Doubleday, Page and Company, 1932.

Weisbord, Robert and Arthur Stein. *Bittersweet Encounter*. Westport, Conn.: Greenwood Press, 1972.

Weiss, Melford. *Valley City, A Chinese Community in America*. Cambridge, Mass.: Schenckman, 1974.

Wells, Henry George. *The Future in America*. New York, reprint ed.: Arno Books, 1974.

Wells, Ida B. *A Red Record*. Chicago: Donohue and Henneberry, 1895.

Wesley, Charles. *Negro Labor in the United States*. New York: Vanguard Press, 1927.

Wharton, Vernon Lane. *The Negro in Mississippi*. New York: Harper and Row Torchbook ed., 1965.

White, Walter. *A Man Called White*. New York: Viking, 1948.

Wilcox, Walter. *The Negro Population*. Washington, D.C.: Government Printing Office, 1904.

Williams, James. *Life and Adventures of James Williams, A Fugitive Slave*. 5th ed. Philadelphia: A.H. Sickler, 1893.

Williams, Lee, and Lee Williams II. *Anatomy of Four Race Riots*. Jackson, Miss.: University and College Press of Mississippi, 1972.

Wilson, Robert, and Bill Hosokawa. *East to America: A History of the Japanese in the United States*. New York: Morrow, 1980.

Wollenberg, Charles. *All Deliberate Speed: Segregation and Exclusion in California Schools, 1855-1975*. Berkeley, Calif.: The University of California Press, 1976.

Woodson, Carter G., ed. *The Works of Francis Grimké*. 4 vols. Washington, D.C.: Associated Publishers, 1942.

Wright, Marion. *Human Rights Odyssey*. Durham, N.C.: Moore, 1978.

Wright, Richard. *Black Boy.* New York: Harper, 1945.
Wu, Cheng-tsu, ed. *"Chink!"* New York: Meridian, 1972.
Yin, Robert K., ed. *Race, Creed, Color or National Origin.* Itasca, Ill.: Peacock, 1973.

ARTICLES

Albig, William. "Opinions Concerning Unskilled Mexican Immigration." *Sociology and Social Research* 15 (1930): 62-72.
Aptheker, Herbert. "The Souls of Black Folk: A Comparison of the 1903 and 1952 Editions." *Negro History Bulletin* 34 (January 1971): 15-17.
Bagnall, Robert. "The Spirit of the Ku Klux Klan." *Opportunity* 1 (1923): 265-67.
Bamford, Edward. "The Mexican Casual Problem in the Southwest." *Journal of Applied Sociology* 8 (1924): 363-71.
Bauman, Mark. "Centripetal and Centrifugal Forces Facing the People of Many Communities." *Atlanta Historical Journal* 23 (1979): 25-54.
Beals, Carleton. "Valerio Trujano: Black Joy." *The Crisis* 38 (1931): 153-54, 174.
Bernardy, Amy. "Immigration to the South." *Boston Transcript*, March 28, 1908.
――――. "Italians in Our South." *Boston Transcript*, November 28, 1906.
Berthoff, Rowland. "Southern Attitudes Towards Immigration, 1865-1914," *Journal of Southern History* 17 (1951): 328-60.
Betten, Neil, and Raymond Mohl. "From Discrimination to Repatriation: Mexican Life in Gary, Indiana During the Great Depression." *Pacific Historical Review* 42 (1973): 373-88.
Bond, J. Max. "The Japanese in California." *The Crisis* 40 (1933): 133-34.
Brown, William Garrott. "The White Peril: The Immediate Danger of the Negro." *North American Review* 79 (1904): 825-41.
Bruce, Philip. "The Negro Population of the South." *Conservative Review* 2 (1899): 262-80.
Carruthers, Ben. "Spick." *Opportunity* 14 (1936): 239-40.
Cohen, Lucy. "Entry of Chinese to the Lower South from 1865 to 1870." *Southern Studies* 17 (1978): 5-37.
Crouthamel, James L. "The Springfield Race Riot of 1908." *Journal of Negro History* 45 (1960): 164-81.
Cunningham, George. "The Italian, A Hindrance to White Solidarity in Louisiana," *Journal of Negro History* 50 (1965): 22-36.

Davis, David. "Recollections of Atlanta." *Jewish Currents* 32 (September 1978): 14-18.

Fleming, Walter. "Immigration to the Southern States." *National Geographic* 16 (1905): 517-19.

Foner, Philip. "Black-Jewish Relations in the Opening Years of the Twentieth Century." *Phylon* 36 (1975): 359-76.

———. "No Room for Race Prejudice." *Jewish Currents* 34 (February 1980): 4-6.

Fortune, Jessie. "Among the Children of the East Side Jews (1905)." *Jewish Currents* 29 (February 1975): 4-7.

Ginsberg, Louis. "The Jewish Colony at Waterview." *Virginia Magazine of History and Biography* 66 (1958): 459-62.

Goins, Alvin, and Max Meenes. "Ethnic and Class Preferences Among College Negroes." *Journal of Negro Education* 29 (1960): 128-33.

Gray, J. Stanley, and Anthony H. Thompson. "The Ethnic Prejudices of White and Negro College Students." *Journal of Abnormal and Social Psychology* 48 (1953): 311-13.

Hadley, A.W. "The Tontitown Settlement." *Maxwell's Talisman* 5 (1905): 14-16.

Hall, Chatwood. "A Black Man in Red Russia." *Abbott's Monthly* 6 (June 1933): 8-10, 38-40.

Hellwig, David. "Afro-American Reactions to the Japanese and Anti-Japanese Movement, 1906-1924." *Phylon* 38 (1977): 93-104.

———. "Afro-American Views of Immigrants, 1830-1930: A Historiographical-Bibliographical Essay." *The Immigration History Newsletter* 13 (November, 1981): 1-5.

———. "Black Attitudes Toward Immigrant Labor in the South, 1865-1910. *Filson Club History Quarterly* 54 (1980): 151-68.

———. "Black Leaders and United States Immigration Policy, 1917-1929." *Journal of Negro History* 66 (1981): 110-27.

———. "Black Reactions to Chinese Immigration and the Anti-Chinese Movement, 1850-1910." *Amerasia* 6 (1979): 25-44.

———. "Building a Black Nation: The Role of Immigrants in the Thought and Rhetoric of Booker T. Washington." *Mississippi Quarterly* 31 (1978): 529-50.

Hertzberg, Steven. "Southern Jews and Their Encounters with Blacks: Atlanta, 1850-1915." *Atlanta Historical Journal* 23 (1979): 7-24.

Hewe, Leslie. "Tonitown." *Economic Geography* 29 (1953): 125-43.

Holmes, William F. "Whitecapping: Anti-Semitism in the Populist Era." *American Jewish Historical Quarterly* 64 (1974): 245-61.

"How Italians Can Help Negroes." *Southern Workman* 34 (1905): 202.

Johnsen, Leigh. "Equal Rights and the Heathen Chinee: Black Activism in San Francisco, 1865-1875." *Western Historical Quarterly* 11 (1980): 57-68.

Jonas, Franklin, ed. "A Socialist View of the Jews of the South: The Observations of Baruch Charney Vladeck." *Southern Jewish Historical Society Newsletter* 3 (1981): 2-4.

Jordan, G. Gundy, "The Southern Need for Labor." *National Civic Federation Review* 2 (1905): 15-16.

Ken, Sally. "The Chinese Community of Augusta, Georgia from 1873 to 1971." *Richmond County History* 4 (1972): 51-60.

Kinsey, Winston. "The Immigrant in Texas Agriculture During Reconstruction." *Agricultural History* 53 (1979): 125-41.

Lapp, Rudolph. "Negro Rights Activities in Gold Rush California." *California Historical Society Quarterly* 45 (1966): 5-13.

Levy, Eugene. "Is the Jew a White Man?: Press Reaction to the Leo Frank Case, 1913-15." *Phylon* 35 (1974): 212-22.

Loewenberg, Bert James. "Efforts of the South to Encourage Immigration, 1865-1900." *South Atlantic Quarterly* 33 (1934): 363-85.

Meade, Emily Fogg. "Italian Immigration in the South." *South Atlantic Quarterly* 4 (1905): 217-24.

Meenes, Max. "A Comparison of Racial Stereotypes of 1935 and 1942." *Journal of Social Psychology* 17 (1943): 327-36.

Miller, Kelly. "Race Prejudice in Germany and America." *Opportunity* 14 (1936): 102-105.

Moore, Anita. "Safe Ways to Get on the Soil: The Work of Father Bandini of Tontitown." *World's Work*, 24 (1912): 215-19.

Ong, Paul. "An Ethnic Trade: The Chinese Laundries in Early California." *Journal of Ethnic Studies* 8 (1981): 95-113.

Osthaus, Carl. "From the Old South to the New South: The Editorial Career of William Tappan Thompson." *Southern Quarterly* 14 (1976): 237-60.

Pei. M. A. "Facts and Comments." *United America*, 2 (July 3, 1926): 5.

Pinckney, Alphonso. "Prejudice Toward Mexican and Negro Americans, A Comparison." *Phylon* 24 (1963): 353-59.

Pollack, Herman. "A Forgotten Fighter for Justice: Ben Goldstein-Lowell." *Jewish Currents* 30 (June 1976): 14-18.

Polos, Nicholas. "Black Anti-Semitism in Twentieth Century America." *American Jewish Archives* 27 (1975): 8-31.

Pozzetta, George. "Foreigners in Florida: A Study of Immigration Promotion, 1865-1910." *Florida Historical Quarterly* 53 (1974): 165-86.

Proctor, H. H. "The Theology of the Songs of the Southern Slave." *Southern Workman* 36 (1907): 587.

Reynolds, Alfred. "The Alabama Negro Colony in Mexico, 1894-1896: Part I." *Alabama Review* 5 (1952): 243-68 and "Part II" 6 (1953): 31-58.

Rhoads, Edward. "The Chinese in Texas." *Southwestern Historical Quarterly* 81 (1977): 1-17.

Rippy, J. Fred. "A Negro Colonization Project in Mexico, 1895." *Journal of Negro History* 6 (1921): 66-73.

Rubin, Jay. "Black Nativism: The European Immigrant in Negro Thought, 1830-60." *Phylon* 39 (1978): 193-202.

Rubinow, I. M. "Lessons from Russia." *The Crisis* 4 (1912): 191-95.

Scarpaci, Jean. "Immigrants in the New South: Italians in Louisiana's Sugar Parishes, 1880-1910." *Labor History* 16 (1975): 165-83.

_____. "A Tale of Selective Accommodation: Sicilians and Native Whites in Louisiana." *Journal of Ethnic Studies* 5 (1977): 37-50.

Schappes, Morris U. "Historical Impressions of Black-Jewish Relations Prior to World War II, Another Comment." *Negro History Bulletin* 40 (1977): 890-92.

Schoonover, Thomas. "Misconstrued Mission: Expansionism and Black Colonization in Mexico and Central America During the Civil War." *Pacific Historical Review* 49 (1980): 607-20.

Shankman, Arnold. "The Galveston Movement: Letters of Annie E. Johnson and Jacob Schiff." *Atlanta Historical Journal* 23 (1979): 77-83.

_____. "Happyville, the Forgotten Colony." *American Jewish Archives* 30 (1978): 3-19.

_____. "The Image of the Italian in the Afro-American Press, 1886-1936." *Italian Americana* 4 (1978): 30-49.

Slayden, James. "The Mexican Immigrant." *Annals of the American Academy* 93 (1921): 121-25.

Speed, Jonathan Gilmer. "The Negro in New York." *Harper's Weekly* 44 (1900): 1249.

Speranza, Gino. "A Mission of Peace," *Outlook* 78 (1904): 129-30.

_____. "Italian Farmers in the South: An Interview with Adolfo Rossi," *Charities* 15 (1906): 185-86.

Spoehr, Luther. "Sambo and the Heathen Chinese: Californians' Racial Stereotypes of the Late 1870s." *Pacific Historical Review* 43 (1973): 185-204.

Stone, Alfred Holt. "The Italian Cotton Grower: The Negro's Problem." *South Atlantic Quarterly* 4 (1905): 42-47.

_____. "The Italian Cotton Growers in Arkansas." *American Monthly Review of Reviews* 35 (1907): 209-13.

Supple, Barry. "A Business Elite: German Jewish Financiers in Nineteenth Century New York." *Business History Review* 31 (1957): 130-48.

Terrell, Mary Church. "What It Means to Be Colored in the Capital of the United States." *The Independent* 62 (January 24, 1907): 181-86.

Trask, Robert. "Mobility and Occupational Structure on the late Nineteenth Century Urban Frontier: The Case of Denver, Colorado." *Pacific Historical Review* 47 (1978): 189-216.

Tropp, Mina. "Memoirs Mostly About a South Carolina Childhood." *Jewish Currents* 34 (February 1980): 10-15, 29-31.

Ward, Robert DeCourcey. "The Agricultural Distribution of Immigrants," *Popular Science Monthly* 66 (1904): 166-75.

_____. "How Shall We Select Our Immigrants?" *Charities* 14 (1905): 906-12.

_____. "Immigration and the South." *Atlantic Monthly* 96 (1905): 611-17.

_____. "The Immigration Problem." *Charities* 12 (1904): 141-42.

Washington, Booker T. "The Race Problem in Arizona." *Independent* 71 (1911): 910-11.

Williams, Oscar. "Historical Impressions of Black-Jewish Relations Prior to World War II." *Negro History Bulletin* 40 (1977): 728-31.

Woodson, Carter G. "Economic Conditions Among Negroes in the South." *Journal of Negro History* 64 (1979): 267-72.

Wright, Marion. "Two Southerners Who Made a Difference." *Jewish Currents* 31 (1977): 22-26.

UNPUBLISHED WORKS

Baiamonte, John. "Immigrants of Rural America: A Study of Italians in Tangipahoa Parish, Louisiana." Ph.D. dissertation, Mississippi State University, 1972.

Booker, Henry. "Efforts of the South to Attract Immigrants." Ph.D. dissertation, University of Virginia, 1965.

Capeci, Dominic. "The Harlem Riot of 1943." Ph.D. dissertation, University of California at Riverside, 1970.

Diner, Hasia. "In the Almost Promised Land: Jewish Leaders and Blacks, 1915-1935." Ph.D. dissertation, University of Illinois at Chicago Circle, 1975.

Dudley, Julius. "A History of the Association of Southern Women for the Prevention of Lynching," Ph.D. dissertation, University of Cincinnati, 1979.

Ellis, Ann. "The Commission on Interracial Cooperation." Ph.D. dissertation, Georgia State University, 1975.

Fishel, Leslie. "The North and the Negro, 1865-1900." Ph.D. dissertation, Harvard University, 1953.

Gaston, Edward. "A History of the Negro Wage Earner in Georgia, 1880-1940." Ph.D. dissertation, Emory University, 1957.

Hellwig, David. "The Afro-American and the Immigrant, 1880-1930." Ph.D. dissertation, Syracuse University, 1973.

Hertzberg, Steven. "The Jews of Atlanta, 1865-1915." Ph.D. dissertation, University of Chicago, 1975.

Hill, Adelaide. "The Negro Upper Class in Boston." Ph.D. dissertation, Radcliffe, 1952.

Marinbach, Bernard. "The Galveston Movement." Ph.D. dissertation, Jewish Theological Seminary of America, 1976.

Pettus, Mildred Louise. "European Immigration to South Carolina, 1881-1908." Master's thesis, University of South Carolina, 1954.

Scarpaci, Jean. "Italian Immigrants in Louisiana's Sugar Parishes." Ph.D. dissertation, Rutgers University, 1972.

———. "The Italian Immigrant: An Answer to Louisiana's Post War Plantation Labor Problem." Unpublished paper presented at the Citadel Conference on the New South, Charleston, S.C., 1978.

INDEX

populations in, 33-34
Louisiana, 89, 95, 102, 128
Lovenstein, William, 125
Lower California, Mexican Land
  and Development Company,
  66-67
Lum, Gong, 22
Lynching, 75, 86-87, 124, 125-26,
  141 n.26, 145 n.54, 154-55

Mack, Julius, 154
Madden, W. S., 121
Mafia, 86-87, 95, 102
Magazines, Afro-American, xi-xiii
Man Farthest Down, The (Wash-
  ington), 90-91
Mapimi, Mexico, 62-64
Margaret, Ala., 99
Marshall, Louis, 164
Martin County, N. C., 129
Marx, David, 125
Meade, Emily Fogg, 95-96
Meier, August, 150
Mexican Land and Development
  Company, 61
Mexican Land Corporation, 62-65
Mexican War, 60
Mexicans: Afro-American antipathy
  to, 70-72, 75-76; religion and
  morals of, 68-70, 80 n.41;
  repatriation of, 74, 76
Mexico: Afro-American views on,
  60, 63, 67-69, 75-76; proposed
  for Afro-American immi-
  gration, 60-67; proposed for
  Japanese immigration, 48
Mexico City, 68
Miami, 129
Middleton, R. Izard, 9
Miles, W. R., 10
Miller, Herbert A., 163
Miller, Kelly, 115, 119, 121, 122,

124, 160, 164
Miller, Stuart Creighton, 8
Mississippi, 87, 111, 132, 135;
  Chinese in, 21-22, 156; Italians
  in, 100, 102, 155; Jews in,
  142 n.35
Modell, John, 53 n.1
Morse, Josiah, 125
Mosely, Jesse, 65
Moskowitz, Henry, 124
Mount Carmel, Pa., 93

NAACP. *See* National Associ-
  ation for the Advancement of
  Colored People
Naples, 90-92
Natchez, Miss., 142 n.35
National Association for the
  Advancement of Colored
  People (NAACP), 43, 46, 52,
  69, 131, 162, 169 n.46
National Conference on Social
  Work, 124
National Council of Jewish Women,
  (NCJW), 125
National Democratic Club, 9
National Labor Convention of
  Colored Men, 7
Naturalization, 6, 15, 43, 45, 46
NCJW. *See* National Council of
  Jewish Women
Needleman, Joseph, 129
Negroes. *See* Afro-Americans
Nella, A. P., 97
Neufeld, E. M., 128
Nevada, 4, 9
New Albany, Miss., 87
Newberry, S. C., 136
New Deal, 49
New Orleans, 86-87, 92, 103
Newspapers, Afro-American, xi-xiii
New Testament. *See* Bible

New York (city), 37, 92, 93,
121. *See also* Harlem
Nisei. *See* Japanese
North Carolina, 128, 129, 146 n.65

Oakland, Calif., 49; minority
populations in, 33-34
Obrégon, Alvaro, 66
Occupations, 151, 160, 166 n.8. *See
also names of specific occupa-
tions or groups of workers*
Oklahoma, 66, 78 n.20
Orientals. *See* Chinese; Japanese

Painter, Nell, 11
Palermo, Sicily, 89
Park, Robert, 90
Parks, R. S., 102
Pasquale, Luigi de, 169 n.40
Peddling and peddlers, 111, 114,
120, 135, 138 n.3, 160
Pei, M. A., 87
Pennsylvania, 93
Percy, LeRoy, 96
Periodicals, Afro-American, xi-xiii
Petruzella, Colerga, 99
Phagan, Mary, 129
Philanthropy, 124-26, 163-64
Phoenix, Ariz., 16, 22
Pickens, William, 46, 69
Pinchback, Pinckney B. S., 115
Pine Grove, Nev., 9
Plessy v. Ferguson, decision, 83
Polier, Shad, 125
Powdermaker, Hortense, 132-33,
134-35
Prejudice. *See* Racism
Press, Afro-American, xi-xiii
Professions. *See* Occupations
Prowd, John, 65
Public Law 89-236, 165
Publications, Afro-American, xi-xiii

Pullman Company, 19, 49
Purvis, Charles, 52, 162

Quackenbos, Mary Grace, 158

Racism, 76, 81 n.47, 81 n.49, 100,
120, 145 n.57, 155. *See also*
Anti-Semitism; Ku Klux Klan;
Schools, segregated
Railroad porters, 19, 22, 124. *See
also* Brotherhood of Sleeping
Car Porters
Railroads. *See names of specific
lines*
Randolph, Asa Philip, 49
Rayner, J. B., 94
Raynor, Isador, 132
Reconstruction, 150
Religion. *See* Bible; Roman
Catholicism; *see also under
names of specific national-
ities or ethnic groups*
Republican Party, 131
Retail trade, 111, 113-14, 160-61
Richmond, 129
Roberson, Mason, 16-17
Rogers, J. A., 129-30
roman Catholicism, 68-69, 153
Romero, Matias, 61
Roosevelt, Franklin, 49
Roosevelt, Theodore, 41-42,
53 n.7, 155
Rosedale, Miss., 22
Rosenberg, Samuel, 132
Rosenwald, Julius, xiv, 124, 164,
169 n.42
Rossi, Adolfo, 96
Rubin, Charles, 133
Russo-Japanese War, 35, 50

Sacramento, 4
Saint Cloud Sugar Plantation, 89

ABOUT THE AUTHOR

ARNOLD SHANKMAN is Professor of History at Winthrop College, Rock Hill, South Carolina. He is the author of *The Pennsylvania Anti-War Movement,* editor of *Human Rights Odyssey,* and the author of numerous articles on black, Jewish, ethnic, and Civil War history.